NAVIGATING THE AGE OF CHAOS

A Sense-Making Guide
to a BANI World That
Doesn't Make Sense

Jamais Cascio, Bob Johansen,
and Angela F. Williams

Berrett–Koehler Publishers, Inc.

Copyright © 2025 by Jamais Cascio, Bob Johansen, and Angela F. Williams

All rights reserved. No portion of this work may be reproduced or transmitted in any form or by any means, electronic or mechanical, including photocopying and recording, or by any information storage or retrieval system, or be used in training generative artificial intelligence (AI) technologies or developing machine-learning language models without permission, except in the case of brief quotations embodied in critical reviews and certain other noncommercial uses permitted by copyright law. For permission requests, please contact the Copyright Clearance Center at marketplace.copyright.com/rs-ui-web/mp.

Berrett-Koehler Publishers, Inc.
1333 Broadway, Suite P100
Oakland, CA 94612-1921
Tel: (510) 817-2277
Fax: (510) 817-2278
bkconnection.com

ORDERING INFORMATION

Quantity sales. Special discounts are available on quantity purchases by corporations, associations, and others. For details, please go to bkconnection.com to see our bulk discounts or contact bookorders@bkpub.com for more information.
Individual sales. Berrett-Koehler publications are available through most bookstores. They can also be ordered directly from Berrett-Koehler: Tel: (800) 929-2929; Fax: (802) 864-7626; bkconnection.com.
Orders for college textbook / course adoption use. Please contact Berrett-Koehler: Tel: (800) 929-2929; Fax: (802) 864-7626.

Distributed to the US trade and internationally by Penguin Random House Publisher Services.

The authorized representative in the EU for product safety and compliance is
EU Compliance Partner, Pärnu mnt. 139b-14, 11317 Tallinn, Estonia, www.eucompliancepartner.com, +372 5368 65 02.

Berrett-Koehler and the BK logo are registered trademarks of Berrett-Koehler Publishers, Inc.

Printed in the United States of America

Berrett-Koehler books are printed on long-lasting acid-free paper. When it is available, we choose paper that has been manufactured by environmentally responsible processes. These may include using trees grown in sustainable forests, incorporating recycled paper, minimizing chlorine in bleaching, or recycling the energy produced at the paper mill.

Library of Congress Cataloging-in-Publication Data
Library of Congress Control Number: 2025015187 ISBN 9798890571212 (hardcover) | ISBN 9798890571229 (pdf) | ISBN 9798890571236 (epub)

First Edition
33 32 31 30 29 28 27 26 25   10 9 8 7 6 5 4 3 2 1

Book producer and text designer: Happenstance Type-O-Rama
Jacket design: Ashley Ingram

Contents

Preface v

Introduction: The Age of Chaos 1

PART I: The BANI World
1. BANI: A Spectrum of Chaos 15
2. Brittle: Things Fall Apart 27
3. Anxious: Under Pressure 41
4. Nonlinear: Out of Control 57
5. Incomprehensible: Stop Making Sense 69

PART II: Positive BANI
6. Bendable: Resilient Clarity 87
7. Attentive: Active Empathy 105
8. Neuroflexible: Practical Improvisation 119
9. Interconnected: Full-Spectrum Thinking 135

PART III: BANI in Action
10. BANI Worlds: Mapping New Realities 153
11. BANI Leadership: Charting the Course 167

Conclusion: BANI and Our Futures 187

Discussion Guide 195

Notes 203

Bibliography	215
Acknowledgments	227
Index	229
About the Authors	239
About Institute for the Future	243
About United Way Worldwide	245

Preface

This book introduces a new way of thinking about our future and how we can best engage the accelerating upheaval.

Navigating the Age of Chaos offers a lens through which we can identify the various ways in which our present and future chaos will manifest, allowing us to recognize and focus on possible paths forward through that chaos.

This book opens our eyes and helps us understand the new phenomena and pivotal changes in the world, see their impact and trajectory, and learn what actions we need to take now. Even more so than before, the future is uncertain—and yet we must act.

Chaotic disruption is well on its way to becoming the new normal. We need better language to make sense out of a world that is changing in ways that the old terminology can no longer capture. The BANI framework—Brittle, Anxious, Nonlinear, Incomprehensible—is that new language.

Developed at the end of the Cold War, VUCA was a good start in understanding the emerging future: Volatile, Uncertain, Complex, and Ambiguous. The term proved useful as a sense-making framework over recent decades. But VUCA isn't VUCA enough anymore. VUCA doesn't describe the emerging future with enough clarity or provide the guidance we need to navigate. We've entered an unruly period where patterns dissolve and events unfold without predictable order or control. The kinds of mental models and strategic paradigms that seemed forward thinking in a VUCA world will be too cautious and insufficient for the new age.

The lead author of this book, Jamais Cascio, is a scenario-planning futurist and the original creator of the BANI concept. In this book, he and his coauthors will explain and expand upon the idea, bringing both greater clarity to the framework and a better understanding of how today's leaders can use it to illuminate events and guide strategy.

Jamais and coauthor Bob Johansen, Distinguished Fellow at Institute for the Future and a leadership futurist, worked together to create a "positive BANI," a way to take the BANI logic and show the kinds of responses and approaches that create the best path forward in a chaotic, BANI world.

Jamais, Bob, and coauthor Angela F. Williams, visionary on-the-ground nonprofit leader and CEO of United Way Worldwide, dig into real-world examples of BANI environments and how we can respond.

The three coauthors worked together to draw out leadership lessons for the BANI Future. They aim to help people recognize this emerging age of chaos in their personal, social, and organizational lives, including the following:

- Leaders and rising-star leaders: Use this book to encourage more human, humane, productive, and sustainable practices for thriving in a BANI world. Trust is at the core of leadership, but BANI bleeds trust. In this world, trust will be hard to develop but easy to lose.
- Individuals: Use this book to help cope and even thrive with psychological stress even while living day to day in an increasingly chaotic world.
- Corporations: Shareholders, board members, executives, and other stakeholders can use this book to identify strategies for surviving and thriving.
- Nonprofits: Use this book to understand the external future forces within which you will need to achieve your mission.
- Communities and governments: Use this book to guide elected officials and policymakers in creating future-friendly incentives and regulations.

In a BANI world, **Brittle** systems will not fail gracefully—they will shatter. We can counter Brittle by being **Bendable**, as in flexibility and resilience, with resilient clarity. **Anxious**—*anxiety*—is the engine of BANI. Anxiety will be baked into everything. If you're not at least a bit anxious today, you're not paying attention. Anxious can be countered by being **Attentive**, with empathy for what others are experiencing. **Nonlinear** means basic beliefs about cause and effect no longer hold true. The future is unlikely to unfold as you expect. In response, we must be **Neuroflexible**: improvise, think critically, and reject scripted responses. **Incomprehensible** means being unable to decipher the "why" of an event, phenomenon, or process. We witness incidents and decisions that seem illogical or senseless, whether because the origins are too long ago, or too unspeakable, or just too absurd. But we can push back against the Incomprehensible with **Interconnection** of multiple perspectives and ideas.

We conclude with seven core leadership strategies for navigating the chaos of the BANI Future, set in the discipline of possible future scenarios:

1. Think futureback: from the BANI Future back to present choices.

2. Tell great stories that confront BANI but flip it positive.

3. Develop specific leadership skills (included in this book) matched to BANI challenges.

4. Organize with great clarity of direction—but flexibility of execution.

5. Track and map signals from today that hint at BANI Futures.

6. Work within moral, ethical, and legal bounce ropes—not rigid guardrails.

7. Practice frequent scenario gaming of BANI variants.

Creating a positive BANI will require us to reexamine our assumptions, overcome embedded or habitual behaviors and ideas, be aware of our environments, and be nimble in our strategies. Ultimately, a chaotic world means that we must deepen *clarity* but let go of *certainty*.

BANI is a powerful lens for understanding our path. It gives a name to what we are experiencing and a framework for clarifying our options. We can't see where we want to go in the future if we can't say accurately where we are.

This book offers practical ways for people—especially leaders of corporations, nonprofits, and government—to understand the chaotic BANI world and to map the way to better futures. To become pathfinders for a better world.

INTRODUCTION

The Age of Chaos

In the mid-2010s, everything started to get a little crazy.

Imagine a history book looking back at the period from 2015 to 2025. What would be the core story, the theme of the chapter? The relentlessly lingering COVID-19 pandemic and the political backlash against vaccination? The most significant cross-border war in Europe since World War II, in parallel with catastrophic and horrific violence in the Middle East? The weakening and potential collapse of an almost eighty-year-old alliance? The seemingly sudden rise of generative artificial intelligence technologies, with impacts on everything from employment to dating to political stability? The rapid spread and empowerment of oligarchy and authoritarianism, and the simultaneous breakdown of democratic norms? The acceleration of the climate emergency, with its succession of fires, storms, and hottest years ever (so far)? The metastatic growth of economic inequality, both within and between nations? The *Cordyceps*-like infection of social media into every facet of our lives?

How about all of these happening at the same time?

The BANI framework—Brittle, Anxious, Nonlinear, Incomprehensible—emerged from a necessity to find a better language to describe what so many people had been experiencing from the mid-2010s onward. It wasn't an academic exercise; it was a visceral need for the right words. For billions of people around the globe, the world was changing in a way that the previous language could no longer capture.

In principle, much of what has happened since the mid-2010s has been of a kind with things we've experienced throughout recent history. Arguably, nothing happened that hadn't been written up, gamed out, or otherwise examined, *in isolation*. In reality, the simultaneous dangers—call it the *polycrisis*, or *omnicrisis*, or (a favorite) *metapocalpyse*—combine and intersect in ways that push far beyond anything we've seen. Problems hit faster and harder, with greater intensity and impact. Familiar systems misbehave. Unexpected events are somehow more devastating. And they just keep coming.

For those of us who make a practice out of watching, synthesizing, and making sense of the world in ways that help illuminate what might come next, this moment has been disorienting. The patterns and norms that we've come to see as part of the structure of the times have become weakened, lost, or dead. Never before has it been this difficult to understand the bigger picture, and never before has it been this important that we do so.

We are in an age of chaos, an era that intensely, sometimes violently, rejects legacy structure. Chaos is an environment that regularly ignores and violates expectations, patterns, and norms. It isn't simple instability; it's a reality that seems to actively resist efforts to understand what the hell is going on. It vividly demonstrates the need for a way of making sense of the world, the need for a new method or tool to see the shapes this age of chaos takes. The methods we have developed over the years to recognize and respond to commonplace disruptions seem increasingly, *painfully* inadequate when the world appears to be falling apart.

A Farewell to VUCA

One commonplace method used to understand disruption is the "VUCA" concept. VUCA is an acronym meaning *Volatile, Uncertain, Complex,* and *Ambiguous*. The US Army War College in Carlisle, Pennsylvania, introduced the idea of VUCA in 1987, building on the leadership theories of Warren Bennis and Burt Nanus.[1] VUCA offered a language for framing the disorder of the geopolitical environment emerging from the end of the Cold War and the rapidly expanding internet. The fall of the Berlin Wall and the collapse of the Soviet Union had disrupted the old, bipolar world order. Instead of a rather stable bipolar rivalry between the United States and the USSR, leaders had to navigate through multipolar uncertainty and prepare for threats from unexpected places.

VUCA was a *framework* for more precise descriptions of a rapidly changing world, a consistent set of terms and concepts that could illuminate the dynamics of change in the new era. There was no implicit theory behind the term; VUCA didn't tell you *why* the world had become volatile, etc. It didn't have an agenda. What it provided was a method to articulate the various ways in which we experienced a changing world. It was a tool for assigning structure to a world that was increasingly disordered.

Although first taking root at the US military, the VUCA framework began to trickle into the language of political analysts and business consultants through the 1990s. But for many of those charged with thinking about the world, 9/11 and its consequences marked the point that VUCA became a fundamental part of how we think about change.

Phenomena like the political uncertainty among the great powers, the cultural and moral questions of the global war on terror, and the accelerated growth of the World Wide Web as a source of information (and misinformation) offered clear examples of a world becoming increasingly volatile, uncertain, complex, and ambiguous. The VUCA framing gave a consistent name and conceptual model for what we were experiencing.

We shouldn't dismiss the importance of a consistent language for a changing environment. Often, debates about correct responses or wise courses of action amid evolving conditions end up stuck on disagreements about the descriptions of those changes. A common language, a widely recognized and generally accepted model, helps to move arguments past definitions into the real subjects at hand.

The term VUCA has proven to be a useful sense-making framework for the world over recent decades. It underscores the difficulty of making good decisions in a paradigm of frequent, often jarring and confusing, changes in technology and culture. From the late 1980s to the late 2010s, VUCA was a useful way to describe a world of increasing disruption, intensifying a focus on risk management and preparedness within the framework. Being ready for an increasingly VUCA world was the goal.

But VUCA, while highlighting turbulence and confusion, assumed that the world was fundamentally knowable. The various developments underway in the first decade of the new millennium were disruptive and dangerous, to be sure, but they were explicable. The path leading us to that point was relatively clear, even if the eventual consequences were uncertain.

That "knowability," however, is fading. When we look at the present world, and especially when we look ahead to 2035 and beyond, VUCA is no longer enough. Leaders don't just need agility and vision; they need new ways of making sense out of what is happening around them. We are no longer facing just volatility—we are experiencing brittle systems prone to collapse, often seemingly out of nowhere. We are no longer facing just uncertainty—we are experiencing rampant anxiety, particularly from young people, a growing dread coming from a lack of visible options. We are no longer facing just complexity—we are experiencing nonlinearity where expected outcomes cannot be assumed. We are no longer facing just ambiguity—we are experiencing incomprehensibility where even full datasets fail to make sense.

Massive events like 9/11 and the financial crisis of 2008 could be understood through the VUCA lens. They were unpredictable but understandable shocks. In contrast, when the COVID-19 pandemic hit, the limits of knowable VUCA became clear. Certainly, the potential occurrence of a pandemic had been forecast by some (including by Institute for the Future), but the actual manifestation of a pandemic was not just a volatile event—it was a wave of brittleness events. It exposed systems that had looked strong but shattered under pressure. Responses were not just uncertain; they were anxious with misinformation and political instability that compounded the crisis. The virus spread nonlinearly, defying containment models. The global economic impacts confounded even the best experts, who struggled to make sense out of what was happening. This wasn't just about an ambiguous lack of clarity; it was about outright incomprehensibility. VUCA served a purpose, but the world had moved beyond it. The need for a new frame was becoming clear.

To borrow a concept from chemistry, there has been a *phase change* in the nature of our social (and political, and cultural, and technological) reality—we're no longer happily simmering; the boiling has begun. But if it's a new paradigm, it needs a new language.

A World Turned BANI

In thinking about the kinds of changes underway by 2018, whether in technology, politics, the climate, and more, veteran futurist Jamais Cascio saw that disruptions had started to hit harder and seemed to be much less predictable than before. Consequently, those disruptions would lead to greater and greater difficulty in decision-making based on expected behavior (of technologies, of other countries, etc.). There were recurring themes in these disruptions—systems unexpectedly on the verge of collapse, developments triggering great stress, surprising implications of disproportionality, and events, behaviors, and changes that simply made no sense. Global systems of all kinds seemed to be tipping toward chaos.

Jamais created BANI—the acronym combining Brittle, Anxious, Nonlinear, and Incomprehensible, in an intentional parallel to VUCA—as a way of describing what this new chaos felt like. Although he saw the value of quantitative analysis, over the years of working with narrative foresight it had become evident to Jamais that myth and culture matter to the conveying and understanding of a changing world even more than numbers. BANI can illuminate systems, but it operates at a human level. It is not a technical analysis; there's no math that defines brittle versus nonbrittle, for example. It's visceral and experiential. But it serves to depict the nature of the moment, and moments to come, in a way that seems to resonate for a great many people.

The emergence of a BANI world will continue to be fraught:

- Fraught with opacity, as the very frames we use to describe the world are breaking down.

- Fraught with discomfort, as we are forced to abandon the illusion that what is going on makes sense.

- Fraught with tension, as we realize that the more we try to control the future, the more brittle our systems become.

- Fraught with resistance, as many people cling desperately to old assumptions of predictability and control. The more data we collect, the more anxious we feel.

This is not just a shift in conditions; it's a shift in how we must think. The word "fraught" summarizes the shift we must all go through from VUCA's now-familiar instability to BANI's unsettling new quagmire of unknowability.

In a BANI world, a belief in "knowability" can be problematic, even dangerous. A BANI environment is particularly hostile to arrogant ignorance: the certainty that one knows more than one really does, even as the lack of real knowledge undermines any ability to recognize one's own failings. Sometimes called the "Dunning-Kruger effect," such arrogant ignorance often manifests as absolute certainty by overconfident but underinformed individuals.[2] Whether it's a specialist in one discipline deciding that they are experts across the board, or someone who has watched a handful of online videos declaring that they've "done their own research," the people who have unwarranted confidence in their own expertise are spectacularly dangerous in a BANI world—especially if they become leaders.

A BANI Future demands a new perspective on the world, one that recognizes that uncertainty isn't a lack of knowledge; it's an awareness that our "possibility space"—the variety of potential outcomes and consequences of change—is larger than we had thought. That, in turn, means that our options for how to respond to change have fewer limits than we had feared. It also makes us more willing to see when our decisions are flawed and need to be changed. Successfully navigating an uncertain future requires that we be willing to accept when we are wrong.

The risk of embracing a BANI perspective is that, when we focus too much on the catastrophe, we lose sight of our own agency.

Consequently, we've developed a "Positive BANI" or "BANI+" parallel framework, speaking directly to the kinds of perspectives and methods that counter the dynamics of the "negative BANI."

What we are experiencing in the age of chaos cannot be summed up as *problems*, with corresponding *solutions*. A world that's brittle, anxious, nonlinear, and incomprehensible cannot be fixed and returned to a simpler time. There's no Return to VUCA.

There will undoubtedly be a point when a different language, a different meaningful acronym, may better describe what we will have come to experience. But for now our focus needs to be on what we can do to respond to a BANI world. We can do so in ways that help to mitigate its worst elements, ameliorate many of its harms, and—with effort—strengthen us against their recurrence.

While the first half of *Navigating the Age of Chaos* details the meaning of BANI as a way of describing a chaotic world, the second half explores this more hopeful concept of Positive BANI.

We counter Brittle with **Bendable**, as in flexibility and resilience, such as alternative sourcing and disaster plans. Anxious is met by **Attentive**, empathy for what others experience and an attempt to not use anger and fear to respond to anger and fear. Nonlinear needs us to be **Neuroflexible**, the capacity to improvise, think critically, and reject scripted responses. And we can push back against the Incomprehensible with **Interconnection** of multiple, diverse perspectives and ideas. At the heart of the Positive BANI concept is that we must reexamine our assumptions, push past embedded or habitual behaviors and ideas, be aware of our environments, and be nimble in our strategies. Ultimately, a chaotic world means that we must seek *clarity* rather than *certainty*.

We finish the second half of the book with a look at useful perspectives for thinking about BANI: BANI-inflected scenario foresight, enabling us to imagine different outcomes in a BANI Future, and a dive into how organizational leaders must recognize and respond to a BANI world.

Global BANI

Names have power. Being able to give a name to the conditions in which we find ourselves is useful. It's a starting point to figuring out how to move out of such conditions, or at least adapt to them, and gives a common language to work with others who may find themselves in the same type of conditions. Differentiating between forms of chaos in a BANI world (i.e., Brittle, Anxious, etc.) further allows the person amid the chaos to recognize recurring patterns and better focus on useful responses.

Jamais first offered the BANI framework in a talk for Institute for the Future, at its fiftieth anniversary event in 2018. It received a positive response, especially from the attendees from the Global South. However, the COVID-19 crisis starting in early 2020 opened up the minds of a much wider audience to the BANI idea. Jamais took the material he had created and turned it into an article, "Facing the Age of Chaos," published on *Medium*.[3] From there, the concept took off, spreading rapidly around the world.

That points to one of the most striking aspects of the overall response to BANI: just how *global* it is. The vast majority of that interest in BANI over the course of its first few years came from people in the Global South; Jamais spoke about BANI (remotely) to audiences in locations like Brazil, Mexico, and Sri Lanka. Over subsequent years, the idea has spread quickly—as of early 2024, there were over 1.5 million results on Google on the combination of "BANI" and "brittle." The places talking about BANI are remarkably varied, including the *Vatican News*, CNN Türkiye, HBR China, and the Brazilian military.

As of this writing, many discussions of BANI come from India and Indonesia, and across Southeast Asia. We also see regular articles on BANI in China, Russia, and Ukraine. And some of the most insightful uses of BANI come from consultants and social theorists in places such as Australia, New Zealand, Sweden, and Czechia. Generally speaking, the most interest in BANI can be found in the parts of the world in the midst of a chaotic present: places experiencing civil uprisings, cross-border wars, authoritarian takeovers, economic precarity, and much more.

In nearly every case, their core use of the BANI concept is as a way of articulating and giving name to how they experience chaos. Around the world, BANI provides a language to talk about why the present feels so different from past periods of crisis.

Navigating the Age of Chaos

All of this leads inexorably to this book. *Navigating the Age of Chaos* encompasses three core elements, each playing to the strengths and experiences of the coauthors. Jamais focuses on the basic question of what BANI (both negative and positive) and the "age of chaos" mean—what are the underlying ideas and concepts going into these terms? He also dives into the ways in which these concepts interact with foresight work and what we like to call "futureback" thinking. Angela F. Williams offers a more grounded perspective, talking about how real people around the world grapple with a BANI environment and the age of chaos. It's critical for us as authors to keep the human beings living in chaos at the forefront of our thinking. Bob Johansen examines what kinds of strategies, both personal and organizational, can best help us thrive within the age of chaos and the BANI Future.

So let's take a closer look at what this book holds.

In the first part of *Navigating the Age of Chaos*, we illuminate the immensity of the challenges we face now and will face in the future, emphasizing that the difficulties they present come not just from their individual attributes, but from the combination and intermixing of these disruptive forces. A brittle system presents a dilemma not just because it's brittle, for example, but because it's brittle amid a larger environment of the anxieties the endangered system triggers, the nonlinearity it displays, and the utter incomprehensibility of the situation. In other words, it's not just that the world is Brittle; *the world is BANI.*

- **BANI** describes the world and future where expected patterns fail, and the illusions we have built about what we can do and how we live have been swept away.
- **Brittle** is perilous, is endemic, and will not fail gracefully. It matters because we experience its consequences; it can do real damage to real people.
- **Anxious** is the engine of BANI, the measure of the chaos we experience. It's the inescapable feeling of being crushed by the visible consequences of choices.
- **Nonlinear** is the imbalance between cause and effect. We see it in the environment, our economies, and especially in the hoarding of power.
- **Incomprehensible** is confusing, even ridiculous. It's absurd and unthinkable. It's the language of a world that has simply stopped making sense.

In the second part of the book, we flip the story to show the kinds of strategies, beliefs, and perspectives that let us respond to, even push back against, the stresses of a BANI world. We cite examples of both individuals and organizations successfully facing BANI-like conditions. BANI+ isn't just a collection of strategies; it's a paradigm shift. When you adopt a BANI+ approach, you alter your understanding of how the world works.

- **BANI+** describes a way to disrupt the disruption of BANI. These are active measures we can take and perspectives we can adopt to push back against disaster.
- **Bendable** is adaptive and resilient. Bendable recognizes the scale of the challenges we face, but it asks us not to resist until we break but to evolve past the crisis.
- **Attentive** is empathetic and aware. It's the recognition that others are experiencing the enormity of a BANI world, too, and seeks outcomes that can be shared.
- **Neuroflexible** is improvisational and experimental. It shows us that established behaviors and scripted responses can worsen a crisis in a BANI world.
- **Interconnected** is inclusive of a multiplicity of perspectives. When we seek out different sources of knowledge and ideas, we can see crises in new ways.

The third part of the book covers two different ways in which the BANI/BANI+ lens can focus how we work and live. The first chapter looks at scenarios, asking us to imagine in detail the different ways in which a BANI environment and BANI+ choices can create new worlds. The second chapter looks at leadership, guiding us through the complexities of informing, inspiring, and navigating through a BANI Future that poses unprecedented challenges.

- The use of **scenario world-building** turns the idea of an uncertain future into a usable process. We can investigate and imagine the possible consequences of our choices today, looking for the surprises and nuances that might emerge as our world evolves.

- The skills needed for **leadership** in a BANI Future let us draw a map of intent, the realization of action amid chaos. Our goals as leaders of organizations, communities, even nations must be to build clarity and to set aside any notions of certainty.

Navigating the Age of Chaos illuminates where we are, indicates where we are going, and demonstrates the tools that will enable us to thrive.

If you're wondering whether *Navigating the Age of Chaos* takes an optimistic or pessimistic perspective, the answer is "yes." We hold in a kind of mental superposition the simultaneous concepts that the chaos we're experiencing has a significant likelihood of becoming catastrophic *and* that we have all of the knowledge and technologies we need to make the world a better place. Both of these can be true. The parts of the book that talk about "negative" (Jamais likes "original recipe") BANI may well leave the reader feeling shaken, even despondent, about the state of our futures. The parts of the book that talk about BANI+, and the lessons that leaders and strategists can take from this discussion, however, might just leave the reader feeling hopeful.

The direction the world takes is in our hands. It's only by seeing the reality of what lies before us that we can make informed, *wise* choices about where we go from here.

PART I

The BANI World

"BANI" (we pronounce it like "bonny") offers a one-word term for the combined forms of global chaos that have become increasingly endemic since the mid-2010s. The first chapter of this section dives into what it means, how it gets used, and why it matters.

Talking about the BANI world or the BANI Future, as we do in this book, is a way of focusing attention on the various ways in which human civilization is at risk and—critically—how individuals and organizations react to these risks. In this way, it serves as a lens, allowing us to see with greater clarity the nature of the challenges we face and how they manifest as they combine and evolve.

After that, the four terms making up BANI each get a chapter:

Brittle: Systems that appear strong but can fail abruptly and catastrophically

Anxious: Systems that elicit reactions of fear, anger, and doubt

Nonlinear: Systems that show significant disproportionality or disconnection

Incomprehensible: Systems that are opaque and difficult to explain or understand

BANI is not quantitative or formulaic; it's evocative. It describes the subjective conditions for humans and human society at the present moment and in the imminent future. It provides a platform upon which to build structured narratives about what is happening in the world and how we may respond.

BANI has a parallel framing, BANI+, that uses the same acronym to lay out the kinds of responses that can meet the challenges described in the original term. We'll look at that in part II.

1
BANI

A Spectrum of Chaos

CHAOS: In *Navigating the Age of Chaos*, we talk about chaos not as a mathematical phenomenon, but as something we experience. It's the lack of an underlying structure to the function of the world. It's a lack of consistency or predictability. It's the disruption that emerges from parts of a system clashing, whether because they're broken, absent, or transformed.

It's not simply *change*; it's a kind of change that breaks coherence and makes what comes next harder to understand. When we think about our present and our future, whether in technology, politics, the climate, and more, we see disruptions that hit harder and are far less predictable than before. As a result, decision-making based on expected behavior of critical systems, whether technological or geopolitical, becomes increasingly difficult. Yet there are recurring themes in these disruptions—systemic precarity, overwhelming levels of stress, seemingly broken cause and effect, and a world that has become increasingly incoherent.

Chaos is a paradigm in which our expectations based on past experiences too often fail to warn us of imminent changes. In this new paradigm, we need a new way of looking at the world. BANI is a lens that helps us see with greater clarity through this chaos to our world and our futures.

The Age of BANI

The future is uncertain, and yet we must act. This has always been the fundamental dilemma of life: we must make choices *now* based on what we believe will happen, both as a result of what we do and in the larger environment in which we live. By and large, humans aren't too bad at this. We have evolved various cognitive systems allowing us to make useful projections about the consequences of our actions.

The ability to act now to achieve a consciously intended (but currently unrealized) outcome goes at least as far back as early *Homo sapiens*. Cognitive scientists refer to this as *causal cognition*, a recognition of cause-and-effect processes and the ability to make usable forecasts as to future results of present actions. It appears to have evolved around the same time as our ability to throw with accuracy at a moving target.[1] Both of these are abilities that no other primates have, including our closest relatives: chimpanzees, bonobos, and gorillas. The ability to imagine the future is intrinsic to what makes us human.

That doesn't mean that we always get it right, of course. Sometimes the ball we throw at a running teammate misses its target; sometimes what we envision as the outcome of our actions is seriously mistaken. But getting it wrong can teach us, letting us try to understand how we need to change our action to fit an existing, repeatable process—a pattern. We rely on repeated patterns to help us get more accurate, whether in ballistics or forecasts.

But what happens when the patterns that we perceive and understand lose coherence and functionally stop working?

The BANI framework describes such a world, where expected patterns don't work as well, and sometimes don't work at all. We often can't rely on our assumptions about our strength, our ability to shape outcomes, our capacity to foresee changes, at times even our basic understanding of reality. The world no longer seems to work the way that we thought it did.

BANI derives from four concepts—Brittle, Anxious, Nonlinear, Incomprehensible—that describe a world, an *age*, of chaos, one that we arguably entered in the mid-2010s and will very likely persist for years, even decades.

The four categories of BANI chaos are not mutually exclusive; rather, they often appear together, with events or systems demonstrating multiple kinds of chaos—being both Brittle and Nonlinear, for example, such as the 2024 CrowdStrike crisis (see chapter 2). This underscores one of the key drivers of the BANI era, interaction (even interdependence) between multiple chaotic processes. We frequently talk about the climate emergency in our discussions in this book: it's not just because it hits all four elements of BANI; it's also because the climate emergency is tightly woven into other chaotic systems like global inequality, desperate migration, military conflict, and more. And while climate is arguably the biggest cross-BANI issue, it's not the only one.

The BANI world, and the BANI Future, describe a planet where this sort of chaotic interweaving is everywhere—and all signs point to it increasing.

The BANI World

The core of the BANI story is this: Since roughly the mid-2010s, the world as a whole has become less predictable—not in the crystal ball sense, but in terms of behavioral and functional consistency. The outcomes we expect and the outcomes we get often diverge quite radically. Systems that we have come to rely on—global trade, communication media, democracy—fail or misbehave in disruptive ways. Many of the illusions that we have built up about how everything functions, based largely on how everything appeared to work in the pre-BANI, even pre-VUCA, years, are dematerializing in front of us.

In a Brittle world, what we believe about the reliability of systems, technologies, and people fails us. We imagine that the world around us works as described, only to find that we've come to rely on fragile monocultures, interdependent entanglements, even hyperefficient processes in which everything must always work exactly right. External forces entirely out of our control put enormous pressure on fundamental systems. We put our trust in elements of the world that don't just bend or break when they stop working; they *shatter*. The strength of the systems we depend on is illusory.

In an Anxious world, our belief about our ability to shape and control outcomes faces increasingly complex technologies and ideologies built to deceive us. Revelation of that loss of control can mean hopelessness and despair. At the same time, our media hijacks basic cognitive processes to make us consume more, click more. We start to see every decision as potentially disastrous. And the more we learn about the world, the worse it all feels. Political systems, economic systems, environmental systems—the dynamics that make the world work are running amok. Our illusion of control is gone.

In a Nonlinear world, basic beliefs about cause and effect no longer seem true. Disproportionality is the rule, whether in scale, scope, or time. Key systems groan under the weight of imbalances of power or wealth. Enormous efforts seem to elicit minuscule results, while haphazard online videos or viral jokes shake up corporate boardrooms and international markets. COVID-19 was an object lesson in nonlinearity but ended up being so enmeshed in political struggles that we risk another pandemic being even worse. Whatever illusions we held about predictable systems and reliable outcomes are gone.

In an Incomprehensible world, we hold onto less and less understanding of why we get certain outcomes. Our world reveals itself to be unthinkable, and senseless, and absurd. We build tools to help us think only to find that they lie to us. We make life-changing decisions driven by ephemeral whims and trends. We are overwhelmed by information without any consistent method of finding meaning. Any capacity we have to think about the future is undermined, relentlessly, by chaotic firehoses of dubious facts and confusing pseudopatterns. Our illusions of understanding what is going on get ripped away.

And yet we must act.

The task that faces us every day is the need to make decisions, big and small, about ourselves, our families, our communities, our organizations, even our nations and planet, in an environment where everything we think we know is contingent, and our ability to trust our technologies and knowledge continues to diminish.

When we talk about a BANI world, we're talking about the daily, personal experience of seeing the institutions we trust and the structures we depend on weaken, twist, and sometimes shatter. But we're also talking about the long-term, organizational, and community experiences of seeing the future we wanted to have evaporating in front of us. This isn't the consequence of a single mistake—no butterflies were harmed sixty-six million years ago to make this happen—it's the cumulative result of myriad choices made every second of every day, choices usually made with the best intentions but rarely with the deepest thought. There's plenty of blame to go around for our reality being BANI.

The BANI Future

The chaotic dynamics that have characterized the world since the mid-2010s don't appear to be going away any time soon. Instead, signs—from climate crises to aggressive social media to political unraveling—point to this age of chaos continuing, even worsening, in the years to come. That's not fun to think about.

But we do have to think about it. At a point in history when structured, deep thinking about the future is the hardest, it's also far and away the most important. Even when we don't know what to do next, we still must act. Simply continuing to do the same thing might work for a while, but in a BANI Future eventually even the most reliable systems can fall apart. Familiar processes suddenly turn feral; comfortable choices produce unintended and usually very much unwanted results.

Over the next four chapters, we'll talk about the details and nuances of how each element of BANI manifests now and how each may manifest in the future. In most cases, the BANI Future explorations end up describing possible events and outcomes that are significantly worse than what is happening today. This is, in part, because the bigger potential dangers are easier to see—they loom above the horizon of the future like a distant mountain. It's also because we want to underscore the immensity of the challenges of the BANI Future.

We see a BANI world and BANI Future because multiple transformative and incredibly disruptive processes are reaching fruition at more or less the same time.

It's not just that the climate emergency is worsening; it's that we're at the last point where we can head off an increase in temperatures above 2°C.

It's not just that artificial intelligence is proliferating; it's that the decisions we make now about how AI is to be regulated (or if it's regulated at all) will be the baseline for a generation or more.

It's not just that social media is everywhere; it's that the hyperactive evolution of social media technologies has done dramatic harm to the trust we have in each other.

It's not just that we're seeing a new Gilded Age of intersecting power and wealth; we're seeing critical—and sometimes irreversible—global decisions made by a very small number of often unelected but always incredibly wealthy individuals.

It's not just that we're seeing an intensification of political rivalries; we're seeing that the political structures built in the 18th and 19th centuries are unable to survive 21st-century technologies and warp-speed communication.

This isn't an exhaustive list (although it may be exhausting to contemplate); feel free to add bullet points around pandemics (past and those to come), war (now and those being planned), migration, oceans, and so much more. These dilemmas are all peaking now or will be in the very near future. Even more importantly, **each will shape how the others happen.**

The most difficult part of thinking about the BANI Future is not letting the intensity and abundance of the chaos turn into fear, anger, or anticipatory capitulation. It's easy to look at the scope and scale of the chaotic forces we'll be grappling with and decide it's all too big, too overwhelming, just *too much*. Honestly, you may well be right to think that way. The hardest part of doing foresight work, whether as a profession or just as a task, is taking in the multiplicity of risks and absurdities without seeing everything as doomed.

Well, maybe we are doomed—*but what are we going to do about it?*

We may not like the world we have; it's incumbent upon us, then, to change it. A frightening future, a difficult future, a confusing future, a *whatever* future is not the end of the story. The world will continue to spin. No matter the possible tomorrows, we need to remember to ask **"and then what happens?"**

The role of BANI, now and in the future, is to provide a language for understanding this omnicrisis and our possible responses. BANI is a cognitive sextant. It's a system built around a lens that lets us figure out how to navigate through the maelstroms.

How BANI Is Used

If the BANI framework is entirely unfamiliar to you, it may be helpful to see how others around the world have employed it. From the outset, BANI was rapidly embraced by people in the parts of the world seeing a multitude of intersecting crises. Business, academic, even religious leaders use BANI as a way of understanding their disrupted worlds and as a way to communicate that understanding. BANI creator Jamais Cascio reached out to some of those who had started to use BANI in their own work. He asked if they could tell him a bit about how they made use of the BANI idea.

What they told him was this:

- **BANI is a new perspective.** Very often those of us who think about the world and try to derive insights get locked into particular mindsets and points of view. They've worked before, why wouldn't they work now? By bringing in a reframing of the situation, one that is simultaneously familiar in structure but novel in perspective, we have an opportunity to look at the set of dilemmas and problems in a new light.

- **BANI offers a distressingly accurate depiction of the challenges we face at present and a likely vision of what the next few decades will hold.** It's not that it tells us something new, necessarily, but it offers a narrative of the world that fits better with what people have been experiencing. It's more than a tool for business consultants and futurists; it's a perspective that can be applied to any structured approach at understanding human behavior amid disruption.

- **BANI focuses on the human, emotional aspects of disruptive change.** BANI is not quantitative or mechanical; it's much more about how people—from leaders to citizens—*feel* about what they are experiencing in a chaotic world. How people feel about their lives is a critical determinant of the decisions they'll make.

- **BANI reflects the sometimes-overwhelming levels of disruption caused by the chaos around us but frames this disruption as being in the form of *dilemmas*, not problems.** Problems can be solved. Dilemmas usually don't have a single solution or answer; more often, dilemmas must be responded to in a way that minimizes harm, even while recognizing that the challenges they pose won't completely go away.

- **BANI acknowledges that what we are experiencing is real.** BANI reassures people that what they're seeing, feeling, living through is real. We are often afraid to express our worries, thinking that we may be exaggerating the problems or overreacting to bumps in the road. But what we're experiencing now and will experience in the years to come does differ from the past.

BANI is a structure upon which we can build a consistent story about what's happening in the world and what may be the result, one that matches the reality of what people are experiencing and—arguably, more importantly—one that matches the reality of how people feel in this world.

BANI Is a Seed for Narratives

BANI can be used as a catalyst for scenarios of what the world might look like or should look like in the years to come. Telling stories and building scenarios based on the structure of possible BANI Futures lets us ask difficult questions about our current circumstances and where they might lead. We'll look more deeply into how BANI can be used to build out scenarios in chapter 10.

BANI also provides a framework for exploration of emerging systems, policies, or movements. It leads us to ask if these developments make us more Brittle, for example, or whether aspects of them are fundamentally Incomprehensible. This is particularly useful when coupled with the Positive BANI framework that we build out in part II.

But more broadly, BANI pushes us to *tell stories*—stories about both the present and the future. When a system proves to be Brittle, our stories need to describe what that means, how it plays out, what it feels like to live in that world. Similarly, if we are being made increasingly Anxious by the changes around us, our stories will need to talk about what preceded this situation, how we got here, and what impact it has on us. Nonlinearity and Incomprehensibility have their own parallel narratives and questions.

As we will explore throughout this book, humans use *narratives* to express our understanding of what's happening around us. We can even think of these narratives as mythic. We have, for millennia, created myths to explain the hidden functions of the world.

As our societies have become more sophisticated, new sciences have helped some of the "myths" to more closely match physical reality. Other myths, those we create about the behavior and beliefs of ourselves and the people around us, may be less scientific, but they remain powerful. All of these myths, these stories we tell about our world, our futures, and each other, have a purpose. When what we see aligns with what we understand, we have a deep sense of agency—**we can most usefully change the world when we know how it works**.

One reason why BANI has taken root is that so much of what's happening around us no longer makes sense; our narratives no longer match our reality. Not only does that undermine any sense of certainty we might have had about our societies and our choices, it undermines our sense of agency. How can we change the world if we don't really understand what's happening to it?

BANI Is a Call to Action

For many of us, the response to learning in detail about the BANI Future is something on the order of "Well, that sucks." When we don't really understand why this is happening, when we have lost our sense of agency and control over our experiences, it's hard to do anything beyond a deep, pained sigh and a slow shake of the head. It's all too big.

We recognize that you'll probably do that sigh-and-shake combination multiple times over the next four chapters. Some of what we detail about the ways in which our existence is Brittle, Anxious, Nonlinear, and Incomprehensible will be highly upsetting. The point is that looking deeply at a world made BANI will inevitably be distressing, especially as you think about what it's like to live in the parts of the world most directly affected by BANI forces. Imagining what a BANI Future will be like for the next generation or two will weigh just as heavily. You should be aware of all of this going in.

But that's not the entirety of the BANI story, both in the book and in reality. The original, negative BANI takes up less than half of the word count; we spend more time talking about how we can and will respond to a BANI world and future. You should see the risks and dilemmas presented over the next four chapters as a list of what we need to grapple with as a planet. A long list, yes, but not an infinite one. When you read in the following pages about cascades of destroyed satellites, stochastic terrorism, or the parallels between nuclear war and the climate emergency, you can sigh deeply and shake your head, but don't let that be all you do. Start thinking about what can be done to reduce the harm created by a BANI Future, and start asking "and then what happens?"

2
Brittle

Things Fall Apart

BRITTLE: In BANI, "brittle" refers to a system that may work properly under normal conditions but is susceptible to sudden and catastrophic failure. It may seem strong, it may function well, but under a certain degree of stress, it breaks down, often in a highly disruptive way. Brittle systems are solid until they're not—brittleness is illusory strength. Brittle systems are nonresilient and may make resilience more difficult by masking growing problems. A brittle system in a BANI world may be signaling all along that it's good, it's strong, it's able to continue, even as it's on the precipice of collapse. That collapse may come from internal failures, external pressures, or even shifts in the structure of its relationship to the external environment. Something changes, possibly a small something, leading to massive consequences.

The Age of Brittle

In the age of chaos, brittleness is endemic. We have witnessed (and will continue to see) a great diversity of systems abruptly going from functional to failed. Note that the pressures that lead to that failure may have been quietly building for some time, or have long been a visible possibility for those paying close attention. But for most of us, the transition from a working system to a broken one feels sudden—it's sometimes difficult to see one's level of precarity from the inside.

If you're familiar with the Jenga game (where players dismantle piece by piece a tower built from many wooden blocks), think of it this way: those who live on the top of a Jenga tower will see their world as stable until it collapses; those who can step outside will see the supporting pieces going away one by one.

Brittle is perilous, projecting both threat and uncertainty, with high stakes for individuals and for institutions. In a BANI world, people and organizations will face conditions that are not just challenging but potentially hazardous or even deadly. Missteps will have personal, financial, organizational, and even societal consequences.

Often, systems are Brittle because the connections they have with their broader ecosystems (of customers, resources, and so on) are themselves brittle. Weak links to a larger world can mean that expected or assumed support won't be there when we are hit by surprising dangers. That unforeseen risk may itself be an indicator of brittleness; organizations disconnected from their environments can be blindsided by unexpected developments.

Brittleness can come from a system experiencing unprecedented stress, revealing long-hidden weaknesses. Systems that rely on norms and socially agreed-upon behavior can swiftly come undone if someone intentionally ignores those norms. The relatively swift flow of traffic depends on drivers agreeing to remain in their lanes, even when the only division between northbound and southbound vehicles is a faded line of paint. Crossing that line is easy but can lead to tragic consequences. The ongoing function of norm-based systems, whether driving or democracy, depends on mutual decisions not to cross the line.

In BANI, Brittle systems do not fail gracefully; they shatter. When the global supply chain collapsed during COVID-19, it did not slowly degrade; it rapidly fell apart. Brittleness at such a vast scale so often arises from efforts to maximize efficiency, to wring every last bit of value—money, power, food, work—from a system. The linkages become so taut, the connections so interdependent, that a failure of one part triggers a rapid total disassembly.

Brittleness can be found in monocultures, where growing a single crop means maximum output, until a bug that only affects that one particular species or strain destroys the entire field. Brittleness emerges from dependence on a single, critical point of failure, and from the unwillingness—or inability—to leave any excess capacity, or slack, in the system. Brittleness arises when deep interconnection becomes deep interdependency. We see brittleness in the "resource curse," when countries or regions are rich with a useful natural resource, so they focus entirely on its extraction . . . and then that resource becomes functionally worthless after a change in technology.

With that in mind, let's talk about guano.

Guano Madness

In the 19th century, guano (primarily bird feces) became the reason for the beginning of the agricultural revolution in Europe and America. It turns out that guano makes an outstanding fertilizer, increasing crop yields dramatically. It was a vital resource like few others before it. Empires were built upon it—but it was a brittle foundation.

In 1813, an internationally best-selling book revealed that crop yields increase significantly when Peruvian guano is used as fertilizer; this led to a massive surge in demand and an ongoing cycle of trade between Peru and Europe—consumer goods in, guano out. In the early 1840s, the Peruvian government nationalized all guano exports, collecting royalties on the sale, making guano Peru's greatest source of income. (Peru used that income to free the roughly 25,000 Black slaves in the country, as well as to eliminate the head tax on its Indigenous peoples; it then replaced its Black slaves with Chinese laborers, convicts, and people grabbed from Pacific islands.[1])

As explorers found guano in other locations, a variety of nations—both major powers and smaller states—engaged in guano imperialism, holding onto any feces-covered islands they happened upon. The United States passed the Guano Islands Act in 1856, allowing American citizens that happen to discover an uninhabited, unowned island to claim it for the United States.[2] Consequently, the United States annexed almost one hundred islands, with several remaining US territories today.

Despite guano being found in other locations, Peru (and, to a lesser extent, Bolivia) seemed to have the greatest concentration, and other nations looked on hungrily (as it were). In 1865, Spain tried to recapture islands owned by former colonies, ostensibly for reparations after previous conflicts. This kicked off guano island wars with Chile, Peru, Bolivia, and Ecuador, wars that lasted between fourteen and twenty years. In 1879, Chile attacked its neighbors Peru and Bolivia, even while still fighting Spain, and by the end of the century Chile controlled the most profitable sources of nitrogen for fertilizer in the world.

All very exciting, to be sure, but why are we talking about bird poop? Because by 1913, the value of all of that guano effectively disappeared. The 1913 invention of the Haber-Bosch process allowed for the creation of cheaper-than-guano fertilizer using globally abundant materials: air, water, and natural gas. Guano went from being a critical resource to functionally worthless in a matter of a few years. Moreover, it wasn't just the collectors of guano that lost everything; the entire chain of wealth and power based on guano collapsed effectively overnight. Dependence upon guano turned out to be a brittle system.

Keep this example in mind when you think about rapid transitions in the use of other natural resources, like fossil fuels.

Brittle Ubiquity

In the abstract, a brittle system is fundamentally one that is believed to be stronger than it really is, and when it fails, it does not bend; it breaks. Both of these elements are crucial. We don't consider something that exceeds its expected life, such as the Mars Exploration Rovers *Spirit* and *Opportunity*, which each lasted for years longer than their planned ninety-day missions, to be brittle when it finally fails, even if that failure is irreversible. Neither do we consider something that fails gracefully and safely, like a circuit breaker, to be brittle, even if that failure happens suddenly.

But brittleness has seemingly become more prevalent in the BANI era, especially as large-scale systems face unprecedented levels of pressure, resulting in abrupt—and very much unwanted and unexpected—failures.

The COVID-19 pandemic revealed that quite a few of our core social and economic systems were far more brittle than believed. National health-care systems, both public and private, were overwhelmed by the crisis; hospitals could not provide mutual aid when every one of them faced similar levels of demand, and secondary systems like postmortem body storage were never designed to face such numbers. Global supply chains collapsed, showing a vulnerability to disruption later echoed by the Suez Canal crisis, where a massive container ship (the *Ever Given*) ran aground and blocked the canal for six days.

While COVID-19 and the *Ever Given* were singular events (at vastly different scales, of course), the global climate emergency is an ongoing process that reveals systemic brittleness over and over, particularly regarding infrastructure. Summer heatwaves in Europe can kill more than 50,000 people annually, due to the lack of cooling infrastructure in homes and buildings never designed for record-breaking heat. The power grid in Texas has repeatedly proven unable to cope with temperature extremes, both cold and hot. Sea level increases have made storm surges far worse, leading to devastating flooding, as with Hurricane Sandy inundating the NYC subway system in 2012 (or Hurricane Ida doing the same in 2021).

Where does all of this brittleness come from? Sometimes, it's due to a radical change in conditions—increases in temperatures or sea level that go beyond what a system was built to withstand, for example. Often, however, it's a consequence of the combination of the elements mentioned previously—monocultures, interdependency, and the like—with a cost- or profit-driven push for hyperefficiency.

At its most basic, efficiency is the process of generating maximal output (of software, of widgets, of educated students) at minimal cost, whether of people and materials or, usually, money. It can manifest as just-in-time production, or the elimination of redundancy, or a focus on the next ninety days with little thought to the next ninety months (let alone ninety years)—whatever action serves to improve the bottom line *now*. Any system that depends on every piece working to spec, then made to work faster or at lower cost, becomes more brittle. As long as this kind of hyperefficiency works, the system can rapidly generate value; when it stops working, for whatever reason, the system can fail catastrophically.

Sometimes the brittleness becomes evident when the users and operators of a functional system discover that there are ways that the strength of that system can be circumvented. Robust computer firewalls and encryption remain subject to "social engineering" of the people on the network. Democratic political systems show surprising brittleness when extremist movements or leaders ignore historical norms, using blatant lies or a refusal to adhere to expected behaviors without significant repercussions. This is most frequently visible in nationalist and protofascist groups, but populist movements against globalization or both for and against climate regulations have also learned the power of ignoring norms.

Brittleness exists where complex systems have a fundamental dependency on a single, vulnerable, point of failure. The deeper in the system that vulnerable point can be found, the more likely it is that the failure would be unrecoverable. Arguably, one of the most dangerous manifestations of brittle in the BANI world is when brittleness leads to a failure that cannot be reversed. These aren't common, but they often have the potential to be absolutely catastrophic. A brittle collapse—a shattering—can alter conditions in a way that makes it impossible to return to previous conditions. When people talk about "tipping points" or say that "you can't unbreak an egg," they're talking about consequences of just this kind of collapse.

Another especially dangerous way for brittleness to show itself is when an initial failure of a brittle system cascades into greater and greater collapse. Among the most frightening of these is the *Kessler syndrome*, a forecast that the number of objects in low Earth orbit (LEO), both active satellites and space junk, is now or will soon become sufficiently dense that the destruction of a moderate-to-large satellite, whether by impact with a piece of space junk or by being targeted in an intentional attack, would lead to a slow-moving but effectively unstoppable cascade of devastation.[3] A 500-kilogram satellite—a common size in LEO—being broken into pieces would produce sufficient debris to destroy dozens (or more) of other satellites in the area, which in turn would produce their own debris, destroying even more satellites, and so forth. Over the course of years, this would make LEO—home to over 80 percent of satellites now in operation—entirely unusable.[4]

As an example of how brittle systems overlap, it turns out that global warming, by concentrating heat in the lower atmosphere, leads the upper stratosphere—which reaches into LEO—to become cooler and contract. When countries or companies retire their satellites, they rely upon atmospheric drag to eventually pull the now-junk material out of orbit. As the upper stratosphere contracts due to global warming, dead satellites will remain in orbit longer than expected, increasing the potential for an accident.[5]

Although it is a frightening prospect, a Kessler event is still just a possible scenario. But a very real, albeit far less catastrophic, example of a brittleness cascade is from this last decade, with the CrowdStrike incident in July of 2024.[6]

Cascade of Catastrophe

The basic story is this: CrowdStrike's Falcon software, which was part of a server-level cybersecurity system, was built to run during the Windows startup process. When an update broke the application, Windows computers using that program—nearly all of them found at medium to large organizations around the world—could no longer start, or "boot." Consequently, any services or processes depending upon those computers couldn't function, either. Moreover, because the faulty software interfered with the boot procedure, getting into the computer to remove the bad patch couldn't be done remotely; it required on-site, hands-on work.

As these systems provided critical services, thousands of businesses and organizations all over the world were unable to function, from airlines to 911 emergency networks to the NHS. As a consequence of *this*, millions of people couldn't get to a meeting or a loved one, couldn't report a fire, couldn't get help for a medical emergency, and myriad more situations where the failure at the end of a chain of computer hardware resulted in very human consequences.

According to Microsoft, around 8.5 million devices globally were hit by this crash.[7] But that was just the tip, as it doesn't really reflect the hundreds of millions of people who relied on those services, from passengers to patients, and who had no alternatives. Billions of dollars, and potentially some lives, were lost. Most companies recovered within a few days, but for some people, the impact lasted far longer.

The software patch, in and of itself, was simply a failure; the resulting damage to globally connected networks of devices and to services that ran on those devices was a cascade of brittleness.

The CrowdStrike incident combined multiple drivers of brittleness: a near-monoculture of cybersecurity systems; the single point of failure of the update process; the lack of a robust automatic recovery; the lack of proper testing of the patch and the resulting rush to deployment; and most importantly, the lack of redundant or backup systems—not just for the devices running CrowdStrike, but for the millions of computers *not* running CrowdStrike but dependent upon servers that did, and for the various services those computers provided. There are many good reasons for not building out redundancy at that scale. Still, the lack of that capacity resulted in a brittle system, no matter the cause.

But this episode was, from a wider perspective, a blip—a one-off, fixable, event. The collision of massive network interdependence and the push for hyperefficiency means we'll see many more of these blips. Of greater concern is the example of brittleness that comes from many years of accumulated pressure on systems upon which everyone on the planet depends: the brittle climate.

WAIS and Means

The climate emergency is probably the most BANI phenomenon on Earth. Every one of the BANI terms can be illustrated by something happening because of human-caused, or *anthropogenic*, global warming. Moreover, many climate dangers and global warming consequences cover more than one element of BANI: "brittle" and "nonlinear" are givens, and if you aren't feeling overwhelming anxiety about probable climate dangers, you should be. And what else can you call the repeated unwillingness to take sufficient action but "incomprehensible"?

But let's focus on "brittle" for the moment. Phenomena we think of as brittle are susceptible to abrupt transformation from functional to broken. Bear in mind that "abrupt" has a somewhat different meaning when we talk about climate. Geophysical systems typically change over the course of hundreds of thousands of years. If a climate-related process takes seventy years, it may feel slow from a human perspective, but in planetary terms it's terrifyingly rapid. It may be helpful (if unpleasant) to remember brittle can also mean cascading and irreversible.

The West Antarctic Ice Sheet (WAIS) is an expanse of ice covering a bit under two million square kilometers of the Antarctic continent, running one to two kilometers thick. It rests on bedrock that's just below sea level; it's melting, gradually, and if nothing else changes will probably add another 11 centimeters to sea level by the end of the century. But that "if" is looking increasingly optimistic.

Multiple models and ongoing direct study make it highly likely that the current melting of the WAIS is accelerating; moreover, the WAIS is already locked in to melt *completely* over the course of a few centuries, if not sooner, based just on the warming that has already happened.[8] A complete melt of the WAIS will raise global sea levels by at least 3.3 meters, about 10 feet, inundating coastal cities around the world. Stopping that would require bringing Antarctic temperatures down 1°C below preindustrial levels, not just stopping climate change but reversing it to make Earth *colder*.

But all of these dangers could happen much faster if warming continues as projected. The WAIS is held in place in part by the Thwaites Glacier, a mass of ice about the size of Florida. There are early signs of possible collapse, which would greatly accelerate the melting of the WAIS.[9] If that happens, the Intergovernmental Panel on Climate Change (IPCC) Sixth Assessment Report puts the likely sea level increase *by the end of the century* at 41 to 57 centimeters, or 16 to 22 inches. Of course, that's only the effect of the WAIS melting; a world in which the Thwaites Glacier collapses is one where other locations with at-risk glaciers, such as Greenland, also pour megatons of water into the seas.

Much of the wider discussion of this jumps to a later point in the process, where the glacier has collapsed, the ice has melted, and sea levels have risen. A 10-foot increase in sea level from the loss of the WAIS would be catastrophic for hundreds of millions, likely billions, of people around the world; a 20-inch increase wouldn't be quite as bad but would still be economically and socially devastating for millions. However, we should not ignore what happens along the way.

Even a comparatively small increase in sea level has dramatic effects on storm surges, allowing seawater to reach places that had once been protected. In nature, coastal ecosystems can be ruined, flooding areas not adapted to high salinity with seawater. The effect on human infrastructure can be just as serious. When Hurricane Sandy flooded the New York subway system in 2012, it was the worst disaster to ever hit the transit network; subway-station flooding during big storms is now a regular occurrence. The ongoing increase in sea level has also helped to push insurance companies out of states and regions at growing risk. As the sea level slowly rises, homes along the coasts will rapidly go from millions-of-dollars valuation to functionally unsellable.

Brittle Norms

"Norms" are shared standards of acceptable behavior, whether based on a factual description (e.g., drunk driving is dangerous) or an assertion of what one ought to do (e.g., do not drive drunk). While they can be codified into regulations and law, often they are enforced largely by social disapproval. Norms are informal ways of maintaining social or organizational order.

Recent years have seen multiple examples, around the world, of high-profile figures and political leaders ignoring or explicitly violating norms concerning ethical behavior. What makes this BANI, however, is the overall lack of major consequence for those violations. It turns out that our political systems rely heavily on extremely brittle norms for leaders.

In 2021, Professor Veronica Root Martinez, then at Notre Dame Law School and now at Duke University School of Law, examined "The Role of Norms in Modern-Day Government Ethics" for a symposium on the ethics of government service.[10] In her article, she argues that failure of political leaders to adhere to established basic norms and ethics comes, at least in part, from the rise of social media undermining the stigma associated with such violations. The lack of social opprobrium, in turn, reduces the pressure for legal intervention.

A desire to ignore norms is not unusual; Martinez cites multiple examples from the 21st century, across party lines. It's driven by a basic combination of a pursuit of power and "plain, old arrogance." What's novel is the way in which *social media* could amplify the voices of support for norm-breaking behavior while quieting those calling for repercussions. Rather than facing disapproval from a narrow set of colleagues and constituents, political leaders found that they would often receive political benefit from parts of the larger populace by refusing to stick to normative rules.

It didn't take long for examples of leaders facing little consequence for violating norms for massive norm breaking to become commonplace. With social media becoming a critical way for adults to consume news—Pew Research found that 33 percent of American adults regularly got their news from Facebook, while 54 percent at least sometimes gathered news from social media in general[11]—the ways that social media can highlight the most polarizing voices (explored in the next chapter) can make it very hard to see a strong pushback against the violation of norms.

Martinez's set of potential interventions—formal sanctions and legal consequences; "doubling down on the public good" within leadership culture; and private pressure, largely from sources of money—all require the cooperation of the very people finding that toothless norms make their pursuit of power and "plain, old arrogance" much easier.

Brittle People

When we talk about brittleness, we cannot forget that the most brittle systems with which we regularly engage are our fellow human beings. We appear strong, often truly are strong, but we can be put under enough pressure that even the strongest of us are at risk. Any of us can be stressed until we break, and for a great many people, the path from where we are at present to that breaking point is unhappily quite short. But even broken people have to keep going; the pressures and demands of a chaotic world will continue to grind us down, even if we're already shattered.

Brittleness is a significant hazard for individuals. Brittle personalities are detached from others. They are often lonely and at risk in terms of their mental and physical health. The peril for both individuals and organizations is to mistakenly equate stability with strength. Sometimes, stability will mask fragility. Disconnected systems and people are often brittle, even if they look stable.

Of course, brittleness isn't just an individual experience; the stresses of a BANI world can shatter relationships, even communities. This is especially problematic because a fundamental part of being able to respond to a BANI world is being able to work together. As we'll see later, there are dynamics at work in the BANI world that increase tension. But even without those outside drivers, an individual reaching a breaking point can become a cascade of brittleness for a relationship, a family, or a community.

All of this is made worse when brittleness arises out of choices made by those we depend upon, including ourselves. Or out of the choices made by a powerful but narrow group, with consequences that hit more widely. There is a slogan (or cliché) in Silicon Valley, supposedly coined by Facebook's Mark Zuckerberg, celebrating disruption: *move fast and break things*. But "things" are often interconnected with people, meaning that very often that slogan should be articulated as *move fast and break people*.

Brittleness matters because we experience its consequences. Kessler cascades or software failures of critical systems matter not because satellites are expensive, or air travel is crucial to our transportation infrastructure (or whatever), but because the loss of these *things* can do real damage to *people*. When people break due to the overwhelming stress of a world of chaos, it does real damage to other people in their circles. Brittleness in a BANI Future, in a BANI world, *has real consequences for real people.*

And that can make us rather anxious.

3

Anxious

Under Pressure

ANXIOUS: In BANI, "anxious" refers to a pervasive feeling of dread or hopelessness in the chaotic environment. It's relentless worry about events and processes over which we have no control, or about situations where there are no good responses. It's not directly quantifiable and can often be difficult to describe. It's the inescapable feeling of being crushed by the visible consequences of choices and fearful about the possible consequences that we don't see coming. Every decision appears to be potentially disastrous. Of the elements of BANI, it is by far the most personal.

In many people, being anxious can manifest as decision fatigue, where the need to make multiple choices in a short period of time becomes emotionally exhausting; in others, it manifests as decision paralysis, where the overwhelming variety of choices, with all of their various implications, renders us unable to move forward. It's contextual, with some environments and communities lessening the feeling of being overwhelmed, and others making everything worse. Modern media often tap into the neurological components of anxiety, hijacking it to grab and hold onto attention.

The Age of Anxious

Warning: This chapter may be upsetting. Be mindful of your reaction, and take a break from it as needed. Seriously.

In many ways, Anxious—*anxiety*—is the engine of BANI. The impacts of a BANI world come down to our responses to it, and those responses are very often driven by the stress triggered by chaotic conditions. The consequences of a system being brittle, or nonlinear, or incomprehensible, are significant not just due to their objective reality, but due to how they make us react. Our anxiety is the measure of the chaos.

It's tempting, in a book about dramatic changes to social, economic, or technological conditions, to emphasize the objective, to be dispassionate about the levels of disruption we experience. There is a perceived seriousness about neutrality; readers often see cold discourse about the end of the world as somehow being more professional. But the authors are not outside the context. We experience the Anxious in BANI as much as anyone, and to pretend that we can be wholly objective is misleading at best.

Much more importantly, attempting to talk about BANI anxiety from a distance implicitly diminishes its emotional and experiential weight. We can't talk about hopelessness or dread or worry as a quantitative force. There is no calculus of anxiety.

In our experience, anxiety is the element that comes up by name most frequently in discussions about BANI around the world. The multitude of events and processes often linked to the BANI framework, such as the climate emergency, wars in Europe, Africa, and the Middle East (and looming threats of war elsewhere), artificial intelligence, authoritarians seeking or gaining power, and economic instability, all engender anxiety for millions, if not billions, of people. Too often, that anxiety can become near crippling.

In some cases, we can't help but worsen our own fears. For many of us, the urge to understand a chaotic world means that we're constantly scanning news sources, waiting for the next shoe to drop, dreading to see what horror shows up next. For this group, doomscrolling is as habitual as breathing.

Such action seems almost inescapable when the intersection of uncertainty and consequence is at its peak—when a disastrous situation takes a turn for the worse, for example, or in the days before a critical election. This anxiety influences our decision-making, our ability to analyze the situation we're in. Thoughts about the future—short term or long—are colored by the fear we feel in the moment.

In other cases, we may do our absolute best to avoid any and all sources of news about the world. We skip over potentially critical reports and information because we simply can't take another headline about that genocide, or this new AI model, or some elected official.[1] If our work requires us to pay attention to the details of a changing world, actively avoiding these anxiety triggers can feel like a dereliction of duty.

Anxiety can drive passivity, because we can't make the wrong choice if we don't choose, right? Or it can manifest as a horrified realization that we missed the chance to make a critical decision, and we won't get another opportunity. Or as that awful gut feeling that there's a very real possibility that people we depend on will make a bad decision that will leave us all far worse off than before.

Generally speaking, anxiety in the BANI world comes largely from a sense of the world being out of control. Our ability to understand what is happening, why it's happening, and what might happen next is undermined in the BANI environment. It's not just a situation where the future is unknowable; it's a world where we are repeatedly deceived by the apparent or expected nature of things, which in turn makes us doubt the stability of everything else. It's as if we no longer have a firm grounding to build our futures upon.

Too great a number of us respond by taking a permanent way out. We see suicide increasing in frequency globally, but especially among those who discover that the seemingly good choices they've made over the years were actually wrong, were dead ends, or were even, in retrospect, evil. Hardworking, honest people that once considered themselves in control of things, discovering that, no, they aren't . . . and they probably never were. Not necessarily because someone or something else was actually in control of things, but because control was never possible to begin with. That can be a terrible realization.

For so many in the world, Anxious becomes Despair.

Despair

Despair is more than just sadness. It is a relentless feeling that there are no pathways out of a miserable situation. Sometimes it includes a belief—justified or otherwise—that we are the root cause of our own misery: *if we'd only chosen differently, or not said what we said, or took that chance*. Even if our situation is no fault of our own, we feel despair when we believe that there's nothing we can do to make things better.

The drivers of despair in a BANI world are numerous. It's very easy to feel like there is no way out of the climate emergency, for example (and the various examples of climate-related BANI elements cited in this book don't help with this). Or perhaps it's more personal than systemic, like a belief that a changing institution or industry will leave us broken and in poverty, and that there's nothing we can do to stop it. Despair isn't the only manifestation of anxiety in a BANI world, but it's arguably the deadliest.

In 2015, economists Anne Case and Angus Deaton published a research article in the *Proceedings of the National Academy of Sciences* examining midlife mortality among White non-Hispanic American men.[2] In a 2017 follow-up article, they used the term "deaths of despair" to encompass the causes of mortality shown to be increasing in the population being studied. Even as rates of heart disease, previously a leading cause of death, declined, mortality from suicide, alcoholism, and drug overdose increased significantly. Moreover, this shift was especially pronounced in men without a college education. Over time, researchers have widely embraced the term "diseases of despair" to refer to these outcomes.

Despair crosses demographic groups. Suicide—one of the diseases of despair on the rise—is the third leading cause of death for fifteen- to twenty-nine-year-olds worldwide, while suicide rates for older American men (fifty-five and up) increased significantly between 2001 and 2021.[3] And it's not purely a postindustrial-world phenomenon. Globally, three-quarters of suicides happen in low- and moderate-income countries.[4]

Opioid abuse, another disease of despair, is a global problem, but it is particularly acute in the United States. Of the approximately 600,000 drug-use deaths worldwide in 2019, the World Health Organization estimates that opioid overdose caused about 120,000 of them.[5] In that same year the United States recorded a bit over 70,000 opioid overdose deaths—more than half of the global total.[6] In comparison, in 2019 over 2.6 million people died from alcohol consumption worldwide, with a comparatively low 145,000 in the United States that year.[7] Unsurprisingly, in the United States those numbers jumped significantly in 2020 and 2021; anyone who lived through those years knows just how apocalyptic they often felt.

While the concept of "deaths of despair" emerged from research focused on White, working-class populations in the United States, despair as a social and psychological condition is not exclusive to any one group. In fact, for many communities of color, despair is often not a *new* condition, but a chronic and deeply embedded response to systemic injustices that have persisted for generations. Structural racism, economic exclusion, environmental injustice, and overpolicing have long shaped the lived experience of despair for Black, Indigenous, and other marginalized communities in the United States. The experiences of minority and oppressed populations in countries around the world can be even worse.

These forms of despair may not always show up in the same mortality data as opioid overdoses or suicides—but that does not mean they are any less acute. The emotional and psychological toll of living in a society that routinely devalues your life and safety—through discriminatory housing, unequal education, wage disparities, and state violence—can create a profound sense of futility. In a BANI world, brittle support, disproportionate power, and incomprehensible policies compound this systemic anxiety. The despair experienced by marginalized groups is not just reactive but all too often inherited and intergenerational.

Across a BANI world, there are abundant reasons to despair—even as some elements of our living conditions have never been better. There's often a deep schism between the state of our fundamental, planetary systems and our day-to-day experiences. This split can be disorienting, especially in nations like the United States, where we are simultaneously immersed in signifiers of material wealth even as our perceptions of the world darken. These dark perceptions aren't just cynical posturing—the crises and disasters, problems and dilemmas that provoke our anxiety are, in most cases, very real. In a BANI Future, anxiety will continue to be a perfectly rational response.

Despair isn't solely inwardly focused; our empathy for others can be a catalyst for despair, too. It can come from seeing others make choices or act out in ways that objectively will make their futures worse. It's especially sharp if you've been emphatically making clear all along just how dangerous that choice or action would be. The Cassandra complex is relatively commonplace among foresight specialists and futurists, the feeling that you're shouting from the rooftops about an imminent crisis, and nobody is listening. Or worse, they're loudly mocking you for talking about a disaster that hasn't happened yet, calling you a "doomer" or "doomsayer" because you keep trying to draw attention to likely threats. When that disaster happens, by the way, you're probably not going to be thanked for your prescience.

Admittedly, talking in detail about systemic threats really is just heaping more anxiety on listeners. Jamais recalls giving a talk on climate futures in 2019 to an audience of leaders and strategists from across industries. By the end of the talk, multiple members of the audience were crying, and it's likely that most people in attendance saw an increase in their anxiety that afternoon. Jamais says that it left him with profoundly mixed feelings—relieved that he had made his point so clearly, but guilty that he had caused emotional pain for people in the room. Inducing despair wasn't the intent of the talk, but that didn't matter—speaking honestly about the current and near-future state of the global climate can be devastating for the listener. It's not just climate, of course. One of the unfortunate realities of the BANI environment is that it's easy to find myriad examples of a world gone mad.

Rage-Farming

Our tools let us access images, video, and depictions of crises instantly and often without any substantive context. It turns out that we are, apparently, quite eager to consume that material, so our connections just give us more.

Modern civilization has gotten quite good at hijacking biological functions that shape our behavior. Take the consumption of food, for example. Humans evolved such that our growing brains needed more nutritionally dense (but comparatively rare in the prehistoric environment) fats and sugars; consequently, we developed a biological response to consume as much of these as possible when they are available.[8] In conditions where such nutrients are abundant, such as the modern world, the result is overconsumption and endemic health crises. We may know objectively that flavored tortilla chips and gummy bears aren't good for us, but deeply rooted neurobehavioral systems say "more, please."

Our media environment works in quite a similar way, only instead of chips and candy, we are given anxiety and fear, *because that's what our brains respond to.* We get stimulated in ways that provoke us. It's not that we necessarily want to see upsetting things; it's that—for good evolutionary reasons, mind you—our brains are more sensitive to recognizing threats than to recognizing joy. There's a great deal more immediate risk in ignoring signs of a nearby saber-toothed tiger than ignoring the laughter of children. That neural wiring remains, even after the saber-toothed tigers have gone extinct.

Neuroscientists have long recognized that the brain responds to negative emotional stimuli more rapidly than to positive, and media curation algorithms have learned to push that kind of stuff to the top of the queue.[9] In our socioeconomic-technological environment, getting and holding attention is a commonplace way to make money. Digital attention-seeking methods (such as algorithmic feeds in social media) rely heavily on stimulating our anxieties to pull clicks. With good reason: according to a study in *Nature Human Behaviour*, negative words in headlines consistently generate more clicks (hence more money) than do positive words.[10]

There's even jargon for it: "rage-baiting" or "rage-farming."[11] Rage-farming turns out to be fairly profitable—to enrage is to engage.[12] And it's startlingly easy to trigger anger in people online. It's not always "irrational" anger, by the way: some individuals seem eager to be outraged, to be sure, but there are plenty of people who derive joy out of upsetting others and will say whatever they can to cause hurt. Moreover, there are plenty of people who embrace particular positions about social or political issues in part because they insult or offend groups that they hold in contempt.[13] Studies show that negative political commentary in social media is twice as likely to "go viral" than positive statements.[14]

Rage-farming and other forms of click generation and algorithmic manipulation aren't just the tools of socially maladjusted young males and professional trolls paid by a hostile foreign power. Legacy media outlets like newspapers and journals do this, too. Our social and informational universe overflows with sources that grab and hold our attention by making us feel Anxious.

Also, these sources often lie.

Alternative Realities

The BANI Future is one where it's functionally impossible to tell the difference between reality and falsehood. We aren't *quite* there yet, but we will be in the coming years. We are quickly heading toward a world where the conventional mechanisms for determining what's real no longer work. That gives many of us nightmares.

A short example: By the 2010s, it was possible to use various digital media tools to create a photograph or video showing an event that never happened. One common method of verification was whether there were multiple images or recordings of that event—generating a single or small number of digital fakes was plausible, but creating hundreds or thousands, each from a different angle, in a different format, taken at slightly different times, was extraordinarily difficult, even impossible. The more pictures or videos you had of an event, the more you could trust that it actually happened.

With the continued development of generative AI image and video creation, what was once nearly impossible can now be readily done with a small number of personal computers. By the 2030s, it will likely be possible to do with a phone (or whatever replaces the phone). Will it all be believable? We are approaching a point where belief in anything will first depend on what you accept as plausible reality. It will no longer be "If I didn't see it, I wouldn't believe it"; it will be "If I didn't believe it, I wouldn't see it."

The BANI world is surrounded by what we might think of as *malinformation*, a broad category of bad knowledge that encompasses misinformation (which may or may not be intentionally false), disinformation (motivated, intentional falsehoods), hoaxes, exaggerations, pseudoscience, and more. Not all malinformation is consciously hostile. Malinformation may come from a need to be first with a news story (accuracy can be fixed later, but there's only one "first to report") or from incorrect or incomplete sources. It may be a joke gone awry. But malinformation has very much become a way to increase anxiety intentionally. It may come from a desire or need to deceive, to knowingly relay falsehoods in order to discredit an opponent, to boost your own position, or even because, as the saying goes, *some people just want to watch the world burn.*

In coming years, it's possible that the mix of immersive, augmented, and AI-enabled media will require overwhelming levels of skepticism and scrutiny. It's also possible that most of us will just give up, accepting all information and reality as contingent, and going along with whatever fits our mood or ideology. We may even create an environment where the only recordings you can trust are the ones you make yourself, so you have to record everything.

The BANI Panopticon

What do you call a world where just about everyone around you is recording just about everything? In 2004, Jamais called it a "participatory panopticon," referring to the 18th-century idea by British philosopher Jeremy Bentham of the panopticon: a prison where all cells could be constantly watched. In subsequent years, the notion of the panopticon broke out of prison and has become a common term for a society of constant surveillance. But if we're all doing it to each other, Jamais reasoned, it must be a *participatory* panopticon. In 2004, the idea of everyone carrying a constantly networked high-quality video camera was fanciful; today, it's basic reality.

The low-level discomfort about being subject to constant (but largely casual) observation sets the baseline for privacy anxiety in the BANI Future. To a degree, the advent of generative AI image and video technology has *lessened* the impact of surveillance; a single video of an incident offers diminishing value as evidence. We are increasingly under observation by authorities, companies, and our peers, even as it's getting increasingly difficult to distinguish reality from falsehood. But the BANI panopticon is much less about people using ubiquitous cameras, and much more about our digital tools making it possible to see us in entirely new—and often unexpected—ways.

In 2021, a drug dealer in Liverpool, UK, was identified when he posted a picture of his hand holding a block of cheese, allowing the police to scan his fingerprints from the photo.[15] The criminal used methods of avoiding being identified that had worked in the pre-BANI world: turning off location data, not taking any pictures of his face, and using encrypted messaging with a pseudonym. None of these mattered when image analysis could extract fingerprint data from a basic photograph. "His love of Stilton cheese" was his undoing, according to the lead detective—all very amusing, were it not for the implications. What else might we be unintentionally showing in photos—not just new ones, but any pictures we've taken over the past couple of decades?

The BANI panopticon goes far beyond image analysis. There are AI-based processes able to create useful representations of individuals based on entirely "anonymous" data. Tools like probabilistic identifiers rely on patterns found in anonymized collections of data that, in combination, can produce a sketch of a particular individual's behavior. Nothing about these identifiers comes from clear, specific sources of information; it's all based on AI-derived intersections of various behavioral models. The accuracy of these kinds of systems can vary dramatically, with some companies claiming close to 95 percent accuracy.

In a world where even anonymous data can be used to identify individuals, it's not surprising that there's been rapid growth in the variety of tools of digital deception. Although these systems may sometimes be used to explicitly add "noise" to the collection of data about an individual as a form of brute-force privacy camouflage—sometimes referred to as "poisoning the data stream"—users increasingly rely on deception software to craft alternative narratives about themselves.

Tools for altering and masking appearance and voice allow for everything from minor "clean-up" facial fixes to the total substitution of a radically different age or gender. In its simplest form, it's social cosplay. In its more advanced versions, it could be considered making data decoys. This all might make things worse, but at least it keeps some of it under our own control.

AMOC Time

And then there's the climate.

The intersection between anthropogenic climate disruption and the elements of BANI could fill multiple volumes. Many of the consequences of global warming (whether near term or long term) are anxiety inducing, to be sure. Most of those, however, are understandable, with fairly straightforward effects and responses—sea level increase, for example. Definitely a bad thing, but something that's comparatively easy to explain and to think about. To really get to the consequences that keep climate researchers awake at night, you have to look for the impacts that are simultaneously overwhelming in scale and nearly unstoppable, impacts that go well beyond anything we've experienced. Of these, one stands out: the Atlantic meridional overturning circulation, or AMOC.[16]

The global thermohaline circulation ("thermohaline" meaning hot and salty) is the main current in Earth's oceans, moving heat around and spreading salinity. It has two big components: the Southern Ocean overturning circulation, which moves water around in the southern Pacific Ocean, and the AMOC, which operates in the northern Atlantic ("meridional" refers to meridians, lines on maps, but here specifically north–south flow). These circulations move water around but also move dissolved minerals, organic carbon, and oxygen. They are pretty critical for the planet's health.

The one in the Atlantic—the AMOC—has a special added responsibility. It moves warmth from the equator, up the Gulf Stream, below Greenland, then splits in two, with one flow returning to the equator, and the other looping alongside Great Britain and up along the Nordic countries, into the Greenland Sea, then back. The warmer water running up the western side of Europe warms the air, in turn keeping the weather nicer than it would be at those latitudes elsewhere in the world. It's a big reason why London doesn't have weather similar to Winnipeg and Rome isn't like Chicago, despite being at the same latitudes.

The problem is that Greenland ice sheets are melting and dumping cold freshwater into the North Atlantic, on top of the AMOC. There are signs that an increase in meltwater will interrupt the AMOC, either reducing its volume or cutting it off entirely. A total collapse isn't a certainty this century, but some models do support the possibility; the last time the AMOC collapsed, about 130,000 years ago, there were subsequent ice sheets as far south as New York. A significant weakening of the AMOC, however, has a very high likelihood and could potentially happen by mid-century. When it starts, it will be essentially impossible to stop.

If the AMOC heat flow to Europe weakens, what happens? Europe gets cooler, to begin with (although temperatures still won't match other cities at those latitudes unless there's a full collapse). Precipitation rates change and largely decline. Those two changes, right there, would wreak havoc on European agriculture. Storms would likely be stronger and less predictable—with the potential for cyclonic superstorms with near-hurricane winds. This all wouldn't happen overnight, so people have time to move—add Northern Europeans to the list of climate migrants. With all of this, we also have disruptions of supply chains, industrial production, and other more prosaic concerns.

Some models suggest that a disruption of the AMOC would greatly lessen the amount of North Atlantic plankton, a bottom-of-the-food-chain species that every other creature in the northern Atlantic Ocean ultimately depends on. And because climate is a global system, the change in the AMOC would have knock-on effects around the world—the heat that's not going to Europe has to go somewhere. It may even put the Southern Ocean overturning circulation at risk. A weakening of the AMOC would eventually change the timing and location of monsoonal rains that South Asian agriculture depends on.

To be clear, as of the time of writing, the scientific consensus is that the AMOC is not yet showing signs of weakening. But even the scientists arguing that the AMOC isn't slowing now agree that it will happen;[17] not knowing how soon causes its own kind of dread. When the AMOC does start to slow, the cascade of collapse will be irreversible. No amount of electric cars or wind farms will fix this.

And Then It Got Worse

We warned the reader at the outset that this could be a difficult chapter. The BANI world is inherently challenging; we wouldn't be talking about a transition away from VUCA and toward BANI if the dangers of the world hadn't leveled up. Jamais included "Anxious" in BANI precisely because he saw the stress and (too often) trauma so many people, of all ages, around the world, have been experiencing as the result of this chaos. Diving into what that means would never be easy.

But all is not lost. We'll get into the possible responses and strategies—what we're calling "Positive BANI" or "BANI+"—in the latter half of the book. But just as a bit of foreshadowing: in a BANI Future, **hope** remains as present and as important as ever. Not hope in the sense of wishful thinking or belief without evidence, but hope as the recognition that, in nearly every situation we currently and will face in a BANI world, **we know what to do to reduce the harm**. The challenge facing us isn't trying to figure out what steps we should take; it's trying to figure out how to make sure we take them.

The twist here is that, particularly with climate, the amount of effort we put into action to reduce the harm may not match the amount of change that results. At best, it's a confusing reality. Even the most ambitious plans and strategies will have to grapple with the Nonlinear nature of the BANI Future.

4

Nonlinear

Out of Control

NONLINEAR: In BANI, "nonlinear" refers to a system, or interconnected systems, displaying apparently disconnected or disproportionate cause and effect. Perhaps other systems interfere or obscure, or maybe there's hidden hysteresis: enormous delays between the visible input and the visible output. In a nonlinear world, results of actions taken, or not taken, can end up being wildly out of balance. Small decisions end up with massive consequences, good or bad. Or we put forward enormous amounts of effort, pushing and pushing yet with little to see for it.

We may think of nonlinearity in mathematical and scientific terms, but in BANI it's a somewhat more metaphorical concept. It ultimately boils down to there being visible—and meaningful—imbalances in key systems. When small triggers elicit huge consequences, when significant efforts show little result, or when there's unexpected lag between cause and effect, we have BANI nonlinearity.

The Age of Nonlinear

One of the prime characteristics of a BANI world is a recognized imbalance between cause and effect, whether caused by obscure physical systems, overly complex interconnections, blatant hoarding of political or economic power, or something else. Such imbalances are not new; what is novel about the current moment (and the BANI Future) is the degree to which these imbalances shape fundamental aspects of our existence, and the ways in which these imbalances—these nonlinearities—interweave with other manifestations of BANI in our lives.

Although the term itself may be less familiar, nonlinearity is a well-known concept. Most of us are aware of the notion of the "butterfly effect," the idea that a small change, such as the flapping of a butterfly wing, can lead to enormous consequences, such as a hurricane or tornado. Alternatively, it can refer to the 1952 Ray Bradbury story "A Sound of Thunder," in which a time traveler steps on a prehistoric butterfly back during the Age of Dinosaurs, thereby transforming all of subsequent history. This wasn't the original use of "butterfly effect," but it is equally relevant. Some might remember the proverb from Benjamin Franklin's *Poor Richard's Almanack* (and other poets and writers) about nails and battles:

> For want of a nail the shoe was lost;
> For want of a shoe the horse was lost;
> For want of a horse the battle was lost;
> For the failure of battle the kingdom was lost;—
> All for the want of a horse-shoe nail.[1]

Although this may seem like a failure cascade (as described in chapter 2), the critical difference is the *divergence of scale*. The cause (a lost horseshoe nail) and the effect (a lost kingdom) differ enormously in scale, but the chain of causation in the story remains clear. In reality, something like this would very likely go unrecognized, and the changing of the political status be blamed on military strategies, the king's policies, or (depending on the time and culture) divine preference.

Unfortunately, the BANI framework denies us the luxury of attributing unexpected and unwanted outcomes to the supernatural.

Nonetheless, nonlinearity remains a much more recognizable phenomenon than we might expect. We're surrounded by it, and it has played a major role in recent history.

- The COVID-19 pandemic was a nonlinear experience, one that biologists and epidemiologists had long warned us about; the concept of "flattening the curve" is inherently a war against nonlinearity.

- The pervasiveness of social media and its outsized influence on emotions (as talked about in the previous chapter) have run roughshod over social, political, even business norms.

- The political impact of a very small number of people with very large amounts of money has become more visible and often more callous, even vindictive.

- The structure of modern postindustrial/market capitalism increasingly demands a nonlinear unending growth.

- Most seriously, the recent era has made abundantly clear the global differences made by a seemingly very small increase in average temperature: we see around us, with growing intensity and frequency, real-world examples of the impacts of global warming–induced climate change . . . and we're barely up 1.5°C over preindustrial levels.

Living with Nonlinearity

Let's put this in the BANI context. In a nonlinear world, causes and effects are not proportional or consistently predictable. Small actions can trigger surprisingly wild outcomes. Chain reactions and unexpected feedback loops will become disturbingly common. Seemingly minor issues can ripple through nonlinear systems and create counterintuitive havoc. Logic will fail but will do so unpredictably. Expectations must be tempered. Even the best predictive models will be suspect. Predictive forecasting with consistent accuracy will be essentially impossible.

Nonlinearity is often quite hostile to conventional organizations. It can be overwhelming and confusing and lead to fragmented or contradictory decisions. Fragmented decision-making and nonlinearity in isolation can lead different parts of large organizations to become entangled and out of sync. Because nonlinear systems often involve delayed consequences where the impacts of decisions take a long time to materialize, it can be difficult to attach actions with outcomes. People who change their behavior but see no results within what they perceive as a reasonable timeframe will become frustrated.

In nonlinear systems, resource needs may shift unpredictably, meaning that leaders could allocate too much or too little to key areas of impact. What seems like a low-priority area may suddenly become critical.

Nonlinear can be seen as a partner to Brittle, in particular with the idea of a cascade of failure. As the previously mentioned "want of a nail" proverb suggests, a greater collapse can be the inevitable result of a very small mistake. The nonlinearity seen when a small cause has massive, cascading results seems to be a common part of the age of BANI. This isn't a surprise; global society is deeply cross-connected, and many critical systems are entirely interdependent.

Nonlinear is just as linked to Anxious, as the discontinuities inherent to nonlinear systems—and the unexpected changes that result—are often profoundly unsettling. We tend to think in terms of linear relationships, where cause and effect are both evident and clearly related. When a tiny change has a catastrophic result, or (arguably worse) when enormous effort has very little consequence, we worry that we've done something wrong. Very often, we can't see the larger web of connections that might make a system behave in unwanted ways.

Nonlinear will frequently lead to Incomprehensible results. If a system has seemingly always behaved in a linear fashion, but suddenly offers up nonlinear outcomes, we can find that baffling, even frightening. A system shifting from apparently linear to apparently nonlinear often represents something fundamental changing in the drivers of that system. It may be a change in technology and culture leading to an actual evolution of that system; it may be that those changes lead to a superficial linearity evaporating, exposing that the underlying system has always been nonlinear.

Pandemonium

Nonlinearity is ubiquitous in biological systems. The growth and collapse of populations, the effectiveness of vaccination, swarm behavior, and the spread of pandemics—all of these have a strongly nonlinear aspect. From outside, they're fascinating to watch; from within, they're staggering to experience, as we have discovered.

Jamais first introduced BANI to the world in the midst of a crisis of nonlinearity with COVID-19. The scale and scope of this pandemic went far beyond everyday experience, and the speed at which the infection spread over its first few months was, for many, shocking. For a disturbingly long time, the increase in worldwide cases trended toward the exponential. Images like residents locked into apartment buildings in China and refrigerator trucks used as storage for corpses in New York compounded the fear.

And while science and governments eventually controlled COVID-19 (at least as compared to its early days), the chances of a new pandemic emerging are just as great as, possibly even greater than, they were pre-COVID. H5N1 bird flu is a perennial threat (and may even become a serious problem over the lifetime of this book), but other pathogens (both viruses and bacteria) abound, evolve quickly, and can take us by surprise. It just takes the right swap of nucleotides to enable an animal virus to infect humans, itself an example of disproportionality of power.

At a basic level, pandemics and epidemics offer a manifestation of nonlinearity recognized widely enough that we use it as a metaphor for a sudden and rapid uptick in popularity—a video or post "going viral." We see how quickly something can whip through a classroom or workplace. Just one or two people getting it, at first, then many more, then (just about) everyone. Exercise for the reader: Did the last two sentences refer to colds or memes?

We've even seen the remarkable emergence of a deadly pathogen in an entirely digital setting. In 2005, the massively multiplayer online game *World of Warcraft* had an event that remains a fascinating case study of infection.[2] A new "boss" fight included an attack on player characters called "Corrupted Blood." Although the damaging effects of the attack would eventually stop, any other player character near the initial target would get infected by the attack, too, then spread it to others nearby. For the very high-level characters meant to be involved in the fight, the attack was dangerous but not catastrophic.

But when the infection was brought (accidentally, at least at first) to crowded noncombat settings like cities, it would spread rapidly through the hundreds of characters there at the moment, few of which were high-enough level to survive the attack. Shopkeepers and other nonplayer characters could be infected but not die, effectively becoming asymptomatic carriers, passing the disease to any player character that walked by. Most people avoided crowded spaces (in game) in order to avoid accidentally contracting Corrupted Blood; some players used characters with healing abilities to serve as de facto "first responders"; a few people would get infected and bring the disease to previously clear locations, because they found it funny or simply didn't care.

This may have been just an amusing pre-BANI event, except it turned out to have real epidemiological value. Most models of pandemic spread rely on large-scale averages of human behavior. With Corrupted Blood, researchers could see in detail the various ways in which people would behave in a deadly outbreak. In subsequent years, the Corrupted Blood event helped researchers working on the spread of SARS, and it served as an important way to understand behavioral choices in the early days of COVID.[3]

Corrupted Blood gave us a preview of the social and cultural impacts of a pandemic like COVID-19, a foreshadowing of a BANI world with colorful graphics and cartoon monsters.

Follow Me

Online nonlinearity isn't restricted to massively multiplayer games. We see nonlinearity on a daily basis in social media, from the viral spread of cat videos to the "critical mass" swarming of social media platforms. In some cases, the impact of nonlinear connection online isn't limited to comment sections or even medical journals.

Time and again, individual posts to social media networks can catch the right combination of timing, audience, and popular mood to go quickly from an offhand comment or short video to a message examined closely in boardrooms, news desks, and academic conferences. The post need not be serious or truthful; it just needs to be infectious—catchy, even. The situations that enable a casual post to go viral are capricious and very hard to replicate. Moreover, exposure to similar messages can easily trigger a resistance to them—we might think of these as memetic antibodies.

Although it's been hijacked to mean "an amusing image, usually with ironic text," the word *meme* has a somewhat more complex history. Created in 1976 by the evolutionary biologist Richard Dawkins, the meme was meant as an analog to the gene: a core unit (of mind rather than body) that could combine and replicate.[4] An impressive landscape of ideas emerged from that notion, one of memeplexes and narratives and cognitive ecologies. Still, as a science, memetics remains less like chemistry and more like alchemy.

That doesn't mean it's all random. As we've noted, algorithmic curation can take great advantage of how the human brain responds to various kinds of stimuli and, in doing so, elicit changes to behavior. Individual creators on TikTok and similar social media platforms, even those with relatively small followings, have driven unexpected corporate shifts—such as altering food menus or sparking product redesigns.

Algorithm-driven platforms amplify small inputs unpredictably. A sixty-second TikTok can produce millions in sales or provoke a PR crisis. That is to say, social media platforms are nonlinear amplifiers. Small, random posts can go viral and have massive consequences, while carefully crafted messages might be ignored. Algorithms often boost polarizing content, creating self-reinforcing cycles.

But algorithms, while powerful, are not always required. Human swarms online can have unanticipated results. In 2021, a Reddit group triggered an unexpected, disproportionate surge in stock prices, particularly GameStop, catching hedge funds and Wall Street by surprise.[5] So-called meme stocks became a market in and of themselves, expanding to include meme-based cryptocurrencies. One of these "memecoins" even became the unlikely icon of a major effort to dismantle much of the American government.[6]

Some Are More Equal Than Others

The difficulty that humans have in really understanding disproportionality can have serious sociopolitical consequences. Multiple studies across the 2010s and into the 2020s have shown that, although most Americans believe that there's too much income inequality in the United States,[7] their assumptions about what that looks like are seriously mistaken. People massively underestimate just how much wealth inequality exists in America (with similar findings globally[8]), even in comparison to what they see as "ideal."

A 2014 study is representative.[9] The people surveyed in the United States stated that the ideal ratio of CEO pay to unskilled laborer pay is 7:1, and they estimated that the reality was more like 30:1. The actual ratio at that point was 354:1. A 2024 study (on estimates of top 1 percent income) referred to this repeated misperception of outsized income as "scope insensitivity"—after a certain size, everything is "big" or "rich," and the objective material differences tend not to matter as much as the relative differences.[10] Both 30:1 and 354:1 are too big when the ideal is 7:1, even if the difference in reality is dramatic.

This imbalance of wealth has practical implications. In early 2025, research by the financial information firm Moody's Analytics found that, in the United States, the top 10 percent of earners—those making $250,000 or more—accounted for just under 50 percent of all spending. In comparison, three decades ago they accounted for about 36 percent.[11] The bottom 80 percent were much more conservative with their spending. Consequently, any significant disruption that prompted the wealthiest Americans to curtail spending would have a disproportionately large impact on the national economy.

Outsized income inequality has been with us for decades, and the remarkable underestimation of high wealth levels predates the BANI era. What is very much an element of the BANI world are the novel ways in which that high wealth exerts political power. Wealth has always meant power, but it hasn't always meant *this kind* of power.

For decades, we've seen large-scale donations to political campaigns; we've seen the political power wealth can have over media platforms (*New York Journal* publisher William Randolph Hearst, allegedly, to a reporter on the eve of the Spanish-American War: "You furnish the pictures, and I'll furnish the war"[12]). Rarely, however, do we see people with multiple levers of control over commerce and ideas take an active and visible role in shaping government policy, even while maintaining a position in charge of information distribution (with control over national newspapers and social media technologies). Or shape the tactics in a war halfway around the planet, as with Starlink and the Russian invasion of Ukraine.[13]

Nonlinearity in the form of disproportionate cause and effect is clearly visible across the world of politics, especially international politics. How much did the Russian hack on the US elections of 2016 cost, compared to the impact it had on the world?

We might even think of terrorism as nonlinear warfare, in terms of the money and effort required to undertake it versus the money and effort spent to spot it, prevent it, and/or avenge it.

But arguably the most disturbing example of nonlinearity in politics, as well as an example of what happens with disproportionate social power, is seen in *stochastic terrorism*. The term emerged in the pre-BANI era but rose in visibility with the 2016 US presidential campaign, with one candidate musing about "Second Amendment people" should the other candidate win.[14]

There's no formal definition of stochastic terrorism, but the common understanding is this, as described by Heather Timmons in 2018: "The use of mass communication to incite random actors to carry out violent or terrorist acts that are statistically predictable but individually unpredictable. . . . Someone, somewhere, would react—it's just hard to predict who and when."[15] A person with a highly visible platform does not need to give specific instructions to have their goals carried out, only imply that they might be pleased if something caused it to happen.

This is not a new idea, of course. In the late 12th century, King Henry II wondered aloud, "Will no one rid me of this turbulent priest?" regarding the archbishop of Canterbury Thomas Becket. Although it was never given as a direct command, four knights subsequently traveled from Normandy to Canterbury and killed Becket.[16] However, leaders (and other high-visibility people) have far greater platforms today with which to grumble about opponents. Merely being mentioned in a negative way by a high-profile political figure is enough to cause multiple incidents of doxing, swatting (calling in a police emergency that might result in the victim being killed by heavily armed SWAT officers), and other forms of distributed harassment.[17]

Wait for It

Stochastic terrorism may hit a little bit too close to home for some of us, so let's pull back to a big-picture view.

We'll start with a reality that is unsurprising when looked at closely but probably not that obvious to the wider populace: **stopping the anthropogenic emission of carbon won't make Earth cooler**. Generally speaking, we seem to assume that if you stop doing something bad, the bad consequences go away. When problems don't just disappear, we look for someone to blame. Take inflation: when the post-COVID global spike in inflation settled down, many people in the United States and elsewhere appeared to assume that prices would "go back to normal"—that is, go back to preinflation levels. The reality is that a decline in inflation means only that prices stop increasing so quickly. However, the ignorance—or rejection—of the reality that prices did not and would not come down had serious political consequences.

Along those same lines, carbon dioxide takes thousands of years to cycle out of the atmosphere with normal processes; the carbon that's there will continue to work to retain atmospheric heat. Doing everything we can to cut carbon emissions to zero will not bring temperatures back down in this millennium, no matter how fast or how thoroughly we do it. But it's actually more complicated, more *nonlinear*, than that.

One of the initial triggers for the inclusion of nonlinearity in what became BANI was the obscure (but important) idea of "climate hysteresis." Hysteresis is the term for a disconnect between evident cause and evident effect. The cause and effect are still there, still real, but there's a lag between them. That's hysteresis. Hysteresis is sometimes used in parallel with "path dependence." The critical aspect of this concept is that, regardless of any delay, the connection is locked in—the cause *will* lead to the effect, no matter the lag.

To put it simply, there is a delay between changes in concentration of greenhouse gases in the atmosphere and changes in surface temperature and precipitation.[18] The lag seems to be more pronounced for scenarios in which changes in concentration are stopped or reduced. An increase in greenhouse gas concentration (e.g., the parts per million of carbon dioxide) forces an increase in temperature, but that increase might not fully happen for around a decade. Stable or even reduced concentrations have an even slower lag in results: temperatures will keep *increasing* for years, possibly decades, even if we stop adding greenhouse gases to the atmosphere.

What does all that mean? There are all sorts of geophysical implications, particularly around polar temperatures and global levels of precipitation, but let's focus here on the human consequences, like the political impacts. As seen with inflation, this kind of nonlinear change is wickedly difficult for political systems to grapple with. Any actions we undertake to reduce, eliminate, or even reverse global carbon emissions won't see a change in temperature trajectory for years. This is politically problematic in ways that humanity hasn't had to deal with at this scale.

Imagine the kinds of social and economic changes necessary for a cessation of carbon emissions: the elimination of fossil fuels; changes to food consumption, including the likely elimination of meat from ranched animals; increased living density, allowing for more energy and transit efficiency; elimination of or massive reductions in air travel; elimination of or massive reductions in cross-ocean shipping; the list goes on.

Now imagine convincing a large majority of the planet to make these kinds of changes, but then temperatures keep rising and climate conditions continue to worsen. How will people respond? What kind of backlash are leaders likely to experience in that kind of situation?

For many people, the idea that *stopping the bad thing doesn't make things better* is simply incomprehensible.

5
Incomprehensible
Stop Making Sense

INCOMPREHENSIBLE: In BANI, "incomprehensible" refers to being unable to decipher the "why" of an event, phenomenon, or process. We witness events and decisions that seem illogical or senseless, whether because the origins are too long ago, or too unspeakable, or just too absurd. We look at a process and find it too densely interconnected to be able to easily see its core logic. We try to find answers but the answers don't make sense. *How* the situation works—the mechanical components, the political balance, the underlying software—may be functionally understandable, but the motivation, reasoning, or logic remains elusive.

In this situation, additional information is no guarantee of improved understanding. More data—even "big data"—can be counterproductive, overwhelming our ability to understand the world, making it hard to distinguish noise from signal. Incomprehensibility can be, in effect, one end state of "information overload."

The Age of Incomprehensible

The last element of BANI, Incomprehensible, is arguably the most confusing. Many people immediately reject the idea that something cannot be understood. From that perspective, the argument that we can't comprehend a concept, a process, or an event is implicitly insulting, both to the individual and to humanity in general.

Although science regularly discovers new facts about the universe that may not be initially explainable, the discussion of "incomprehensible" in BANI does not really refer to things that cannot yet be empirically understood. In BANI, incomprehensible means events, processes, or behaviors where the underlying driver does not make sense. We may rationalize it by arguing that the driver in question is extremely complex, or hidden, or counterintuitive, but in the end the things we call "incomprehensible" are the things that make us stop and say "What the [heck]?"

Let's start with something comparatively innocuous. A common manifestation of incomprehensibility is with systems and processes that appear to be broken, but still work, or are nonfunctional without any apparent logic or reason. It's a programmer cliché to encounter software that operates only when an apparently nonfunctional, seemingly unrelated line remains in the code. Take it out, the program crashes or doesn't compile. Leave it in—even though it doesn't *seem* to do anything—and the program works. Logically, there is some underlying process or interaction between routines that forces this outcome, but those causes are too complex or diffuse to discover readily with the tools and knowledge at hand.

How about something more complicated? Incomprehensibility may be a root cause of the political divisions in the United States and elsewhere. A recurring theme in discussions with voters across the political spectrum in the United States is the fundamental inability to understand *why* the other side behaves, believes, and votes as it does. One consequence of this lack of comprehension is the frequent assertion that the other side is simply "stupid" or "evil."

This incomprehensibility may be tightly woven into our political system. The proliferation of supporters of a person or party who behave in ways that, at best, act like team sports rivalries, and at worst seem like cults, seems frustratingly inexplicable. Or the recurring question of why voters in a given area or in given socioeconomic conditions would vote for a candidate or party that repeatedly causes them harm. For many observers, it's utterly irrational.

And if "incomprehensible" is still too loaded a term, think about similar phrases we see with alarming frequency: *senseless, absurd, ridiculous, unthinkable*. This is the language of a world where things have stopped working the way we expect them to, a world that has stopped making sense. The age of incomprehensible is a point where the senseless is commonplace and the ridiculous has become almost banal.

This is a problem for individuals and organizations alike. In an Incomprehensible world, the sheer volume and ragged ambiguity of information can lead to paralysis, poor decisions, and fragmented patterns of response. Leaders must confront and communicate the reality that not everything can be understood—something all the more important and difficult when that reality is not acceptable to significant portions of the people being led. Inevitably, some demagogues will claim that they can comprehend the incomprehensible, delivering a message that is temporarily comforting but treacherous in the long run.

One fundamental risk in this is the pervasive danger of information overload and of misinterpretation of data. Complex systems will produce patterns that are confusing and all too easy to misunderstand. Incomprehensible systems will bombard us with more data than we can process. Conflicting or incomplete data will inevitably lead to us doubting our decision-making. Incomprehensibility is a catalyst for an Anxious world.

In an Incomprehensible world, leaders will be tempted to rely too heavily on experts, algorithms, or AI systems to help them make sense of the dilemmas they face. While potentially useful, such tools and expertise will be limited in value, for myriad reasons. In many cases, it boils down to the information sources these experts and systems rely on having become out of date much more quickly than anticipated. Chaos makes planning based on past patterns nearly impossible.

In this environment, the stories we tell ourselves about our world—our *narratives*—are incredibly important. These narratives are how we make sense of things, but amid chaos, it will be particularly difficult for leaders to control the narrative about their organization and its clarity of direction. Everyone will be struggling to make sense of confusing, complex, and competing storylines growing out of current experiences. If leaders lose their compelling narrative, they lose trust. The fundamental dilemma for leaders will be how to lead, even when they cannot fully comprehend.

If it's hard to understand what's happening, if it's difficult to create a meaningful narrative about your world and your goals, *if the present simply doesn't make sense*, it's staggeringly difficult to think usefully about the future. Imagining and planning for complex possible futures is challenging enough in normal times. In a BANI world of relentless chaos, imagining the future is almost unthinkable.

Unthinkable

Herman Kahn's 1960 book, *On Thermonuclear War*, brought the term "thinking the unthinkable" into (relatively) common discourse, and his 1962 follow-up book of that very name drove the point home. Herman Kahn was a physicist, a futurist, and one of the inventors of scenario-planning methodology. He spent much of the 1960s imagining the consequences in detail of global thermonuclear war, the conditions that might lead to the use of nuclear weapons, and the resulting aftermath. In the decades since, the term "unthinkable" has seen wider use but is nearly always applied to the (usually) unwanted consequences of a massive violation of fundamental norms.

The destructive power of nuclear weapons truly goes beyond what most of us can envision, even when surrounded by high-definition video of massive explosions and other consequences of war. As memories fade of what it felt like at the height of the Cold War nuclear arms race, it's possible to start thinking of nuclear weapons as being just a bigger boom. The 2020s will see the deaths of the last people who might have adult recollections of the news of the bombing of Hiroshima and Nagasaki. Even those who witnessed an atmospheric nuclear test are diminishing in number; the partial test-ban treaty of 1963 moved all nuclear tests underground. For the vast majority of people on the planet, our understanding of the scale of destruction coming from nuclear weapons derives from grainy historical footage and movie special effects of varying quality and realism.

But the risk of nuclear war is greater than ever before. The *Bulletin of the Atomic Scientists*, which has since 1947 operated the Doomsday Clock, set the clock to ninety seconds to midnight in 2023, then bumped it to eighty-nine seconds in 2025—the closest to catastrophe they've ever seen.[1] But as our remembrance of nuclear things past grows hazy, it's all too easy to imagine that using a nuclear weapon or two might be useful, even potentially a dramatic way to get everyone to calm down. That's called "escalate to de-escalate," and it's a real strategy.

Over the lifetime of this book, it's entirely possible that a limited use of nuclear weapons may happen. Even the most restricted battlefield use of small nuclear devices (still several times larger than the bombs dropped at the end of World War II) would have enormous environmental, economic, and humanitarian consequences. If nuclear weapons—even just one—hit a populated region it would be an unprecedented global disaster, with repercussions that would last decades.

The logic of nuclear deterrence, simply put, is "If you try to destroy me, I will destroy you, too." To the surprise of many, this threat has worked since 1949 (when the Soviets built their first atomic bomb); the world has successfully avoided the post–World War II military use of a nuclear weapon, despite the best efforts of saber-rattling leaders, excitable demagogues, and mistaken satellites (see chapter 8). Specialists in the field debate as to how likely it is that deterrence will continue to hold true. It's unsettlingly easy for the leader of a nation armed with nuclear weapons to order their use.[2]

But there are, as of this writing, a bit more than 12,000 nuclear weapons available around the world. That's a comparatively low figure—in 1988, there were over 70,000 in the world.[3] Even that limited present-day number amounts to upward of three gigatons of explosive power hanging over our heads.[4] That said, on top of everything else that's happening in the world, it seems like very few people actually want to think about the possibility of a nuclear conflict. For most of us, it has become in every sense unthinkable.

"Unthinkable" echoes but is not the same as "unimaginable." The latter suggests that the topic at hand goes beyond what we might normally expect. "Unthinkable," conversely, suggests that the topic is so awful that the rational mind would want to reject it. Attempting to "think the unthinkable," as Kahn tasked himself to do in 1960, means being willing to imagine outcomes that a rational person would not accept—outcomes that are incomprehensible.

Absurd

Unthinkable may be a bit too much to deal with, so let's turn our attention to the absurd. If the BANI era truly flowered with the COVID-19 pandemic starting in 2020, the quintessential manifestation of Incomprehensible must be the large numbers of people rejecting, even demonizing, the creation and deployment of vaccinations against that same virus.

In the midst of the pandemic, some mistrust would be understandable, especially in communities (like African American) with histories of being the victims of unethical government medical experiments.[5] But the explosion of misinformation, outright lies, and sheer paranoia about vaccines, across demographic groups in the United States and elsewhere, went far beyond any plausibly rational response. The spread of antivaccine malinformation was accelerated by social media algorithms, and transformation of vaccine opposition into a partisan stance pushed it further. For many people in the United States and Europe, refusing the COVID-19 vaccines became a signifier of identity.

This had predictable results. In the United States, the number of deaths from COVID-19 in the demographic categories most likely to refuse vaccines was significantly greater than the number of COVID-19 deaths in more vaccine-acceptant communities.[6] What might seem a logical outcome, however, instead became yet more proof of conspiracies. Some partisan pundits even claimed that liberals caused conservatives to die disproportionately because they knew that liberal support for vaccines would make conservatives oppose them.[7]

Absurdities like the conspiracy theories surrounding COVID-19 vaccines have multiple origins. There is sometimes a kernel of rationality in the position, at least early on—in this case, both governments and the global pharmaceutical industry have ethically dubious histories. However, people and institutions with larger agendas can advocate for a position that has nothing to do with the objective reality of the situation and everything to do with gaining or holding onto social power. And perhaps most crucially, echo chambers and both an inability and unwillingness to hear contrary perspectives reinforce the belief over and over again. COVID-19 and vaccine misinformation greatly took advantage of algorithmic curation of social media showing people more of what they want to see and already believe.

Vaccine avoidance existed well before COVID-19, of course, and to the extent it had political salience, it was a particular subset of liberal that was most likely to subscribe to it. Unfortunately, the late-COVID era has resulted in an environment around the world where resistance among conservatives to immunization against COVID-19 has evolved to embrace a larger antivax position. Diseases thought to be dying out, especially childhood diseases, have been making a comeback in places where vaccination numbers have dropped below "herd immunity" levels.[8]

The development of vaccination was unquestionably one of the pivotal advances in human history. Diseases that killed millions could finally be defeated. Pandemics could be stopped before they could ever start. Vaccinations meant that humankind could finally eliminate smallpox, a 3,000-year-old virus that burned through civilizations across history. Throwing all of that away to show group affiliation on social media is the height of incomprehensibility.

Hallucinatory

Incomprehensibility seems to be intrinsic to the kind of artificial intelligence (AI) systems we're creating. As our AIs become more complicated, learn more, *do* more, the harder it can become to understand precisely how they reach their conclusions. This isn't just a technology riddle. As AI software becomes more tightly woven into our daily lives, we have to pay close attention to the ways in which complex algorithms can lead to biased outcomes, misinformation, and utter confusion. Code that learns from us can learn more than the intended lessons and rules.

This book is being written in a particularly wild moment in the development of AI. The pace of evolution of generative AI (and other neural-network technologies) has become so frantic that the AI world of ten years from now could look as different to us today as the AI world of twenty years past does. It's easy for technological speculation to age very poorly, however, so the focus here will be on broader concepts that will likely remain relevant.

Incomprehensibility in AI emerges when what we expect the systems to understand does not match what they produce:

- When the underlying connections in the neural network become so opaque that we end up with outcomes that are entirely "sensible" to the generative AI but seem to come out of nowhere for the human interlocutor

- When the underlying training data is itself problematic—full of human bias, or of very poor quality, or insufficient in scale

- When there are missing perspectives that haven't been fully turned into usable or accessible data, material critical to reaching accurate or less-biased results

- When training data is derived from material that was, in turn, created by a previous generative AI system, a problem referred to as "AI self-cannibalism"[9]

- When the output of an AI system mixes fact and fiction with the same authoritative voice

This last problem, that of generative AI "hallucinations" and "confabulations," may well be solved over the next decade (as might some of the others). Some specialists argue, however, that it's inherent to large language models (LLMs) and can't be eliminated, only adapted to.[10] But even if hallucinations become a nonissue, there's a risk in not knowing what assertions have been forbidden or excised from the system and whether that internal censorship is itself biased. Can the output be "fact based" when the facts in the training data are themselves in question?

The proliferation of generative AI systems offers a cornucopia of BANI stories. The economic challenges, the ethical problems, the underlying questions of ownership and consent, the enormous amount of energy required for even basic generative AI activity, all of these and more have characteristics demonstrating brittleness, triggering anxiety, and relying on nonlinear processes. But these aspects of generative AI aren't always incomprehensible—the "why" can often boil down to market behaviors and short-term profit mechanisms.

Incomprehensibility arises from an overreliance on AI output without fully understanding the parameters of what the systems can and cannot do. That is, it comes from giving AI more trust than is warranted. Humans presently have a bias toward believing AIs over their own conclusions. A 2016 set of experiments at Duke University tested whether people led by a robotic tour guide would, when a fire alarm went off, continue to follow the robot (that claimed it would lead them to safety) or take more obvious paths to escape the supposed fire.[11] In the first experiment, *all participants* followed the robot instead of their own thinking.

In the BANI Future, the evolution of the human relationship to AI may well be a bellwether for how we can adapt to rapid and fundamentally disruptive transformation on an even larger scale.

Rethinking the Unthinkable

But even while we wrestle with the absurd and hallucinatory, the unthinkable remains. Not just the threat of nuclear war, but another category of catastrophe that is far greater than we want to think about: anthropogenic climate change. It's not so much that we collectively don't understand what's causing global warming; it's that our collective refusal to do enough, fast enough, seems incomprehensible. Moreover, the scale and variety of the consequences of the climate emergency can go beyond what most people are able to wrap their minds around.

The previous BANI chapters have each offered an example of how their respective BANI term can be seen in climate change. Brittle talks about the West Antarctic Ice Shelf; Anxious talks about the Atlantic meridional overturning circulation; Nonlinear talks about climate hysteresis. Each of those topics may seem disturbing, but what makes this all so incomprehensible is that the multitude of events and dangers discussed *all happen together*, alongside myriad other challenges that will appear, large and small.

We know how to slow this process and how to stop it from getting worse; we have some good ideas about how we might eventually be able to reverse it. But it would be disruptive, expensive, and difficult. It would necessitate major changes to how we live our lives. It would challenge aspects of our identities and require unprecedented cooperation. We would be entirely uncertain about how long it will take and how much impact we'll have in time to avoid catastrophe.

To drive home how unwilling human society is to embrace beneficial—but highly disruptive—changes to save ourselves, something called geoengineering has moved from a somewhat esoteric and fanciful idea to techniques under consideration around the world. Geoengineering is the broad term for active steps to modify global climate systems in a way that reduces the impacts of climate change. The most well-known form is solar radiation management (also known as thermal geoengineering): blocking a small portion of incoming sunlight to keep temperatures down. The wilder initial versions of this idea included giant space mirrors, but the much more realistic ones being researched now include maintaining perpetual bright cloud coverage of the arctic and global-scale cooling by pumping a constant flow of reflective material into the stratosphere.

Once we begin to do so, however, we would need to continue the program—and expand it over time—until we have completely cleared the atmosphere of excess greenhouse gases. Simply going to zero carbon emissions wouldn't be enough; we would have to remove all of the CO_2 we've added to the atmosphere since the beginning of the Industrial Revolution. If we stopped the geoengineering program before doing so, we would see a rapid and dangerous temperature spike. Moreover, the results of an active geoengineering program will vary by region, with some places faring worse than others—the potential to trigger war is disturbingly high.

If that sounds somewhat insane, you're not alone in that conclusion. Jamais has been investigating the potential consequences of geoengineering since 2005, and it's his experience that the geoscientists and climatologists working on these technologies largely feel the same way. What they argue is we may well reach a point where the alternative is worse. Geoengineering is a tool of desperation—a consequence of ignoring the unthinkable.

That human civilization would decide to go for the radical and potentially dangerous techno-fix (that doesn't actually fix anything, just holds off catastrophe) instead of taking the more difficult—but ultimately more effective—steps to eliminate greenhouse gas emissions is, for most climate specialists, impossible to understand.

Jamais has looked at this topic in depth and even wrote a short book on it in 2009, which led to an invitation to speak on the subject at the US National Academies of Science, among other venues.[12] For those who have an interest in learning more about this topic, one of the better sources to check out is Oliver Morton's 2015 *The Planet Remade: How Geoengineering Could Change the World*.

An Incomprehensible Collision

Finally, the unthinkable idea of geoengineering runs headlong into the absurdity of conspiracy theories with "chemtrails," the claim that the clouds formed behind high-flying aircraft are actually some kind of chemical being sprayed over the populace. This misunderstanding of condensation trails ("contrails") originated in the late-night talk radio fever swamps of the 1990s. One supposed trigger for the theories was a 1996 strategy paper published within the US Air Force titled "Weather as a Force Multiplier: Owning the Weather in 2025," a speculation on the geopolitical impacts of an imagined future weather control technology.

When word emerged in 2013 that agencies of the US government (including the CIA, NASA, and NOAA) intended to fund preliminary research on geoengineering, conspiracy adherents connected the dots and concluded that chemtrails were real and either were a form of geoengineering or were using geoengineering/climate change as a cover for more nefarious doings. Like most conspiracy theories, the chemtrail claim is highly resistant to fact-based debunking, and adherents can be intense. After giving a talk on geoengineering at a conference in Berlin in 2014, Jamais was cornered by a chemtrail believer demanding that he "tell the truth" about the conspiracy. It was an unsettling moment.

What makes this situation ironic is that there *is* a connection between *contrails* and geoengineering, at least in a broad sense: contrails are water vapor, and water vapor plays a complex role in the global climate. The proliferation of high-altitude clouds formed by aircraft serves to both *reflect* heat from the sun and *trap* heat in the lower atmosphere. In the days after 9/11, when the United States grounded all aircraft, geoscientists could measure a distinct change in temperatures, particularly in places that normally had dense air traffic. Daytime temperatures were higher, while nighttime temperatures were lower—an increase in temperature range of about 2°C.[13]

In other words, contrails are an accidental form of geoengineering. Unfortunately, the cooling effect from reflecting solar radiation and the warming effect from trapping heat do not fully cancel each other out. On balance, contrails from air travel have a slight warming effect on the planet.[14]

It's likely that any future adoption of geoengineering-like technologies, by any country, will be met not just with the political fallout of disproportionate effects around the world but by online activists who see such efforts as sinister programs to spread chemicals to do . . . *something*, not as desperate measures to avoid even more dangerous outcomes.

Well, Now I'm Depressed

Congratulations, you've made it through the anxiety-creating half of the book. If you need to take a break, go ahead. The world will still be BANI when you come back (unfortunately).

The underlying dilemma of talking about the BANI world and the BANI Future is how to make a discussion of global brittleness, anxiety, nonlinearity, and incomprehensibility *honest* but *not overwhelming*. This echoes Jamais's ambivalence mentioned in chapter 3, about giving a climate presentation that made some audience members cry. Is it possible to talk frankly about the details of a BANI world without making the reader despondent? Do we need to reassure the reader that everything will be OK, even if we're not sure that's true?

Although we should not try to diminish the enormity of a BANI world and the BANI Future in order to make thinking about them less stressful, neither should we leave the reader with a counter-Panglossian sense that all is lost in this, the worst of all possible worlds.

What we need to do is, to use an old technology slogan, "embrace and extend." That is, offer a full-throated telling of the BANI story, but use that as a foundation for something more: more evocative, more illuminating, more hopeful. It's critical, however, to keep it in the BANI context, to continue to use the frameworks and language of the BANI concept to talk about something better.

So let's talk about Positive BANI.

PART II

Positive BANI

BANI, as initially constructed, describes a dire world. The age of chaos is not a comforting space. But that doesn't mean that the BANI Future can't be looked at from another perspective.

Coauthor Bob Johansen has worked with the VUCA framing for years, and in 2012, he offered a set of "Positive VUCA" terms (*Vision*, *Understanding*, *Clarity*, *Agility*) that would directly counter the more negative framings of VUCA classic. When Bob started using the BANI framing, he saw that there was space for a Positive BANI, too. Bob and Jamais collaborated on its creation.

Positive BANI (or BANI+) consists of four concepts that directly address—and counter—the four elements of BANI. As will be made clear, these are not intended as *solutions* for the challenges described by BANI but *responses* that allow us to remain resilient in a BANI world. The dilemmas brought by the BANI world are often not directly fixable. Perhaps they've gone on too long or are too embedded in global systems. They could be the emergent consequences of choices we can't—or don't want to—reverse. However, we can respond, adapt, and sometimes ameliorate.

The next four chapters will cover each of the countering ideas, in detail:

BANI	BANI+
Brittle is countered by	**Bendable**, with resilient clarity
Anxious is countered by	**Attentive**, with active empathy
Nonlinear is countered by	**Neuroflexible**, with practical improvisation
Incomprehensible is countered by	**Interconnected**, with full-spectrum thinking

The "B" in BANI+ is **Bendable**. Think adaptable, resilient, *flexive*. Not in a floppy, uncoordinated way, but in way that relies on resilience and a clear view of both what you face and what resources you possess. BANI+ Bendable is the ability to withstand stress when possible and bend without breaking when overwhelmed.

The "A" in BANI+ is **Attentive**. Think accepting, aware, *empathetic*. This carries with it both the capacity to focus amid chaos and the capacity to recognize and respond to the pain in others. BANI+ Attentive is the ability to reflect back on your own challenges and use that experience and knowledge in how you work and live.

The "N" in BANI+ is **Neuroflexible**. Think clever, open, *improvisational*. In a world of chaos, following the scripts and embracing the mental models developed before the BANI era is hazardous. BANI+ Neuroflexible is the ability to recognize that knowledge and plans must be contingent and contextual.

The "I" in BANI+ is **Interconnected**. Think curious, welcoming to varied perspectives, *comprehensive*. A recognition that a complex, rapidly evolving, chaotic world can't be understood from a single point of view. BANI+ Interconnected is the ability to ask for and make use of ideas outside of your immediate circle.

Each chapter will dive into details of these concepts and offer up examples—using both organizations and individuals—of what these approaches and strategies can look like in reality. And like the examples in the first BANI chapters that showed how messy and difficult the BANI world can be, the examples in the BANI+ chapters will show how complicated and imperfect—but necessary and important—the Positive BANI world can be, too. If it was easy, everybody would be doing it.

None of the BANI+ perspectives should be taken as meaning that original-recipe BANI has been defeated. What they mean is this: as bad as things can look in a BANI world, as much as we may fear a BANI Future, **we must not see them as inevitable**. We can adapt to and evolve past every challenge we endure, every threat we face, every dilemma that rises to meet us.

The Future is BANI—but it can be more.

> Pessimism is a luxury affordable only in good times. In difficult times, optimism is a duty, because pessimism easily turns into a self-inflicted, self-fulfilling death sentence.
> —NORWEGIAN SCHOLAR EVELIN LINDNER AND AUSCHWITZ SURVIVOR JO LINSER, 2004[1]

6
Bendable
Resilient Clarity

BENDABLE: In BANI+, "bendable" refers to the ability of a system or entity (person or organization) to respond successfully to stressful dynamics demonstrating unanticipated intensity, duration, or timing. Such responses include flexibility (temporary adjustments in behavior or structure to accommodate the added pressure), adaptation (persistent adjustments, usually to respond to persistent pressure), evolution (fundamental changes to the nature of the system or entity to better withstand persistent pressure), even absorption (bringing the added stress into the normal functioning of the entity or system). Other, more specific or narrow responses can be included, as long as they allow the entity or system continued successful function.

Although it is possible to undertake a bendable response as a form of improvisation, in most cases it relies on some measure of preparation. Planned responses need not be specific to a particular threat; emergency planning or preparation, for example, can take into account diverse forms of disaster (such as remote work plans viable in both a pandemic and the aftermath of an earthquake).

The Age of Bendable

To counter brittle, be bendable—with resilient clarity. By bendable, we mean the ability to flex, adapt, and avoid crumbling under stress.

The BANI Future will create more turbulence than we have ever experienced—as well as new kinds of turbulence. With clear direction and an adaptive mindset, organizations and individuals will be able to navigate these turbulent forces without losing their way. It will require more than coping; it will require reshaping ourselves and our organizations for resilience.

The risks of being brittle can be reduced by developing your capacity to withstand sudden shocks. This simple concept can be difficult to achieve, but it's not impossible. Scenario planning and gaming are futures methods for building resilience by practicing responses to high-risk situations in low-risk ways. Thriving people are bendable, not brittle. Bob's mother had a personal motto that expressed bendability: "I'll bloom where I'm planted."

Resilience is, in many ways, a straightforward concept. It can be created and nurtured by having a cushion of emergency supplies, by preparing and planning for disasters, and by reducing reliance on monocultures or single points of failure. Its underlying dynamic is asking "What if?" and imagining what you would need to do as a result. Bendable resilience will come from continuous awareness of possible unexpected challenges.

Resilient clarity combines an explicit sense of direction with persistence. Be very clear about the direction you want to pursue—the intention to which you are committed—but very flexible about how you will act day to day in your pursuit. Persistence will hold you on course, but only if your direction is calling you on clearly and consistently. There are many ways people can and do seek to understand and respond to the new BANI realities described in this book. Some people, for example, draw closer to friends and family; some seek strength and wisdom from their religious faith; some dedicate themselves to service in the hope of making better futures. Bendability alone is not enough. Bendability is weak if it has no shape or direction.

The classic animation figure Gumby was a green character made of clay who could stretch, bend, and reshape himself to escape danger. Gumby had physical flexibility, but his inner storyline was to react to whatever came along. Gumby (along with his pony pal, Pokey) bounced from adventure to adventure without purpose or direction beyond survival. He was bendable in a wishy-washy but funny way. If Gumby had any clarity of direction, it was to be entertaining.

Gumby cartoons demonstrated what the psychologist Martin Seligman first called "learned helplessness," which is passive adaptability and acceptance that lacks purpose or direction.[1] Seligman found that animals, including humans, can develop a passive resignation to adversity if they believe they have no control over their circumstances. This isn't just a problem for animated stories; the BANI era has seen a great deal of learned helplessness (sometimes described as *premature* or *anticipatory capitulation*) in response to difficult developments.

Seligman's work stimulated later developments around psychological resilience, mental health, and positive psychology. Cultivating bendability and resilient clarity will counter the feelings of helplessness that will come inevitably in the BANI Future. Organizations and individuals will be subjected to continuing challenges, and their responses too often won't seem to make much if any difference—at least in the short term. At some point when infected with learned helplessness, people give up and—like Gumby—just flex with whatever happens.

Flexive Futures

BANI+ bendability is purpose driven. We call it *flexive intent*, and it will be critical to thrive in the BANI Future. Flexive intent is the ability to adapt to changing conditions—even the extremes of BANI—within the protective envelope of a clear sense of purpose and direction. Bendability is valuable, but it is not enough. Flexive intent ensures that flexibility is guided by strategy. The goal is to build resilient adaptability with a very clear sense of direction.

The US Army War College's notion of "flexive command" is useful here, since it evolved from command and control—which no longer works well in a BANI Future. In the best militaries around the world, command and control has already been replaced by commander's intent:

> The commander's intent describes the desired end state. It is a concise expression of the purpose of the operation and must be understood two echelons below the issue commander. . . . It is the single unifying focus for all subordinate elements. . . . Its purpose is to focus subordinates on the desired end state.[2]

Bob has been working with the US Army War College since 9/11 and has adapted what he has learned to inform his notions of clarity, futureback thinking (examining a possible future by thinking backward through what made it possible), and flexive intent. This work is described in more detail in Bob's book *Full-Spectrum Thinking* in chapter 8, "Broader Spectrums of Hierarchy."[3]

Both commanders and leaders must be very clear about direction and outcome goals, but the people who follow them should have great flexibility regarding how to accomplish the intent. In a BANI Future, command and control will be brittle and breakable. Bendability will be effective only when it is wrapped protectively in purpose. Bendable organizations are more likely to survive, but to thrive they need to be rooted in clear intent. Flexive intent can become a guiding force that steers adaptability toward meaningful outcomes. It is not about reacting with Gumby-like sponginess but about bending strategically within the envelope of resilient clarity of direction.

Nor is it a crude case of "the ends justify the means." Quite the opposite, in fact. The flexibility about how to accomplish the commanders' goals is constrained within well-understood legal and ethical boundaries. Resilient clarity includes knowing what not to do.

Flexive intent enables clarity. Clarity is the ability to recognize, understand, and express direction of change—ideally as a compelling story. The best leaders are very clear about where they want to go in the future but very flexible about how they get there.

Clarity is all about intent and direction of change; certainty is rigid and resistant to change. Clarity is best expressed in stories, while certainty is expressed in rules and absolutes. Stories of clarity include questions, while assertions of certainty are all about answers. Faith is a lot like clarity; extreme belief is a lot like certainty. Faith can be a superpower in the BANI world; extreme belief will be dangerous.

Unfortunately, our brains want certainty. We seek out explanations for our experiences that are *satisfying*, even if they're not *true*. We feel rewarded when we discover a pattern, something that links disparate pieces. But in a BANI world, that satisfying certainty is elusive and often deceptive. As much as we may want it, we cannot have it, and we should be especially skeptical when we seem to find it.

Economies of Scope

The concept of flexive intent does not depend on knowing ahead of time about a specific challenge or disruptive situation. Although having plans for a particular expected or repeated crisis can be warranted, flexive intent focuses more on conditions where important elements of the situation are unanticipated. Perhaps a known probable crisis happens more quickly than expected or lasts longer than planned. Perhaps a disaster is deemed possible but unlikely, so most systems or entities are not fully prepared.

The COVID-19 pandemic is a recent example of that latter situation. Pandemics—by definition, virulent diseases with a global reach—are widely known phenomena, with one of the most disastrous hitting a little over a century ago. The 1918–1919 "Great

Influenza" saw nearly a third of the global population infected by the H1N1 influenza virus, with tens of millions killed (typical estimates are 18–50 million deaths, or about 1–2.7 percent of the world's population). Its high mortality rate was undoubtedly boosted by the world having just come out of the devastation of World War I.

But even with historical examples (and numerous smaller outbreaks in more recent years of epidemic diseases like Zika), the world in 2020 was not adequately prepared for a pandemic. Fortunately, COVID-19 did not reach the mortality rates of the Great Influenza. But the COVID-19 pandemic brought with it lessons that extended beyond just how to respond to disease outbreaks.

Many of the impacts of the pandemic, especially in 2020 and 2021, had parallels in the consequences arising after other kinds of large-scale disasters, such as earthquakes. This included the loss of supply chains, the overloading of the medical system, and the inability of large numbers of people to engage in centralized, in-facility work. Organizations from the United Nations to Intel to the California Telehealth Resource Center have reexamined their plans to respond to crises like large-scale earthquakes based directly on the lessons of COVID-19.[4]

Systems, infrastructure, and plans built to be able to satisfy multiple unrelated demands, rather than focusing on just one particular situation, are said to offer "economies of scope." Whereas "economies of scale" take advantage of larger systems to be able to do even more than their size would suggest, economies of scope describe systems that are able to do a greater variety of things than they may have been initially planned to do. Economies of scope offer a straightforward example of what bendability can look like.

How Organizations Can Bend Brittle

In an age of chaos, organizations that can bend without breaking will thrive. Brittleness will jeopardize traditional hierarchical organizations in particular. Bendable organizations will see external threats as a call to transform.

The AT Protocol and Social Media's Brittle Turnaround

As we've discussed throughout this book, social media is often an engine of chaos. As of early 2025, 5.24 billion people used social media, amounting to nearly 64 percent of the global population.[5] Raw size is just one determinant of influence, however; comparatively small social networks can have an outsized footprint if their user base contains high-profile or institutionally powerful individuals. Historically, most social media networks have been highly centralized, with decisions made by the network owners shaping everything that the users can see.

In late 2019, one of those network owners—Jack Dorsey, founder of Twitter—announced the creation of an internal research group to build an open and decentralized standard for social media. However, by the end of 2021 Dorsey had left Twitter and the project, the AT Protocol (or "atproto"), spun out into a stand-alone company named Bluesky. Bluesky is now a public benefit corporation, operating a social network that looks quite a bit like pre-X Twitter. The underlying technology, the AT Protocol, is what makes it different and what has allowed it to flip a brittle system.

The AT Protocol is an open standard for distributed social networking services. Although as of the time of writing Bluesky Social PBC owns the technology, it has announced that it will soon transfer ownership to the Internet Engineering Task Force. As an open communication protocol, the AT Protocol allows users a great deal of control over their networks and experience.

Put simply, the AT Protocol lets users construct and share their own rules about who they connect with and how—that is, their own algorithmic feeds and moderation services. Moreover, the system is designed to be inherently flexible: it supports platform interoperability, scalable networks, and—crucially—portability of user data and social network connections. A user could copy or move their entire set of filters, favorites, and friend lists to any other service using the AT Protocol, even if that platform offers entirely different functions (e.g., video sharing rather than text discussions) or is run by a different company.

Bluesky and the AT Protocol saw a rapid increase in use in late 2024, as the owners of the top legacy social networks (Facebook, X, and TikTok) made unilateral changes to the feed algorithms and moderation rules, changes that many saw as highly politicized. Advocates for the AT Protocol argued that such changes would be impossible on systems using the protocol—if any network owner were to attempt such actions, users could very easily and freely leave that platform without losing any of their history and connections.

Mayo Clinic's Brittle Turnaround

Telemedicine has been technically possible since at least the 1970s, although the tools have evolved dramatically since those early days of telehealth. Bob and Institute for the Future did studies of telemedicine on the North Slope of Alaska and in rural Canada during this period, but there was great resistance on the part of health-care institutions, and the technology was not yet ready to scale.

The COVID-19 pandemic dramatically restricted in-person health-care delivery—especially for nonemergency visits. During the crisis, the Mayo Clinic quickly and massively scaled up its telemedicine capabilities for virtual health consultation and remote patient monitoring.[6] Previously, telemedicine at Mayo had been a small part of their offerings, but it was clearly supplemental and not strategic. The new telehealth options provided improved continuity of care for patients with chronic conditions or postsurgical care needs. For example, remote monitoring tools like wearable devices enabled doctors to track vital signs and health data from afar. Sometimes, telehealth replaced the need for in-person visits entirely.

This shift allowed Mayo to continue delivering care despite pandemic constraints on physical appointments. They could even reach patients in remote areas more easily. The staff quickly learned how to blend in-person and virtual care, lessons that have continued beyond the pandemic. They now have a much more flexible patient-centered approach that was forced by the pandemic but has continued as a much-improved service delivery model. Rather than resisting change, Mayo bent the crisis into a transformation. Once the pandemic eased, Mayo evaluated which services should remain virtual and which would be better done in person. Thus, service was improved overall, even as the importance of personalized service and quality outcomes remained.

All the while, the Mayo Clinic stayed true to their mission of delivering the best care to every patient through integrated clinical practice, education, and research. Mayo invested in training their health-care providers to offer compassionate and effective virtual care—sometimes as an option and sometimes as a requirement because of the pandemic or some other reason. They were bendable within the resilient clarity of the Mayo vision and branding, even amid an unprecedented crisis.

How Individuals Can Bend Brittle

If individuals can bend and flex, they can avoid shattering under stress. The following are three extreme examples of people who developed resilience under pressure.

Viktor Frankl's Brittle Turnaround

Dr. Viktor Frankl survived for years in Nazi concentration camps yet was able to retain a strong sense of hope and develop a new form of psychotherapy based on the importance of meaning.

Frankl was bendable with resilient clarity in ways that are almost impossible to imagine—yet somehow, he did it. He had a very flexible but resilient form of faith, not a rigid form of extreme belief.

Nazi Germany's system of human-engineered oppression was an extreme kind of BANI world and Frankl experienced its most ugly manifestations. Frankl's ability to flip a BANI threat positive—to recontextualize and reimagine it—is perhaps the most universal example of individual mindset and behavior that we have encountered. Frankl has so much to teach us all—lessons that are more relevant than ever today. He was able to flip brittle, anxious, nonlinear, and incomprehensible, so for each of the Positive BANI chapters, we will lead with an example of how Frankl responded to his relentless torture.

Frankl's book *Man's Search for Meaning* continues to sell worldwide since its publication in 1946. It has a powerful message of bending without breaking while maintaining an inner sense of hope even when your experience of daily life is horrible. Quoted in the foreword by the historian Martin Gilbert, Frankl described how his mind clung to his wife's image:

> I understood how a man who has nothing left in this world still may know bliss, be it only for a brief moment, in the contemplation of his beloved. In a position of utter desolation, when a man cannot express himself in positive action, when his only achievement may consist in enduring his suffering in the right way—in an honorable way—in such a position man can, through loving contemplation of the image he carries of his beloved, achieve fulfillment.[7]

Frankl endured incomprehensible suffering while still maintaining a clear sense of purpose. A psychiatrist by training, he was moved among several Nazi concentration camps, including Auschwitz and Dachau. His physical and emotional suffering was unimaginable, yet he miraculously adapted without breaking. His ability to bend seems to have come from profound psychological flexibility, which he described as searching for meaning in even the most horrific circumstances. He believed that (perhaps it would be more accurate to say that he had faith that), even when we are being treated brutally, we still have internal abilities to choose how we respond.

At the core of Frankl's resilience was his clarity of purpose: he believed that humans could endure almost anything if they had a reason to live. Even in a concentration camp, he found meaning in the smallest acts of kindness. His resilience came not from avoiding suffering but in choosing how he responded. Somehow, he maintained his purpose throughout his ordeal. He focused on the importance of meaning—even when it comes only in momentary glimpses.

Frankl entered his first concentration camp in 1942, and his final concentration camp was liberated in 1945. He lived another fifty-two years beyond that. Frankl is a deep human example of bending but not breaking, of resilient clarity, and of flexive intent. He lived until 1997, when he died of heart failure at the age of ninety-two.

Stephen Hawking's Brittle Turnaround

Stephen Hawking was diagnosed with ALS (amyotrophic lateral sclerosis) in 1963, at age twenty-one, and was told he had only a few years to live. Instead of breaking, he adapted his outlook to focus on those areas of life where he still had control even as his physical capabilities were breaking down. He focused on his mind and intellect. He passed away on March 14, 2018, at age seventy-six. His longevity and resilience were as amazing as his scientific achievements.[8]

When he was diagnosed with ALS, Hawking was in his final year as a graduate student at the University of Cambridge. He continued his studies after the diagnosis and became a PhD in theoretical physics with a specific focus on cosmology and general relativity. His work focused on the nature of black holes, the origin of the universe, and the fundamental laws that govern the cosmos. Hawking's book *A Brief History of Time* is a landmark exploration of cosmology that reflects his philosophical resilience.

As his physical capabilities declined, he learned to use assistive digital technologies to communicate, work, and achieve some mobility. A speech-generating digital device allowed him to speak. Specialized computer software allowed him to continue his research actively despite his almost complete paralysis. He collaborated closely—though sometimes with great physical difficulty—with students, colleagues, and caregivers throughout his life.

Hawking's clarity of purpose was evident in his dedication to understanding the nature of the universe. He focused his life on unraveling fundamental scientific mysteries. His purpose transcended his oppressive physical limitations.

Walter McMillian's Brittle Turnaround

A Black man from Alabama, Walter McMillian was wrongfully convicted in 1988 of murdering a White woman and sentenced to death—despite compelling evidence that he was at a fish fry at his church at the time of the crime, and despite the jury instead recommending a life sentence. His conviction was based on what was later revealed to be coerced testimony from a convicted felon, even though multiple witnesses confirmed his alibi. McMillian was placed on death row even before his trial, a stark recognition of the brittle and racially biased legal system that was seeking quick resolution over truth.

Attorney Bryan Stevenson represented McMillian through the Equal Justice Initiative on appeal, after McMillian was wrongfully convicted and sentenced to death. Stevenson uncovered witness coercion, prosecutor misconduct, corruption, and racial bias that contributed to the wrongful conviction. McMillian's story featured prominently in Stevenson's memoir *Just Mercy*.[9]

McMillian endured extraordinary hardship without losing sight of his humanity or his hope for justice. For six years, he lived under the threat of execution where he felt isolated by a legal system stacked against him. Somehow, he was able to bend without snapping. He kept his sense of dignity, humor, and quiet defiance of the injustice he was experiencing so deeply—holding onto his identity beyond his cell. His resilient clarity came from his unwavering belief in his innocence and the pursuit of the truth.

When Stevenson took his case, McMillian had tangible hope for and trust in the process of justice—despite years of setbacks and delays. McMillian showed that resilience does not require invincibility—it comes from remaining grounded in community, forgiveness, and grace. After his release, he continued to work with Equal Justice Initiative to speak out against the injustices of the legal system and systemic racism.

Personal Resilience Skills for Bending Brittle

We believe that many—perhaps most—individuals, with preparation and practice, can become bendable in the face of the BANI world, with resilient clarity. Certainly, most people can be better than brittle.

Physical and mental resilience will increase your bendability. This is a lot like stretching exercises for your body, but most of this stretching will be in your mind. Physical fitness, however, is an obvious prerequisite.

Judith Moskowitz is a psychologist at Northwestern University's Feinberg School of Medicine in the Department of Medical Social Sciences. She focuses on how people cope with extremely stressful situations like being diagnosed with HIV, caring for a loved one with dementia or cancer, or working in frontline gun violence prevention.[10] She has synthesized (from varied sources) eight skills for managing stress, and she has done controlled research to show that these skills can reduce stress and increase health in measurable ways. Moskowitz focuses on honing the ability to experience joy and other positive emotions even in the face of nagging negatives. As in BANI, the health challenges she is studying are not problems that can be solved but rather dilemmas that need to be managed.

We have grouped, adapted, and built upon Moskowitz's eight skills: practice mindfulness, express gratitude, name positive events, savor life, employ positive reappraisal, practice self-compassion, notice personal strengths, and set attainable goals. We will discuss each skill according to its relevance for coping with each core element of BANI in the Positive BANI chapters (6–9), beginning with this chapter about countering brittle.

Bending Brittle

The Northwestern University resilience program suggests two coping skills that have both been around for many years, but each of them requires intense practice in order to see the benefits:

- **Practice mindfulness:** Have situational awareness of your current condition and what is going on around you.

- **Express gratitude:** Appreciate what brings you happiness and create a gratitude journal that you use daily to record your gratitude as specifically as possible.

Even small behavior changes sometimes can make big positive changes to our mental health and resilience. While Moskowitz is not a futurist and has not been studying the stresses of the BANI Future, we feel that her work presents a tested set of techniques to cope with BANI-like stresses in the present world that help us anticipate future stresses and imagine additional resilience skills.

These resilience practices build from physical strength. When Bob was president of Institute for the Future, he had an executive coach named Pierre Mornell who used to repeat this phrase enthusiastically in almost every session with Bob: "More stress, more exercise." Certainly, physical exercise is basic to health, as is stretching your body. Mental stretching is at least as important, and the categories of skills we are building on are mostly mental.

We understand that such stress-relief techniques sound ordinary and commonplace to most people. Certainly, most of these tools are not new. But the challenge for each of us is not just to identify those coping skills that might be useful in response to the BANI world but to practice those skills in a disciplined manner that works for us. These commonplace tools require incessant practice.

When Bob played basketball in high school and college, he learned that "free throws" in basketball are not free, even though a free throw is a simple fifteen-foot shot given as a penalty during which nobody can interfere with the shooter. The mechanics of shooting a free throw are ordinary and commonplace, like the stress-coping skills suggested previously. Successful free throwers, however, must practice incessantly. When Bob played basketball, his coach required all the players to shoot and record one hundred free throws before school every morning, in addition to the usual afternoon practice time. Shooting free throws requires the development of muscle memory, but there is also a psychology to it—particularly late in the game. Everyone is watching you as you shoot. Free throws require physical and mental discipline much like the stress-relief practices we summarized. Incessant practice and disciplined repetition are required for success. The martial arts master Bruce Lee said it this way:

> I fear not the man who has practiced 10,000 kicks once, but I fear the man who has practiced one kick 10,000 times.[11]

Coping skills alone feel transactional and routine, like tools in a toolbox. All coping techniques will work better in a climate of hope and trust. Thriving in a BANI world will be an exercise in faith that is beyond just "having" faith. Faith must be an active exercise, an ongoing practice of leaning forward that includes asking questions. Faith implies trust in the tools and your practice even when the outcomes are uncertain and systems fray. Faith implies holding space for hope as fuel for action. Faith is resilient clarity; extreme belief is brittle.

Cognitive Behavioral Techniques

We believe that the psychological methods of cognitive behavioral therapy (CBT) are very relevant to coping with the BANI Future.[12] CBT focuses on identifying and modifying negative thought patterns and behaviors, which abound in the BANI world. The "T" in CBT is sometimes referred to as "techniques" or "tools." CBT has been successful in teaching tool- and technique-oriented coping skills, although intense repetition and practice is required. CBT is grounded in a belief that thoughts, feelings, and behaviors are interconnected—and can be modified with repetition and practice—like shooting free throws.

By flipping negative thought patterns more positive, individuals can improve their emotional well-being and their ability to react constructively to stressful situations. CBT methods are well suited to the psychological stresses that will result from a world that is brittle, anxious, nonlinear, and incomprehensible.

CBT typically starts from identifying negative thoughts and labeling them with terms such as "automatic negative thoughts," "catastrophizing," or "black-and-white thinking." The BANI Future will be a constant trigger for negative thinking that can deepen emotional distress and worsen unhelpful behaviors.

CBT helps people reframe overly negative thoughts into more balanced and more resilient perspectives. It encourages people to engage in positive and rewarding activities that promote healthy patterns of behavior. It emphasizes coping and resilience skills that can be used in daily life such as before going to sleep or when feeling discouraged during the day.

Of course, it is important to recognize that it is very human and even healthy to be stressed by BANI events and experiences. We're not recommending hiding from BANI or pretending that

BANI can always be flipped into something positive. Still, we all will need to at least cope, and it will be even better to figure out how to thrive with resilience.

In summary, here are a few personal practices for bending BANI brittle that build on the Northwestern methods but add a bit to them:

- **Practice mindfulness:** Remain aware of the current situation to help you realize when you are becoming rigid and encourage yourself to relax in the moment to avoid brittleness. Situation awareness in the military is usually focused on avoiding dangers, but it also includes noticing the positives in your daily experience.

- **Notice and express gratitude:** Appreciate what brings you happiness. Gratitude journals are particularly powerful.

- **Be physically fit:** Promote daily exercise, good sleep, and nutrition so you have physical and mental stamina to bend under pressure without breaking.

- **Reframe perceptions:** Reinterpret obstacles or negative events as learning opportunities that allow you to practice flexible responses to disruption.

When you encounter a brittle situation or feel very anxious—a sudden setback or frightening surprise, for example—you can try to reframe the experience rather than accepting only the negatives.

7

Attentive

Active Empathy

ATTENTIVE: In BANI+, "attentive" refers to the ability to recognize and respond to the anxiety in yourself and in others by creating psychological safety. Attentive entities (people or organizations) embrace active empathy toward others—including others they've never met. This means that they will acknowledge and, where possible, adapt their behavior to lessen the anxiety that is felt by others. Active empathy should also be inwardly directed, as the anxiety and trauma experienced by oneself can be used both as a basis for understanding others and as a barrier to that understanding. It's easy to assume that another entity's anxiety precisely mirrors one's own—or is completely unlike one's own. It is critical to talk *with* the impacted people, not just about them. Listen. Listen. Listen. The best solutions are likely to emerge from those closest to the crisis. Trust is seeded before a crisis but blossoms during a crisis.

Arguably, attentiveness is the most difficult of the BANI+ elements to embrace, as it requires both a capacity to examine oneself and a willingness to accept potential losses (e.g., of power, of money, of efficiency) when attempting to lessen harm experienced by others. Active empathy includes the risk of increasing one's own levels of anxiety. Empathy is a powerful response to uncertainty. In times of crisis—hurricanes, wildfires, pandemics, political chaos—the main events are frightening, but the uncertainty lingers and turns into anxiety. Anxiety spreads fastest when leaders go silent, when nobody steps up to provide clarity in a world that doesn't make sense anymore.

The Age of Attentive

To counter anxious, be attentive to the needs of others—with active empathy. In addition, be attentive to your own personal needs. People need the ability to act without knowing all the answers. If you are attentive, you can empathize and engage with expressions of and sources of anxiety. Active empathy means emotional connection and meaningful action that listens for and responds to anxiety.

Empathy is neurobiologically complex. Most neuroscientists describe two primary forms (some expand it to four or five): **emotional empathy**, which involves sharing the emotional response of another, feeling distress when another person is in pain, and feeling compassion for their situation; and **cognitive empathy**, which focuses on recognizing and understanding the situation in which another person finds themselves, accepting and imagining the feelings or experience of another person, and being able to see how another person's negative experience has harmed them.[1] They are by no means mutually exclusive, and both can be active.

Attentiveness and empathy are forms of mental simulation, as they make use of the human brain's ability to model what another mind is doing. The perception of another entity's emotional state and how that affects their behavior is a remarkable cognitive trick. Feeling empathy for another person requires making an accurate model of their thought and emotional processes—and doing so unconsciously, in the moment.

Active empathy asks us to go beyond simply recognizing the emotional state of another person and to engage in behavior meant to lessen the pain the other person feels. This may not always be possible, or possible to a meaningful degree. It's easy to become overwhelmed by embracing another person's—or group of people's—emotional conditions, thereby increasing one's own anxiety. It's critical to be attentive to one's own condition when attempting to help others.

The BANI Future will fuel and be fueled by anxiety, but the level of anxiety can be reduced or managed in many, perhaps most, cases. Resilience will be possible, but it will take more than just coping. There are techniques (explored later in the chapter) to help ameliorate or manage one's anxiety. Moreover, some degree of anxiety can be positive.

One of our favorite book titles is *Just Enough Anxiety*, by Robert Rosen. So often anxiety is viewed only as a mental health condition that must be treated with drugs or therapy. Rosen opens his book with an insightful Nelson Mandela quote: "The brave man is not he who does not feel afraid, but he who conquers that fear." Rosen goes on to say:

> Anxiety is a fact of life. How you use it makes all the difference. If you let it overwhelm you, it will turn to panic. If you deny or run from it, you will be complacent. But if you use anxiety in a positive way, you will turn it into a powerful force in your life.[2]

In a BANI Future, anxiety will be baked into everything. Anxiety will be expected as a normal human response to daily life by thoughtful people. If you're not at least a bit anxious in the BANI world and the BANI Future, you're not paying attention. This may sound like a cliché, but it's not: the greater the awareness of what is happening in a BANI world, the greater the intensity of felt anxiety.

Understanding and adaptability will be key. Instead of letting anxiety spiral out of control, you can ground yourself by being more attentive to what's going on around you right now in the present moment—particularly those things that you can either control or influence. Then, you can engage with others in a spirit of active empathy. Active empathy goes beyond sympathizing;

it involves engaging through direct and purposeful action. It begins with tuning into the needs of others but requires much more. Active empathy requires meaningful supportive behaviors that reflect understanding and attempt to transform anxiety into something more positive.

How Organizations Can Attend to Anxious

Organizations can be more or less anxious. In a BANI Future, organizations will have many reasons to be anxious—but they have the potential to repurpose some of that anxious energy. By reframing uncertainty into attentiveness, organizations can often identify the true sources of anxiety as well as its potential tradeoffs. They can use empathy to scope out both internal and external dynamics. Rather than being paralyzed by being anxious, organizations like Airbnb and United Way Worldwide have demonstrated how anxiety can spark adaptive strategies and even foster trust amid turbulence.

Airbnb's Anxious Turnaround

In early 2020, the global pandemic was making everyone anxious, including those in the travel industry, like Airbnb. Both traveling guests and hosts were severely disrupted as travel halted abruptly—as were employees of the company. Airbnb was attentive to the anxiety all around them and developed responses that demonstrated active empathy.

For example, Airbnb offered easy full refunds to guests who were unable to travel because of concerns about the pandemic. There were immediate mass cancellations, plummeting revenue, and a growing sense of panic among both guests and hosts. They were also attentive to the fact that the hosts in their network were losing income that was often very important to their household budgets. Airbnb established a fund for hosts to help cover the costs of COVID-related cancellations and the Superhost Relief

Fund, which provided grants to hosts that were facing financial hardships.

Airbnb emphasized enhanced communications that eased the anxiety for both guests and hosts. During a crisis like this, communication is vital and silence can make things much worse. Airbnb created a sense of connection between leadership and stakeholders, which reduced psychological uncertainty with transparency—even though the outside global mood of uncertainty loomed. CEO Brian Chesky was deeply human centered and showed considerable empathy for Airbnb's community.

Airbnb also created an enhanced cleaning protocol to address health anxieties. They partnered with health experts to set new sanitation standards for their housing units. This concern also relieved psychological barriers to booking while reinforcing trust for both guests and hosts.

Finally, when travel decreased dramatically and remote-work options increased, Airbnb was attentive to a surge in demand for long-term stays. They pivoted their offerings to accommodate long-term rentals and remote-work-friendly options for flexible living. They listened deeply to stakeholders and redesigned their offerings in ways that were both attentive and pragmatically empathetic.

United Way Worldwide's Anxious Turnaround

United Way Worldwide experienced a nasty taste of the BANI Future during the COVID-19 pandemic. Communities and community support globally were threatened, and everyone was anxious. Angela F. Williams, the United Way Worldwide CEO and coauthor of this book, led a coordinated response that prioritized clear communications and community resilience. The organization launched the COVID-19 Community Response and Recovery Fund, which raised over $1 billion to provide immediate relief to struggling communities. This initiative provided relief for financial anxieties that the local chapters and their partners were experiencing. It also reassured the anxious public that United Way was mobilized to support local communities during the uncharted and frightening days of the pandemic.

United Way showed active empathy by expanding their 211 helpline, the official national dialing code for human services that connected individuals with local resources like food, housing, and health care. Calls to 211 surged during the pandemic, and United Way's ability to respond with attention and empathy was a lifeline for many people. If COVID-19 taught us anything, it is that the need for human connection is not going away. That is particularly true with regard to the type of wraparound support needed to address health inequities—especially during times of crisis. United Way's clarity story is about the trust and effectiveness of neighbors helping neighbors. The effectiveness of United Way at the community level lies in their ability to listen to voices on the ground, identify creative solutions collaboratively, and then share lessons and outcome data globally.

During this period, United Way placed a priority on mental health and well-being resources. This was a form of active empathy for employees, volunteers, and people being served. They also introduced new communications tools and new ways to work and reach people remotely during periods where social distancing was required. Many local chapters provided emergency childcare services for frontline workers, which showed awareness and active empathy for those who kept essential services running while also balancing the challenges of their own family life during this crisis period.

United Way leaders provided frequent communications and great clarity about the directions they were pursuing. This clarity and communication was critical in moderating anxious feelings among employees, volunteers, partners, and people who were receiving services. The leaders listened to the needs of local communities and responded with targeted actions. In 2022, United Way saw a 40 percent increase in calls to 211, which was likely due to inflation and the increased cost of living. In early 2022, their top requests were for housing, utilities, and food. United Way Worldwide is a federated organization that showed shape-shifting versatility during the COVID-19 crisis and beyond.

Angela summarizes a few key lessons of active empathy in this way:

- Center on those impacted: the people closest to the problem are often best positioned to solve it.
- Get creative: exchange of ideas from around the world is critical. Angela likes to say, "We are partners, not saviors."
- Invest in the future: beyond immediate relief, look for lasting impact.
- Stay for the long term: rebuilding takes time. United Way has been around for 135 years, and some of its partnerships have lasted for generations.

How Individuals Can Attend to Anxious

Just as organizations can rechannel anxious energy into positive action, so too can individuals. In a BANI Future, anxiety will be a constant undercurrent, but it can also be a powerful motivator—even in the most extreme situations. The following three individuals all learned how to transform their own anxiety—and the anxiety of others—into a force for change.

Viktor Frankl's Anxious Turnaround

Anxiety was weaponized as a control mechanism in the Nazi society. In his work and life, Viktor Frankl was able to find purpose and meaning even in the horrors of the Holocaust. This experience led him to develop the practice of logotherapy, which frees people to find meaning in suffering. In the concentration camps, Frankl was able to attend to the needs of others during his own personal and family tragedies.

Frankl's personal resilience strategy was rooted in his own mental clarity and unshakable sense of purpose. He was able to transcend his own horrific experience by focusing on the power of meaning-making. He believed that, even in the most brutal circumstances, life can have meaning.

Even very small acts of dignity and humanity can make a difference by reducing anxiety and giving a sense of agency. Frankl encouraged his fellow prisoners to focus on small, meaningful acts such as helping others, maintaining personal hygiene, and performing simple tasks with pride.

With a kind of futureback thinking, Frankl suggested focusing on the future rather than dwelling on the horrors of the present. He projected toward better days and helped people to focus their minds on the future so as to look beyond the overwhelming anxiety of the present. He listened attentively to the fears and anxieties of his fellow prisoners, validating their feelings and encouraging them to find inner strength and imagine a better future. Internal freedom is possible, even with extreme external constraints.

Kate Darling's Anxious Turnaround

Kate Darling is a leading expert in robot ethics and policy at the MIT Media Lab. Her empathic explorations of how humans and robots could interact has led her to draw an analogy between our relationship with animals and our future relationships with robots and varied forms of AI.

While most conversations about robots have focused on their utility and ability to automate tasks, Darling focuses on empathy and ethical treatment. For example, she explores the ethical implications of harming robots, not because they feel pain (we don't think they do) but because harming them would reflect badly on humans—just as treating animals well is about human principles as much as the experience of the animals. She is advocating for a new narrative around robots, one that integrates active empathy rather than reinforcing fear.

Darling has proposed that robots could serve as tools for teaching empathy to humans. In a world where robots and AI are more integrated into homes, workplaces, and medical care, robots may function as emotional learning aids in addition to carrying out mechanical tasks—much like service or therapy animals. Her work suggests fields like eldercare or child development could benefit from creative use of robots to encourage psychological and emotional health for humans. The challenge is to expand our minds about "robots" and "artificial intelligence," and we don't have language to help us do that. Indeed, we already have vivid images of "robots" that may be extremely inaccurate:

> This book questions that image, of robots as quasi humans, and shows that it seeps into how we design and integrate real robots in our world. A lot of the framing here applies to our thinking on artificial intelligence more broadly.... Instead of establishing perfect definitions and rules that universally apply to all thinking machines, this book encourages us to stretch our minds and question our underlying assumptions.... We should be thinking of robots not as our replacements, but more creatively: as a partner in what we're trying to achieve.[3]

Darling's work exemplifies both attention and active empathy by drawing from fields not traditionally associated with technology, like animal ethics. She then applies these ideas to the emerging field of robotics where nonlinear development is assumed, and the future is very uncertain. She blends insights from robotics, psychology, anthropology, law, and animal husbandry. Drawing from animal welfare laws, which have evolved as societies have become more respectful of animals, Darling argues for flexible and evolving ethical standards that will adapt to the unforeseen changes in robot design and capabilities that are coming.

It is far too early for rigid guardrails around robotics and AI. The technologies are evolving so quickly that it could prove difficult to change hard rules to meet entirely new conditions. A better analogy may be the bounce ropes around a wrestling ring—with stanchions that hold the core values in place as the four posts in a wrestling ring do. The ropes keep the wrestlers inside the ring, but the ropes also flex. Ethical bounce ropes could keep technology and humans in a safe legal and ethical space, while also flexing to allow for surprises and to make unintended negative consequences less likely.

Ekapol Chanthawong (Coach Ek)'s Anxious Turnaround

Twenty-five-year-old Ekapol Chanthawong (Coach Ek) was trapped with twelve teenagers from his Wild Boars soccer team in the Tham Luang caves in Thailand.[4] They had ridden to the cave entrance on bicycles after practice and entered the cave for fun. Unexpected monsoon rains flooded the cave rapidly, trapping them deep inside.

A daring international rescue operation claimed global headlines while the world watched in suspense, but the less-discussed personal leadership of Coach Ek was in many ways even more remarkable. Coach Ek was amazingly attentive to the needs of his young players and showed an active empathy that previews what will be needed from leaders to thrive in the BANI Future.

Imagine being alone underground in darkness caring for twelve young boys with little food for over ten days before divers locate you—and then another eight days before your safe rescue. Coach Ek had been an orphan himself and was raised as a Buddhist monk, where he learned methods of meditation, self-control, and mindfulness. Meditation was critical to calming and comforting the boys. The practice he developed attentively with the boys was lifesaving empathy:

- He realized that the water pooling around them was dirty, but the water dripping from the ceiling of the cave had been filtered and would be safer for drinking. Water was more important than food, so he organized tasks around collecting the drops and staying hydrated.

- He gave them a shared goal of digging—even though the chances of actually digging out were very low. Coach Ek realized that people need a task and a driving story to motivate them to carry out the task. His story was to imagine an orange field when they got out, with more food nearby.

- Coach Ek organized their days around the tasks and their purpose. He set one of the boys' watch alarms for 6 every morning so they had a shared schedule. As author Adam Galinsky says, "Coach Ek *inspired* them to survive."[5] He framed their predicament positively by never using words like "trapped" or "stuck." Instead, he framed their challenge as only temporary—a good story that they would tell their families someday in the future. He understood the importance of hope.

- Coach Ek emphasized the connection that they shared. No matter what happened, they must never fight with each other. They must always look out for one another, particularly for the weakest boys. Teamwork was key, as it was when they played soccer.

- Coach Ek himself recognized the importance of being calm, with clarity and courage. When he was a monk in training, he had only one meal a day for nine years. This framing on food and survival helped the boys accept their constant hunger.

- To lift their moods, they would sing. Coach Ek helped the boys regulate their emotions. When someone needed to cry, they cried. If we get depressed, Coach Ek argued, our bodies will fall apart too. If we are mentally strong, our bodies will restore themselves.

Even in the BANI Future, most of us will not be trapped in caves with water rising all around us. Sometimes it will feel that way, though. When it does, think about the story of Coach Ek.

Personal Coping Skills for Attending to Anxious

Anxious can be countered by recognizing, acknowledging, and where possible, responding to the crises faced by other people in your organization or community. Focus on and listen to the specific details of a situation without assuming you already know what people are going to say. The challenge will be in listening through the noise of the BANI Future.

Attending to Anxious

The following are the coping skills for attending to anxious that we adapted from the Northwestern University resilience course:

- **Name positive events:** Notice when positive things, creative ideas, or meaningful experiences happen. Focus on breathing exercises and techniques that cultivate present-moment awareness that helps to manage your anxiety.

- **Savor life:** Relish positive experiences and enjoy even minute elements of life that give you joy. Encourage individuals to focus on positive outcomes and moments of calm amid anxiety. Recognizing small achievements promotes a sense of agency and reduces anxiety. Any sense of control will be elusive in the BANI world.

Attentive active empathy will require being intensely aware of the many varied experiences of life around you—including the experiences of others you have never met. Attention is necessary to even begin to understand anxiety in yourself or others. When someone says or somehow expresses "I see you" or "I hear you," it can make a dramatic difference to others. Being ignored can be depressing. Acknowledging others in your random encounters is a gift we can all give that is often very important for others.

Mindfulness usually refers to being aware of yourself, but we need also to be mindful of others. Are you attentive to others? The military has a similar practice that they call "situation awareness," but they mean it more in terms of being alert to potential danger—potential harm that others can do to you. "Tone deaf" is the opposite, where you are not in touch with what's going on around you.

Cultivate attentiveness through mindfulness and empathetic practices to figure out a way to survive and thrive while you are experiencing anxiety.

Anxiety often emerges from the unpredictability and overwhelming nature of the BANI world. This chapter focuses on developing calm attentiveness and building empathy for others to counter anxiety. Expressing gratitude regularly helps individuals step out of anxious mindsets and foster active empathy toward others, reducing isolation.

When anxiety spikes due to uncertainty, practicing mindfulness can help individuals focus on their immediate surroundings, calming anxious thoughts. Combining this with gratitude for small successes grounds the person in the present.

Optimal Anxiety

In a BANI world, your own anxiety can help you to be understanding of others who feel anxious. The challenge is what you do with your anxiety, and what you do with the anxiety you sense around you. How can you listen to your anxiety and the anxiety of others while still trying to turn anxiety into something positive?

When Bob was in divinity school, he was attracted to Eastern religions. One of his favorite authors was the Zen philosopher Alan W. Watts, who wrote a book in 1951 called *The Wisdom of Insecurity: A Message for an Age of Anxiety*.[6] It is weirdly comforting to think that Watts viewed 1951 as an "age of anxiety," long before the VUCA world—let alone the BANI Future.

Watts described our dilemma as humans going through life in this way:

> As the years go by (that is, as we age), there seem to be fewer and fewer rocks to which we can hold, fewer things which we can regard as absolutely right and true, and fixed for all time. To some this is a welcome release from the restraints of moral, social, and spiritual dogma. To others it is a dangerous and terrifying breach with reason and sanity, tending to plunge human life into hopeless chaos. To most, perhaps, the immediate sense of release has given a brief exhilaration, to be followed by the deepest anxiety.[7]

Anxiety is not new, but some special kinds of anxiety that humans will experience in the BANI Future will be new and will be dangerous. The intense challenge will be to be attentive to that anxiety, with active empathy for others. Using tools like the ones we discuss in this chapter, it is possible to avoid being overwhelmed by peak anxiety. It is possible to thrive with optimal anxiety.

8

Neuroflexible

Practical Improvisation

NEUROFLEXIBLE: In BANI+, "neuroflexible" refers to flexibility of the mind. It's the ability to recognize changing conditions and adjust our actions and choices on the fly. It asks that we not be tied to parameters based on previous conditions, especially if it has become clear that conditions have evolved. It requires that we pay close attention to early indicators that larger developments may be underway, and to keep alternative approaches in mind as we act.

Neuroflexibility asks us to avoid being too closely tied to a particular way of doing things, especially in chaotic environments. It demands that we pay attention when we feel something is off, and that we focus more on achieving the outcomes we seek rather than hewing closely to a list of steps that has diminishing relevance. Neuroflexibility is recognizing that the world we *want*, the world we *plan for*, and the world we *get* can all diverge considerably. We need to be able to adjust intentions to meet unexpected demands. The right small gesture can make a big impact.

The Age of Neuroflexible

To counter nonlinear, be neuroflexible. Essentially, we will need to teach our brains new tricks. Think of it as practical improvisation and learn from improv actors. The techniques of improvisation will prove particularly useful to break out of linear patterns of thinking.

Nonlinear futures won't unfold in straight lines—they'll tangle in ways that will defy logical expectations. The future is unlikely to unfold as you expect, and counterintuitive thinking will often be required. Orthogonal thinking—the skill of seeing things from different angles—will be essential to navigating the chaos. "Common sense" will often be misleading.

Successful responses to nonlinear developments will require extreme flexibility in both thinking and acting. Our expectations are increasingly likely to be wrong, especially if we have grown up in more stable parts of the world where the impacts of BANI are not yet as obvious. Nonlinear futures will be characterized by eyebrow-raising disruptions and consequences. In a BANI Future, change will explode from directions that can be impossible to foresee—and easily could be the opposite of what we expect. A nonlinear world calls into question established balances of cause and effect, or inputs and outputs. We need to prepare for being unprepared.

Neuroflexibility is the ability to adapt one's thinking and learn new cognitive patterns. Expectations of linearity and order will need to be replaced by critical analysis and gaming of alternative paths. We'll need to be light on our figurative feet; this shift will require more than coping—it will require *dancing*.

Being neuroflexible also means being ready to take advantage of positive nonlinearity. Angela notes that Romania's tax policy is nonlinear in a significant way: it allows taxpayers to allocate up to 3.5 percent of their income tax to charitable causes. This is a modest redirection of funds at no extra cost to the taxpayer, but the impact has been profound. The policy roots trace back to Hungary in 1991, as Eastern Europe was emerging from the Cold War and the fall of the communist bloc. The region faced the challenge of rebuilding its economies and societies and saw a need to incentivize taxpayers to give back to their communities.

This approach spread across the region and had disproportionately positive impacts. In 2014, India adopted a similar policy. This is positive nonlinearity in action; the new challenge is how to scale this still-new way of thinking.

Being neuroflexible requires us to be—just a bit—nonlinear, too.

How Organizations Can Go Selectively Nonlinear

"Going nonlinear" used to imply craziness. In the BANI Future, going nonlinear will most often be a signal of realism. A nonlinear environment will very often require nonlinear actions in order to achieve desired outcomes.

In a BANI Future, change will not happen in neat, predictable steps. Rather, change will more often happen in abrupt spasmodic bursts—nonlinear shifts. These mysterious shifts will come from wildly varied sources including technologies, geopolitics, elections, youth behaviors, climate disruptions, or public health disasters like COVID-19. There may be subtle clues as to which of these varied sources is likely to erupt next, but that's not guaranteed. Still, paying attention to little changes—what Jamais sometimes calls the "distant, early warnings"—will often help you get ready to move.

For organizations to thrive, they will need to practice the ability to pivot quickly—as well as adapt with creativity and agility. Clarity of direction will need to hold as steady as possible, but changes could be very rapid indeed within that envelope of clarity. Occasionally even the overall clarity story of an organization will need to change.

Not everything, however, will go nonlinear. Even in BANI Futures, some things will not change and some change will be linear. Some change will even be predictable—but predictability will be the exception rather than the rule. Organizations must remain grounded in their core mission—their own clarity story—while adapting as required to the chaos around them.

Navigating this balance of clarity and chaos will determine winners and losers.

Netflix's Nonlinear Turnaround

Netflix's story of neuroflexibility and improvisation was forced by unexpected changes in their business and the industry around it. Netflix started in 1997 as a DVD-by-mail rental service. As internet speeds increased, however, there was an abrupt shift in capabilities for distributing video content to homes. Industry stalwart Blockbuster was caught off guard, but Netflix jumped ahead of their competitors. In 2007, Netflix introduced streaming video that allowed subscribers to watch movies and other video content online instead of waiting for delivery of physical DVDs. Netflix improvised with streaming while still maintaining their DVD-by-mail option during the transition.

While you could argue that this was a linear shift in transmission speeds and cost, the shift for Netflix was nonlinear. Just ten years after their company was founded, the DVD-by-mail business model that Netflix pioneered was on the verge of being obsolete.

This technology disruption had many implications beyond the rental business. As Netflix shifted from DVD rentals to online streaming, the variety of competition changed to include companies like Amazon Prime Video, Hulu, and Disney+. Netflix's nonlinear strategies were stymied by traditional studios scrambling to enclose content within their own walled-garden platforms. Content became a big issue that still included licensing but increasingly focused on the potential for new-content creation, as well as the use of data analytics.

Netflix embraced these different ways of thinking about their business and prototyped their way to success. It required neuroflexibility on the part of Netflix to leap into the creation of original content such as *House of Cards*, their first original production in 2013. This move allowed Netflix to differentiate themselves and reduce their reliance on expensive licensing arrangements—all within their brand clarity of delivering home entertainment.

As Netflix expanded globally, they also showed remarkable neuroflexibility as they considered varied global markets. Their localized strategy included producing content tailored to local audiences (like *Money Heist* in Spain and *Sacred Games* in India), as well as navigating varied local regulations and pricing models. They even introduced mobile-only streaming plans for regions with low broadband access but high smartphone penetration.

Netflix's own future depends on whether they can continue to be strategically nonlinear in an industry that continues to be chaotic and unlikely to stabilize in the BANI Future.

LEGO's Nonlinear Turnaround

LEGO™, the very successful Danish toy company, experienced a financial crisis in the early 2000s. The company, traditionally known for its iconic plastic toy building blocks, had expanded too rapidly into unusual-for-them new businesses like video games, theme parks, and even clothing. LEGO was spread too thin and became financially unstable.

Jørgen Vig Knudstorp became CEO in 2004, during this crisis that featured early elements of BANI. It turned out that LEGO's traditional structures were brittle even though they looked strong from a distance. Their business culture was disrupted as the market was changing in nonlinear ways. The cause-and-effect relationships that used to be assumed no longer seemed to apply in the same way.

The new CEO recognized that anxiety was being felt at all levels of the company and that this was directly related to their rapid overextension. LEGO had moved away from its original strengths, creating confusion internally and externally. A different mindset was needed for this very different market—even though the core brand was still viable.

First, they refocused on their core product by reinvesting in the iconic LEGO bricks and framing this new initiative around being a global leader in creative play. Authentic clarity relieves anxiety and provides the comfort of a clear and familiar direction forward—despite feelings of crisis. LEGO's clarity—their brand story—is fostering creativity and imagination through play. Knudstorp decided to cut back on product lines that didn't align with LEGO's core strengths. Instead, he emphasized innovative new product sets that built upon the core bricks.

LEGO also listened to employees across all levels of the organization and initiated a culture of transparency where leaders and frontline workers could discuss openly both challenges and solutions. Regular company-wide updates helped alleviate anxiety by ensuring that everyone understood both how things were going and where things were going. They also reached out to customers to better understand their needs and values. They launched a LEGO Ideas platform where fans could submit ideas for new LEGO sets—some of which became real products. They began programs of partnership with other brands that shared both risks and rewards.

The LEGO story combined crisis response, strategic foresight, and long-term growth. Through these efforts, LEGO was able to turn around its financial situation and reduce anxiety within the company. By being attentive and empathetic—both to its employees and its customers—LEGO was able to weather the crisis and reemerge as a leader in global play. It is a model for how organizations can flip the challenges of the BANI Future into opportunities, while still holding the clarity of a robust and powerful brand. But that wasn't all.

LEGO went nonlinear through programs like LEGO Education, which brought the brand into schools to inspire future generations of builders. LEGO Mindstorms is their robotics program, initially designed for children as an educational toy. LEGO Mindstorms introduced programmable LEGO bricks, which allowed users to automate tasks as they created robots.

To LEGO's surprise, LEGO Mindstorms was adopted quickly by universities and research institutions, including MIT Media Lab, where professors and students saw its potential for higher-level education, research, and new-concept prototyping. This game-changing shift led to the use of LEGO products for teaching topics like robotics, artificial intelligence, and control systems. LEGO adapted gracefully by listening to early users so they could integrate new ideas with their products quickly. LEGO became a bridge between theoretical knowledge and hands-on learning. These efforts evolved into the LEGO League and other competitions.

LEGO Mindstorms was not part of the company's original product set, but LEGO saw opportunity in the nonlinear developments brewing in robotics and sought out ways to connect them to creative play. In many ways, LEGO Mindstorms was a clear example of the link between LEGO and neuroflexibility. Plans and blueprints were available, but not mandatory, and very often experimentation in design could lead to amazing insights and understanding.

LEGO Ideas was another nonlinear response to nonlinear shifts in both digital media and consumer behavior. People wanted more personalization, and digital media made that possible. LEGO Ideas is an online platform where fans can submit ideas for new LEGO sets and the most popular are then produced by the company. This kind of crowdsourcing of new products was a nonlinear disruption of the centralized innovation practices at LEGO in the past.

Another nonlinear shift was toward digital and interactive play as physical toys were being challenged by video gaming and other forms of play on screens. LEGO embraced this shift and partnered with others to create new franchises like LEGO Star Wars, which blended traditional LEGO play with digital storytelling and gameplay. They also ventured into augmented reality and mobile apps, such as LEGO Hidden Side, which allowed users to combine physical play with augmented-reality experiences.

In each of these cases, LEGO was able to be neuroflexible in their strategies. Even as they went strategically nonlinear, they stayed with their overall brand story of creative play and creative building.

How Individuals Can Go Selectively Nonlinear

In the chaos of the BANI Future, even the best-laid plans will be disrupted. Individuals must learn to thrive in nonlinear futures with intention, flexibility, and improvisation. Individuals will need mental agility while staying grounded in purpose and meaning. There is an intentional nature to selective nonlinearity, and there are good models for how individuals can manifest this in inspiring ways.

Viktor Frankl's Nonlinear Turnaround

There is a big difference between choosing to go nonlinear and being forced into going nonlinear. In the extreme horrific conditions of Nazi concentration camps, Viktor Frankl demonstrated incredible neuroflexibility by reframing his intense suffering into an inspiring and robust search for meaning.

Frankl's was a kind of mental improvisation as he realized that, while he could not control the horrors of the concentration camp, he could control how he responded to those horrors. His improvisation was in mindset reorientation: instead of viewing suffering as meaningless horror, he reframed the suffering as an opportunity to discover meaning and purpose. He viewed his daily torment as a chance to exercise his own personal freedom to choose his mental response. Frankl was also forced to improvise in dealing with extreme physical hardships such as hunger, pain, and exhaustion. He created mental exercises such as imagining himself after the war giving talks to others about how he learned from his experiences in concentration camps.

In the camps, Frankl often acted as an informal therapist for his fellow prisoners. He helped them find reasons to hold onto life despite the awful conditions. He had an ability to improvise ways to support others who were close to giving up. Somehow, he was able to boost morale by pointing out glimpses of meaning in a sunrise or a smile. His emerging logotherapy philosophy was a form of improvisation as he imagined meaning and purpose at the center of psychological well-being.

Stanislav Petrov's Nonlinear Turnaround

Mutual assured destruction—MAD—is the underlying concept driving nuclear deterrence. The use of nuclear weapons by one side of a conflict has a very high likelihood of triggering the use of nuclear weapons by the other side; consequently, the logic goes, everyone is highly reluctant to go first. The more you dive into the underlying theories of nuclear war, with its "escalation ladders" and "de-escalation by escalation," the more you realize that MAD is nonlinear. Just one act, one mistake, could lead to exchanges of reprisal ultimately resulting in what could be the end of the world. We haven't seen this happen in reality, of course, but we have come uncomfortably close. Too often, survival rests on the back of a single decision to question expected behaviors.

Those of you who remember late 1983 might recall that it was a remarkably tense time in global politics. The Soviet Union had just shot down KAL 007, a Korean airliner that had flown into Soviet airspace.[1] The United States was performing large-scale military exercises within quick reach of the USSR. In Washington, President Ronald Reagan talked about the "evil empire," and in Moscow Soviet General Secretary Yuri Andropov ordered the KGB to get ready for an imminent US attack. The two superpowers threatened each other with nuclear missiles in Europe and shot at each other's proxies in brushfire wars in Central America and central Asia.

Stanislav Petrov wasn't the regular overnight officer on duty on September 25 and 26, 1983, at the Serpukhov-15 Ballistic Missile Early Warning System control post. He came in as a substitute to maintain his skills, expecting that—like every other night since the Oko monitoring satellites had gone into orbit—it would be a quiet evening.

Forty minutes after midnight, September 26, the computer system registered the launch of a Minuteman missile from the United States.[2] Then another launch signal, and another. Within a few minutes, the early warning system registered five missiles on the way.

Petrov had to decide—was this a real launch or a false alarm? The Soviet strategy at the time was massive response: the launch of all intercontinental nuclear missiles the moment an attack from the United States was spotted. Petrov had actually written the policy guide for missile officers that laid out exactly what must be done in the event of a launch warning.

He had just logic and intuition to go on; the policy guide wasn't enough. A real missile attack wouldn't come from just a single base, he reasoned, nor would it comprise just five missiles. Moreover, he did not trust the computer system identifying the threat. With good reason, as it turned out—the Oko satellite that had sent the alert had been confused by the infrared signature of the sun reflected off high-altitude clouds.

If Petrov had obeyed the script that he himself wrote, followed policy and alerted the Kremlin, a global thermonuclear exchange would have almost certainly been the result.

As thanks for not following the rules and triggering World War III, Petrov was chastised by his superiors for not detailing the event properly in his logbook, and he was very nearly jailed; in the end, he left the military without the usual honors and commendations.

Although this story isn't from the BANI era, its lessons have become all the more relevant. In an era replete with hypersonic missiles and cheap weaponized drones, we're at a point where the time between mistake and cataclysm could be astonishingly short.

Tammie Jo Shults's Nonlinear Turnaround

At 32,000 feet, Captain Tammie Jo Shults was flying Southwest Airlines flight 1380 when her left engine exploded catastrophically and fatally sucked a passenger halfway out of a window at row 14.[3] This BANI-like experience was unscripted and had never before been simulated or practiced in her training—even as a former Navy fighter pilot. Passengers panicked. One hundred forty-eight lives were at stake.

In an experience that felt to those inside the plane like free-falling, Shults and her first officer Darren Ellisor were able to stabilize the plane and identify the closest airport with a long runway, which happened to be Philadelphia. At this point, Shults said the following over the intercom and changed the emotional framing of this awful experience for everyone: "We are not going down. We are going to Philly."[4]

Afterward, passengers expressed how that simple message made all the difference. Her voice was calm and matter-of-fact, in spite of the terrifying circumstances. When Shults was examined after the plane was on the ground safely, the medical personnel said she didn't even have an elevated heart rate. Calm in crisis.

Once on the ground in Philadelphia, Shults went back into the cabin and slowly looked each passenger in the eye and asked if they were OK. Like when she made her simple announcement during the crisis, she communicated calm and clarity.

Shults demonstrated neuroflexibility—the ability to think, feel, and act dynamically in response to a high-stakes nonlinear shock. In the BANI Future, where disruption will be inevitable, leaders will need the ability to pivot and perform. With only minutes to decide, Shults was forced to deviate from the standard flight procedures that she had been taught through decades of experience in training, spending hours in flight simulators, and captaining real flights. She had to teach her brain new tricks on the fly and in the crisis.

The years of experience did help her stay calm under this extreme pressure. Simulation and gaming is a proven way to prepare for chaotic high-risk situations in a low-risk way. She had internalized all the key decision-making processes that were viable, but she was flexible enough to think outside her experience and create a viable exit path to safety.

A final aspect of this rescue was coordination with her first officer. Both pilots had extensive training. Shults was able to rely on Ellisor to manage important details while she focused on the delicate landing of the plane. Their training allowed them to act cohesively even in this nonlinear crisis. The BANI Future will require teamwork.

Personal Skills for Thriving in a Nonlinear Future

Nonlinear challenges don't follow predictable patterns, and they require individuals to develop mental agility and neuroflexibility. Essentially, even as our brains are seeking certainty and expecting a linear world, we all have to teach our brains new tricks—and keep doing so.

Going Nonlinear

The following are the coping skills for nonlinear that we adapted from the Northwestern University resilience course:

- **Use positive reappraisal:** Seek out positives, even in apparently negative or neutral situations. Look for ways to reframe in authentically positive ways. Look for ways to forgive.

- **Practice self-compassion:** Be kind and soothing to yourself. Enjoy very specific experiences whenever possible.

In a nonlinear world where unexpected changes are frequent and there is little sense of stability, it is essential to develop mental skills to adapt and stay emotionally grounded. Positive reappraisal is the ability to reframe challenges and find silver linings—even in difficult situations. Essentially, this is the skill of reinterpreting adversity as an opportunity for growth, learning, or new possibilities. Viktor Frankl's experience finding meaning in suffering while in a concentration camp is an extreme example, but it highlights the robust potential of human resilience. It doesn't deny the negative aspects of a situation, but it does prioritize the search for positive possibilities. Frankl's experience shows that we can—even in extreme situations—reappraise our situation, develop agency, and move forward with clarity.

Fred Luskin's long-term research program at Stanford University on forgiveness provides a practical set of tools that can result in a positive mindset shift. He argues that forgiveness is not about excusing harm but about reclaiming personal peace of mind and agency. Holding onto resentment from past harm can create a kind of cognitive lock-in that is the opposite of being neuroflexible. Forgiveness is an act of improvisation by letting go of the past in order to create a better future. It fosters resilience by easing paralysis from past grievances. In a BANI Future where disruption will be inevitable, the ability to forgive will release past burdens and help people adapt to new realities.[5] Luskin observes:

> There is a world of difference between negative certainty and uncertainty. It can mean the difference between healing and depression.[6]

In a BANI Future, uncertainty will be a constant, but negative certainty will be a choice—usually a bad choice. The BANI Future will punish certainty because certainty is brittle and brittle breaks, but negative certainty can do more than break—it erases hope. Forgiveness will relieve negative certainty and help imagine possible paths forward.

Self-compassion and self-soothing can help in the reappraisal process, since our instinct in difficult situations is often to be self-critical, which can make things worse. In nonlinear environments, setbacks are inevitable. Self-compassion teaches the brain to respond with a nurturing, encouraging voice, rather than a critical or cynical one.

Positive reappraisal and self-compassion are both about building mental flexibility and emotional resilience. These skills allow us to find meaning, purpose, and growth in the face of continuing BANI challenges. Within this mental frame, change can be both a threat and a chance for new possibilities.

When you are confronted with a nonlinear challenge—such as an unexpected shift in a work project—practice mental improvisation to enable rapid brainstorming of creative solutions, using a positive mindset to stay open to change. Promote improvisation exercises to encourage mental flexibility, such as real-time role-playing scenarios that push people out of their comfort zones.

Theater improvisation techniques offer a powerful set of tools for fostering neuroflexibility that can improve your ability to thrive in a nonlinear world. In theatrical improv, people engage in unscripted scenes and are taught to respond spontaneously to fellow actors in real time. Here are a few BANI-relevant techniques derived from theatrical improv:

- **Yes, and . . . :** Accept whatever the scene or your partner gives you, building on an openness to the unknown to create a collaborative flow.

- **Think on your feet:** Respond quickly to whatever is presented, trusting your intuition without a predetermined plan.

- **Listen deeply:** Pay attention to every word, gesture, and cue, looking for signals and possible directions without assuming you know.

- **Collaborate spontaneously:** Cocreate in real time based on trust in others.

- **Embrace failure:** Accept that failure is part of the process and learn to move through failure.

- **Suspend judgment:** Focus on creating momentum without analyzing or evaluating.

Improv allows you to practice in low-risk ways for nonlinear futures and unpredictable environments.[7] In this sense, improv is a form of gaming where it is possible to create a safe space for exploring various what-if possibilities and practicing how you might respond.

Angela likes to tell the mythic "elephant and rope" story, which harkens back to a time when baby elephants were trained by tying them with a flimsy rope only strong enough to constrain a baby elephant. As the story goes, baby elephants pull on the rope at first and it doesn't break. Even as the elephant grows more powerful, however, it keeps assuming that the rope is an unbreakable constraint for its movement. Supposedly, the grown elephant never tests the rope again, even though if it did, it could easily break free. What are the "elephant and rope" constraints that each of us assumes we could not break because we haven't tried to break them?

United Way Worldwide experiences nonlinear disruptions frequently, such as a storm that destroys a community and its infrastructure. One day, it is sunny and bright; the next day, the community is in ruins. In a matter of a few hours, years of progress can be destroyed by a single storm. In these crises, we need to break out of our constraints. Even small acts of kindness can change someone's world and provide reason for hope. Nonlinear times will require us to break out of our old ways of thinking, teach our brains new tricks, and imagine new possibilities. When life doesn't follow a straight line, neither should our thinking.

9
Interconnected
Full-Spectrum Thinking

INTERCONNECTED: In BANI+, "interconnected" refers to being able to mutually communicate with a network of minds diverse in perspective, location, life experiences, culture, and more. It's not a question of sheer numbers; a smaller array with varied points of view is more useful than a large army of like-minded thinkers. Mutuality is important; just as you are able to ask questions, you should be available to answer questions in return.

The purpose of interconnected minds is not to provide final answers (although that may sometimes happen) but to provoke you into seeing the dilemmas you face in a new way. Moreover, the structure of the interconnection should be more weblike than hub and spoke: part of the value of the interconnection comes from the various parts sharing ideas and perspectives with each other.

The Age of Interconnected

To counter the incomprehensible, be interconnected with a full spectrum of perspectives.

In an Incomprehensible BANI world, the issue isn't just whether you've asked the right *questions*; it's whether you've asked the right *people*. Something incomprehensible to you may not be incomprehensible to someone else. The explanations and answers you seek may in fact be available, but not from the people in your current circles. Who might help you make sense out of what is incomprehensible to you?

For example, the "black swan" concept hit the big time in 2001, with the publication of Nassim Nicholas Taleb's book by the same name. It was a long time coming—the first recorded use of "black swan" to illustrate a larger point was by the Roman poet Juvenal in the 2nd century, where he used black swans as an example of something nonexistent. By the 16th century, Londoners, referencing Juvenal, used "black swan" to indicate impossibility. In the late 1600s, however, Dutch explorers spotted real-life black swans in Australia. Consequently, "black swan" took on the meaning of something thought impossible only to be revealed as real.

By 2001, when Taleb's book was published, the term "black swan" was being used as a more colorful but historically inaccurate way to describe what professional futurists had for years called "wildcards" (low-or-uncertain-probability events that—if they did occur—would have a high impact). The use of the term "black swans," as fueled by Taleb's book, was assumed to mean something shocking because black swans were (mistakenly) thought to be impossible.

But the Aboriginal people were very aware of black swans long before the Dutch arrived. Black swans (*Cygnus atratus*) are featured prominently in Aboriginal stories, symbolizing transformation and resilience in some traditions. The real lesson from the black swan story is that we should listen widely, beyond our usual circles, to try and understand emerging futures that look impossible to us. We may just not be asking the right people.

People in power may assume that they are the dominant authority and discount any ideas that don't fit their mental construct. Nontraditional pathways, however, may yield more insight in nonlinear and incomprehensible situations. A story from Angela's family is revealing: while walking down an urban street one night, Angela's husband encountered a drunk homeless person who gave him this advice: "You don't want to start drinking." This was wise advice from a subject-matter expert: he knew what he was talking about.

In the BANI Future, assumptions about sources of knowledge can be dangerous. One of the most problematic assumptions people often have regards their own levels of expertise; this can be a particular risk when someone with that assumption has a significant level of political, economic, cultural, or organizational power. As noted back at the very beginning of this book, "arrogant ignorance" often demonstrates a level of certainty that isn't just unwarranted, it's actually dangerous.

Conversely, too often people assume that their own personal journey to knowledge is the only legitimate route. Some of the most brilliant, innovative businesspeople don't have high school degrees, don't have traditional professional pathways, and because of their upbringing in low-income communities, have a street savvy that gives them insights and experience completely outside the worldview of conventional thinking.

In the BANI Future, not every incomprehensible moment will have explanations and answers, but even so, a more inclusive, diverse network of people will do a better job of chipping away at the incomprehensible. Often, it can be the intersection of distinctly varying points of view that can result in a new understanding. The "friction" of divergent ideas running into each other can be remarkably productive.

This is visible in the natural world as much as in human systems. The intertidal, or littoral, zones along shorelines see constantly changing evolutionary pressures, resulting in rapid species evolution and adaptations.[1] Rocky intertidal zones go from submerged to dry multiple times daily (with accompanying temperature shifts); undergo physical stresses from moving water and rocks; see abundant predation from sea, land, and air; and more. This puts enormous evolutionary and adaptive pressure on the species that live there.[2] Anthropogenic climate change has only accelerated this process.

In biology and culture both, the intersection of diverse systems can produce extremely rapid changes. Conflicts (and disagreements) can occur, but even these can be creative. Human minds can adapt more quickly and more fully when surrounded by a wide variety—a full spectrum—of ideas.

If organizations or individuals can include multiple viewpoints and ways of thinking, they will begin to make sense out of situations that may not make sense at first. Full-spectrum thinking will require looking beyond the labels and categories of the past to define a future that is beyond our current ability to comprehend. This kind of inclusivity can encompass but will go well beyond traditional approaches to DEI—diversity, equity, and inclusion.

Incomprehensible can be countered by embracing a wider variety of perspectives and inputs—ideally from a varied range of sources. *Full-spectrum thinking* means imagining the future across gradients of possibility, while resisting the temptations of the categories and labels from the past. We must resist binary choices and polarized thinking.

Outside points of view can often spot patterns or discontinuities that insiders miss or gloss over. Inclusive, full-spectrum thinking asks us to listen humbly to other points of view from circles of people other than our usual circles. We must continue to ask: Are we engaging with the right people in what we do and how we do it?

How Organizations Can Wrestle with the Incomprehensible

In an increasingly incomprehensible future, organizations will be confronted regularly with challenges that seem illogical, senseless, or impossible to grasp. In situations like this, additional information will be no guarantee of improved understanding. Whether it's disruptive technological change, unanticipated social unrest, or market surprises, the ability to flip the incomprehensible into something positive will become essential for both survival and growth.

If you cannot comprehend fully, a good starting point is to comprehend partially. This may seem a straightforward assertion, but it carries with it subtle dilemmas. When Bob was first getting started in his career as a futurist, his best corporate clients used "the 80/20 rule," which meant that they would proceed with a decision when they had 80 percent of the information they wished they had before making the decision. In the BANI Future, it will be more like the 60/40 rule or the 50/50 rule. You need to balance the risks of judging too soon and the risks of deciding too late. Even in a BANI world, you still need to make decisions. As we said at the outset, the future is uncertain, and yet we must act.

Which leads to a fundamental question: When an organization is unable to decipher what's going on, what does it do? The answer is to listen as widely as possible. Resist defining the unknown future by the categories of the past. Be inclusive, especially regarding different mindsets—embrace full-spectrum thinking across gradients of possibility, but resist the temptations of certainty, mindless categorization, and thoughtless labeling.[3]

When Angela visited Puerto Rico in 2023 after a series of heartbreaking humanitarian crises from hurricanes and their aftermath, she learned that local United Way leaders shared on-the-ground challenges with the Board of United Way Worldwide. One board member worked for an appliance manufacturer and remembered old plans that were never pursued for a washing machine that didn't require power. After hearing the crisis stories from Puerto Rico, the board member found a way to produce 170 manual washing machines and deliver them to families who needed them most. For incomprehensible challenges, it is critical to connect to people who have solutions you could not imagine on your own. The global network of United Way Worldwide expands ways of thinking about challenges based on the insight and experiences of others in the network. Building and maintaining strong relationships within the network makes it possible to nurture the needed consensus for collaboration.

Organizations must see beyond the obvious to tap into a broader range of perspectives, ideas, and possible ways forward. By expanding the boundaries of their thinking and making room for an array of voices, organizations can turn confusion into clarity, uncertainty into opportunity, and the incomprehensible into the actionable. The following are examples of organizations that have all taken something incomprehensible and flipped it into a catalyst for innovation.

Wikipedia's Incomprehensible Origin

When Jimmy Wales and Larry Sanger launched Wikipedia in 2001, the idea of creating a credible source of knowledge analogous to the encyclopedia through crowdsourcing was incomprehensible. Traditional encyclopedias were carefully curated by experts who had impressive credibility and credentials.

Wikipedia's open-contribution model is remarkably comprehensive of varied points of view and varied definitions of expertise. Anyone with internet access can create, edit, and improve articles. This open model means that knowledge comes from a vast range of cultural, geographic, and personal perspectives. The knowledge circles in Wikipedia are extremely wide—just the kind of inclusiveness that is necessary to engage with the incomprehensibility of the BANI world. Wikipedia is a global crowdsourced marvel that had never been imagined before. Wikipedia was impossible, until it happened.

Wikipedia uses full-spectrum thinking by breaking down the categories and knowledge silos of the past. It covers an incredibly wide range of subjects, including quantum physics, obscure local histories, and niche hobbies. Wikipedia's design doesn't prioritize certain subjects over others. It invites exploration across domains rather than within specialties. It encourages making connections across seemingly unrelated topics.

Wikipedia is structured as a self-regulating, shape-shifting organization. It has a robust set of guidelines, and community moderation ensures that the information remains credible and as unbiased as possible. The content comes in over 300 languages, which allows marginalized people to participate on a more equal footing. In this way, Wikipedia democratizes knowledge in ways that traditional encyclopedias could not have imagined. Their model is inherently flexible, so it continues to evolve as new data or perspectives emerge.

Wikipedia is accessible to anyone, from students to researchers to the simply curious. It has become a trusted source for the early stages of research projects—but not as a sole or final trusted source. In the early stages of an inquiry or research project, Wikipedia helps a seeker conduct an initial exploration—but it is not the best place to look for a final answer. It has become one of the most visited websites globally and has reshaped how knowledge is gathered, shared, and analyzed. It embraces inclusivity and thinking in full-spectrum ways.

The Special Olympics's Incomprehensible Origin

The Special Olympics is based on what used to be an incomprehensible idea: that people with intellectual or cognitive disabilities could excel at athletics. Intellectual disabilities include people on the autism spectrum and people with Down syndrome.

Before the Special Olympics, people with intellectual disabilities were excluded from mainstream sports and their athletic potential was rarely even considered—but implicitly denied. Eunice Kennedy Shriver, the founder of the Special Olympics, was a full-spectrum thinker who saw beyond limiting labels like "handicapped" and "disabled." These are people first, people who are different and have special needs. Categorizing and labeling them can be very debilitating. Indeed, all of us have limitations—and some of those limitations grow as we age. In our conversations around the broader topic of people with disabilities, a phrase we've heard to describe people without cognitive or physical impairments is "not yet disabled" or, sometimes, "predisabled."

As an organization focused on people with intellectual disabilities, the Special Olympics shows that athleticism can thrive across a wide spectrum of people, performance abilities, and intellectual capabilities. Also, the Special Olympics includes care providers—not just the athletes. It creates a community where people with special needs are celebrated rather than marginalized. This inclusivity allows them to develop self-esteem, communicate with people from varied backgrounds, and develop leadership skills to expand their own potential. Indeed, the very concept of "ability" is expanded to emotional resilience, teamwork, and leadership. Athleticism goes beyond speed and strength to expand human potential.

The Special Olympics now operates in more than 190 countries, in many different cultural contexts. This is global full-spectrum thinking that recognizes the varied intellectual disabilities across societies. The desire to connect, compete, and achieve is universal and has many side benefits.

Beyond the athletic arena, the Special Olympics is actively engaged in advocacy and education to influence policy, rights, and health access. They practice full-spectrum thinking to transform public perception of people with intellectual disabilities and to address the broader systemic barriers they face.

Programs like Unified Sports expand the Special Olympics vision to pair athletes with and without disabilities. This creates a bridge of empathy and respect for everyone involved. It broadens our concepts of comprehensibility and possibility. These programs also make intellectual and cognitive disabilities more understandable to a wider public.

How Individuals Can Wrestle with the Incomprehensible

As the BANI world expands, some individuals have already figured out personal strategies for coping and thriving in spaces that are incomprehensible to others. These people are the early BANI explorers who embraced incomprehensibility and flipped it into something much more positive. These individuals are the groundbreakers for the rest of us. They all have clarity of purpose, they are all inclusive in their analysis, and they employ full-spectrum thinking to get beyond the categories and labels of the past.

Let's consider three extremely varied examples: Viktor Frankl, Kizzmekia Corbett, and Malala Yousafzai.

Viktor Frankl's Incomprehensible Turnaround

Nazi Germany was morally and intellectually incomprehensible for Viktor Frankl and so many others—especially those locked in the concentration camps. How could an advanced society choose voluntarily to systematically exterminate millions of people? Frankl was able to embrace meaning-making and use the suffering of this deliberate atrocity as a lens for transcendence of evil into his budding concept of logotherapy based on purpose and meaning.

The proto-BANI world of Nazi Germany was driven by human-engineered oppression where meaning was stripped away through brutality and fear, and Jews were targeted as a primary source of Germany's problems. Human cruelty became a way of life, and kindness was applied only to those of your own kind. Frankl had a different model, a different mindset.

The BANI world of today is driven by institutional brittleness, accelerated anxiety, systemic nonlinearity, and overall incomprehensibility. Still, Frankl's lessons remain timeless: meaning is something we all must create—we will not simply find it waiting for us. Meaning is possible, even in the most incomprehensible situations. Our ability to reframe our experiences will determine our capacities to endure, adapt, and thrive.

Kizzmekia Corbett's Incomprehensible Turnaround

Dr. Kizzmekia "Kizzy" Shanta Corbett-Helaire is an American viral immunologist who played a pivotal role in developing the Moderna COVID-19 vaccine. While at the National Institutes of Health (NIH), she was the scientific lead of the Vaccine Research Center's coronavirus team, where her work was instrumental in the development of mRNA-1273, the vaccine candidate that became the Moderna COVID-19 vaccine.

Corbett didn't just help develop a lifesaving vaccine; she helped reshape the process of science communication and interconnection in the midst of a global crisis. She is a prominent science communicator and advocate for vaccine awareness—particularly in communities of color.

The pandemic was an incomprehensible global crisis that overwhelmed systems worldwide. In a world flooded with misrepresentations and outright lies, Corbett became a steady and open source of information for communities that were skeptical of the system. She sought out interconnected solutions, including working with scientists who were normally much more protective of their own research. She wove together approaches that combined innovation, trust building, and equity.

Corbett's breakthrough work on the COVID-19 vaccine was a scientific achievement, but it was also a model for interconnected leadership and full-spectrum thinking beyond the categories and labels of the past. She was able to integrate multiple fields of knowledge, build bridges of public trust, and work closely with local communities. The COVID-19 pandemic wasn't just a medical crisis; it was a global systems crisis that exposed brittle healthcare infrastructure, anxious public sentiment, nonlinear disease spread, and incomprehensible misinformation. Corbett worked at the intersection of molecular science, immunology, and public health. To succeed, she had to combine science with scalability and public communication. She spoke directly to Black communities where vaccine hesitancy was high. She didn't work in silos like so many scientists. She used deep interconnections to push back against the incomprehensible.

Malala Yousafzai's Incomprehensible Turnaround

At age fifteen, Malala Yousafzai was shot by the Taliban for advocating education for girls. Her response was to transform her own very personal trauma through activism. She became an even more powerful voice for education, using her platform to advance the very cause that provoked the Taliban to try to kill her. As she was recovering from her gunshot wound, she said it this way in her book *I Am Malala*:

> I realized what the Taliban had done was make my campaign global. While I was lying in that bed waiting to take my first steps in a new world, Gordon Brown, the UN special envoy for education and former prime minister of Britain, had launched a petition under the slogan "I am Malala" to demand no child be denied a school.[4]

In the BANI Future, some stories will spread virally—and some changes will happen quickly. At the same time, the BANI Future will be too much for many people, and outdated ideas will be dangerously comforting.

Malala's story is one of remarkable resilience, empathy, and attentiveness in the face of horror. As a young girl growing up in the Swat Valley of Pakistan, she became an outspoken advocate for girls' education in a region where the Taliban had banned education for girls. Her attentiveness to the needs and struggles of other young women, combined with her own active empathy for others, led her to become a public figure—despite the risks to her and her family. The Taliban's attempted assassination did not silence her, however; it amplified her message of change to a global scale.

Combining attentiveness and empathy, Malala has established the Malala Fund to provide education for young girls in underserved areas. Her own experience of fear and anxiety was fuel for her global activism. For most of the world, it is incomprehensible that the Taliban would resist education for women. For the Taliban, it is incomprehensible to accept a world outside their own extreme religious beliefs, a polarized form of incomprehensibility.

Malala flipped the incomprehensibility into a personal mission that emphasized the individual right for girls to have access to education. By framing her cause inclusively, Malala expanded her advocacy beyond herself and her local community in Pakistan. She framed her inclusiveness globally, connecting with girls and young people worldwide. The Malala Fund partners with local educators and activists in a wide range of locations where girls face barriers to schooling and learning. This inclusive approach isn't just about telling her story; it is about using her story to empower others.

Malala's programs combine education, poverty reduction, and gender equality. Education for girls isn't an isolated issue; it is a full-spectrum issue with interconnected challenges. Education is a foundation for economic empowerment, health improvement, and social stability. Malala is building bridges across political, cultural, and religious divides—but she is keeping her own story focused clearly on the value and the values of education. Her message appeals especially to global youth, but she has multigenerational appeal. By inspiring younger people, she is creating a vision that will go beyond her individual influence. Malala is making education accessible, especially in marginalized communities.

Malala has flipped the incomprehensible by making her cause inclusive and connected to broader causes. The localized incomprehensible act of violence against her activated a global force for positive change.

Personal Skills for Wrestling with the Incomprehensible

Trying to get your mind around something "incomprehensible" feels so lonely, so stark and heavy—like standing on the edge of something too vast to grasp. Even the best thinkers will be forced to settle for tiny shreds of insight and small moments of clarity. Foresight feels utterly impossible in the face of the incomprehensible, leaving us feeling as if we are standing alone in the cold, with wolves sniffing at our feet.

Mental agility will be necessary, but our bodies must be adaptable as well. When confronted by BANI incomprehensibility, our bodies can stiffen, our breathing can go shallow, the stress can lock us into rigid thinking. There are tools that can help, such as somatic therapy—essentially being more aware of your body and how to keep it in a zone of resilience rather than hyperarousal.[5]

Neuroflexible leaders will know how to regulate in real time. They will breathe more deeply and their heart rates will steady as they focus. Somatic interventions don't just calm the body; they teach the brain new tricks for adaptability. The best leaders will reset quickly, recover from setbacks, and remain engaged with incomprehensibility. The body itself can become a medium for clarity and resilience. The challenge is to be at our best when we are threatened.

The following are the coping skills for the incomprehensible adapted from the Northwestern University resilience course:

- **Notice personal strengths:** Recognize and appreciate your own abilities—even when others do not notice. Doing something is usually better than doing nothing. Focus on the things you do well.

- **Set attainable goals:** Create to-do lists that are achievable, and reward yourself when you accomplish them. Even small progress is far better than doing nothing at all.

Incomprehensible situations feel overwhelming and chaotic, often defying logic. Individuals will need to develop comprehensive thinking to embrace other perspectives, and full-spectrum awareness to navigate these complexities.

Interconnectedness requires community—and not just your own community. Nobody should have to wrestle with incomprehensible situations alone. Building strong connections can help individuals gain perspective from diverse viewpoints.

As we were finishing this work, a new book was published by Carla Fernandez called *Renegade Grief: A Guide to the Wild Ride of Life after Loss*.[6] Although she was writing about the grief of losing a loved one, the human experience of the BANI world very often includes grief for simpler times—even if those times were not really as simple as we remember them. Fernandez stresses the importance of community in grieving so we can pause and reflect while also regathering our energy for the challenges of this increasingly chaotic future. The BANI Future will require us to experience a kind of grief.

> *Renegade Grief* is my attempt to introduce folks to a bunch of different pathways in, with stories from real people who've tried it, too, and a widening of the lens from outside of the Western world's constipated relationship to grief. It reminds us that humans have handled times of extreme change and loss for millennia, and while these particular times are unprecedented, we have what it takes to ride this wave.[7]

The healthy embrace of grief relies on practices that are similar to those for stress relief. Grief is loaded with stress and anxiety. Just as we've drawn in this book from the methods of Judith Moskowitz and her team to relieve stress and cope with medical traumas, we need to draw on and adapt those tools that seem to help with BANI-world stress.

Having a sense of purpose that grounds you, even in chaotic environments full of the unthinkable and the absurd, will give you a better chance to make sense out of a world that doesn't make sense.

People—leaders in particular—will need to seek out and value other perspectives to widen their lens on incomprehensible situations. Intellectual and cultural breadth can expand their thinking and offer new ways to approach complexity. Faith can play a positive role here for many, offering a way to imagine possibilities that are not yet apparent. Even in a BANI Future, clarity of direction will be possible. Certainty will be alluring, but it can erase hope.

In a situation where someone feels overwhelmed by an incomprehensible situation, relying on community support and diverse perspectives can help provide clarity, inspiration, and sometimes even solutions that an individual might not see on their own. Leadership in the face of incomprehensibility is particularly difficult. When the world makes no sense, seeking out new dots to connect can create new possibilities.

PART III

BANI in Action

THIS FINAL PART of *Navigating the Age of Chaos* offers two different perspectives on using BANI as a lens for understanding the world and how we can grapple with the transformations now underway. Neither should be considered a final statement; it's likely that, in subsequent editions of *Navigating the Age of Chaos*, this section will see the greatest number of updates. But these chapters should be thought of as a jumping-off point for translating the ideas of BANI into useful, usable action.

The first of the two chapters, "BANI Worlds: Mapping New Realities," looks at the ways in which BANI can be employed as a framework for building out relevant scenarios and forecasts of the BANI Future. It goes into detail about the purpose of scenario development and offers examples of what a BANI-centered approach to scenario building might look like.

The second of the two chapters, "BANI Leadership: Charting the Course," discusses how organizational leaders can use the BANI lens as a way to better understand their stakeholders and the world in which they operate. The BANI world directly undermines conventional wisdom in leadership. How we operate in the remainder of the 21st century depends on how well we can adapt to the new realities.

After the conclusion, "BANI and Our Futures," we offer another key resource: a set of questions to ask yourself and your organization in order to develop a BANI perspective, along with discussion questions suited for classroom conversations about the BANI world, the BANI Future, and our role as people trying to thrive in a chaotic system.

10
BANI Worlds

Mapping New Realities

SCENARIOS: Scenarios are structured narratives (often, but not always, written stories) designed to illuminate details and implications of possible future outcomes. They can vary dramatically in length, depending on the information needed by the audience to understand the core logic of that future. Scenario creators will typically provide a set of three to five narratives of different possible futures all arising from the same starting point. The differences between these futures depend on the various possible ways in which critical elements of the future can unfold.

Scenarios are not meant as *predictions* but as *provocations*. If it's a stand-alone scenario, it will focus on the less-obvious consequences of one or more big changes over the coming years. If it's a set of multiple possible futures all coming from the same origin, no single one will be the "official" vision of the future. The purpose of scenarios is to provide new perspectives on what may happen and to elicit new realizations about possible outcomes. A good scenario (or set of scenarios) can be a catalyst for a greater understanding of our BANI Future.

The Age of New Realities

We started this book with the statement "the future is uncertain, and yet we must act." The pages that followed detailed the ways in which and reasons why the future is even more uncertain than usual, as well as the ways in which and reasons why we can still act in new, insightful, and hopeful ways. There is, however, a step along the way to help move us more easily from uncertainty to action: we can imagine possibilities.

For many people who use BANI in their work and research, the concept is descriptive—a term to give a name to the changes taking place in a chaotic world. This is good! As we talked about earlier, names have power. Being able to give something a name, being able to identify it as its own thing, goes a long way toward understanding what can be done in these new circumstances. We can't see where we can go if we can't say where we are.

But that's not the only use of the BANI framework. As we suggest in chapter 1, we can also use BANI as a seed for scenarios that let us explore possible outcomes in a BANI environment. In turn, that will let us test different strategic or behavioral responses to those possibilities. BANI-informed scenarios can be a catalyst for new understanding of our changing world and how our systems combine and clash.

Discovering New Realities

The future is uncertain, but it is not opaque. We can see the many dynamics underway today that will have visible and meaningful influence on what our futures might hold. The resolutions of these ongoing processes are not certain, but we can have a bit of clarity about the forms those resolutions might take. Not because of brilliant prescience or mystical clairvoyance, but because of history.

Jamais has long argued that what is usually known as "futurism" could often be more accurately referred to as "anticipatory history." The same processes and dynamics that we can see shaping the course of the past still apply when we look ahead. Foresight specialists are historians of the possible.

The future is uncertain; we can't know what will happen. But because we have some clarity about the forces that affect the future, we can explore what *could* happen. We can create narratives—scenarios—in which we examine possible (ideally, plausible) outcomes arising from those forces. The question is not whether the resulting scenarios (and other foresight methods) are *right*; the question is whether they are *useful*. Can we learn something new?

We believe that BANI **is** useful in this way. We can look at the present chaos and ask what happens if *this* brittle process breaks, or how we respond if *that* nonlinear system produces a far-greater-than-expected (or far-smaller-than-expected) outcome. Done well, these scenarios can be a catalyst for discovery, an opportunity to reveal unexpected but plausible outcomes, possible futures that would otherwise take us completely by surprise. By crafting scenarios of our possible futures, we get a glimpse of possible realities. The BANI concept (as well as its not-evil twin, BANI+) gives us a clearer lens with which to understand the forces that come together to create our present chaos and, importantly, to recognize the nature of the chaos to come.

Humans have imagined plausible visions of future outcomes for millennia—remember *causal cognition*? Foresight specialists formalized this process and have been using narrative scenarios to illustrate and illuminate possible futures for over a half-century. Herman Kahn, mentioned in chapter 5, originated a form of scenario planning back in the late 1950s, with documentary descriptions of the future crafted as if they were stories written by people living in that future.[1] In the 1960s, a variety of groups in the United States and France started using similar techniques, and the oil giant Royal Dutch Shell formalized a process of scenario planning in 1971.[2] In the 1980s and 1990s, companies like Global Business Network popularized the process as a tool for organizational planners and consultants.[3] Using BANI as a scenario seed continues this evolution.

The resulting foresight narratives aren't meant to tell you what **will** happen, but to alert you as to what **might**. In doing so, they can help us make plans, test strategies, and look for unexamined consequences or novel combinations of forces. They can sensitize us to possible outcomes, helping us recognize the early indications that a particularly disruptive change is emerging. They can let us imagine living in different possible futures, different possible realities.

This Is a World in Which...

We should emphasize the word "possible" here. Foresight narratives should be stories of possibility grounded in the real world. This doesn't mean that new things can't happen in scenarios, but it does mean that, when new things do happen, they should be a logical consequence of what has come before. The "anticipatory history" framing is appropriate here: Can you imagine how the events of a forecast might be described in a future history book?

Most foresight narratives are written, but they don't have to be. They can take the form of sets of divergent scenarios, but also of terse reports, image-laden slide presentations, video shorts, and more. But the underlying truth of all of them is that they're *stories*.

Futurists are storytellers. We use narrative to make sense of and give structure to the chaos of anticipated history. We use story to give meaning to and illuminate the logic of the futures we describe.

Many foresight specialists are uncomfortable with this particular observation. It seems too unserious. There's much more gravity in saying that we're doing "strategic wind tunneling" or "contingency analysis" or "preference-agnostic outcome projection."

But there's no shame in telling stories. Using a narrative structure to illuminate subtle, confusing, or distant aspects of the world is something we, as human beings, have been doing for quite some time. As we observed all the way back in chapter 1, humanity creates myths to make sense of the ineffable. We use a narrative of the imaginary to reveal the deep structure of the world.

Jamais specializes in the creation of detailed foresight scenarios, narratives that describe a possible future based on the premise that such a future is real. Scenarios of tomorrow show plausible outcomes based on the forces at work in the present day. When Jamais created BANI, he did so knowing that the tension between the four elements would be catalysts for all sorts of possible scenarios of what may come.

Scenarios are just another iteration of mythmaking. Scenarios are essentially myths intended to reveal the nature of the coming world as it emerges from the present. They're explicitly stories of how the world works. This is especially clear in the introduction, the *incantation*, that begins many written scenarios: *This is a world in which* . . .

One of the most powerful phrases in the English language is "Once upon a time." It immediately tells us to see reality as contingent. *This is a world in which* . . . is the futurist's version of "Once upon a time." It's a phrase that reveals the storyteller's intent: you're about to hear the tale of another reality, one that builds a new tomorrow based on our collective today. It's a fairy tale, too, at least of a sort. There may be a bit more logic and sensibility, but the fantastic elements are unmistakable—not in the shape of giants and beanstalks, or grandmother-devouring wolves, but as digital systems that supercharge our thinking (or take our jobs), radical changes to our planet (and our transformative responses), and even conflicts between forces that could turn the world to ash.

The phrase "This is a world in which . . ." immediately puts the reader in the mindset of "This is a different world"; moreover, it forces the writer to adopt that perspective as well. All assumptions about the way of things come under scrutiny. What element of this world does the futurist want to highlight? How does this world differ from the here and now? What is the story of this world?

When futurists are writing scenarios, even if they don't always use that exact opening phrase, the incantation is implicit. *This is a world in which* a consumer's desire for convenience dovetails with a government's desire for oversight, giving surveillance technologies new power. *This is a world in which* the patterns of our behavior can reveal secrets, no matter how well hidden, using increasingly powerful technologies. *This is a world in which* intimate connections can travel along a path of ether and bit just as much as whisper and touch, creating all-new forms of emotional entanglement. *This is a world in which* we can see our own lives, reflected in a funhouse mirror.

This Is a BANI World in Which . . .

As observed back in chapter 3, our brains evolved to be naturally biased toward paying attention to things that frighten, anger, and otherwise upset us. It's as true for stories of the challenges that could face us in years to come as it is for prehistoric worries about saber-toothed tigers.

Generally speaking, there are two schools of thought about immersing oneself in the details of possible oncoming disasters. Those focused on achieving outcomes argue that we can't figure out what to do if we don't know what we're facing. Those focused on how we act in crisis argue that being overwhelmed by fear is more likely to lead to giving up than acting fast.

Both of these perspectives are likely true. But foresight thinking, scenario thinking, *BANI* thinking, cuts across those differences. We're not mired in the details of a singular catastrophic future; we're actively exploring our potential futures, specifically to figure out what we can do about them.

As we've discussed, the human brain is superbly tuned to create and learn from stories. We recognize subtle patterns, teasing meaning out of noise. We create fictions that let us explore questions of "What happens if . . .?" or "What would have happened if . . .?" We entertain unrealities in order to understand possibilities.

The BANI Future demands that we aren't the passive victims of history. A BANI narrative puts imminent disasters and overwhelming catastrophes in a new context: not as final statements of reality, but as elements in stories—forecasts and scenarios—that let us imagine what we might do in response. To turn a conclusion into a question.

But "a world in which" has another, even more critical, role. "This is a world in which . . .," whether stated or implied, demands that we pay close attention to the shape of the paradigm, not the inner conflicts of the characters. Simply put, the focus isn't on the plot but on the setting. The world in which.

This all may sound like we're talking about science fiction. But although scenarios and science fiction may have surface similarities, they aren't the same; in an important way, they're actually opposites. For the science fiction writer, the *world in which* is a basic foundation, a stage upon which the actual story transpires. Science fiction writers often try to show only the absolutely critical gears and mechanisms of the world, trusting the reader to figure out the larger structure.

With scenarios, the larger structure is kind of the point.

With scenarios, revealing *a world in which* is the very heart of the narrative, and any characters or plots that may show up do so entirely to highlight important parts of that world. Scenario writers leave as little hidden as they can, including everything that the allotted space will allow to explain how the world works and why it works in such a way. A scenario narrative may sometimes tell a single story, but the scenario world contains multitudes.

One characteristic rule of scenario-based foresight is that the scenarios should not advocate for or against a particular kind of future. The admonition against "normative scenarios" is something relentlessly drilled into the heads of aspiring scenarists. There is a very real risk that advocacy scenarios will—consciously or otherwise—leave out elements that should be there, ultimately undermining the strength of the position being trumpeted.

But too-close adherence to absolute neutrality often results in scenarios written from a perspective that philosopher Thomas Nagel approvingly calls "the view from nowhere," a phrase later used by critic Jay Rosen to disparagingly describe the bloodless pseudo-objectivity of American journalism.[4] It's a perspective that is meant to assert impartiality and a lack of bias but can come across as superficial or, worse, disconnected from lived reality.

In part as a result of this, futurism as practiced around the world tends to focus on technology. This can appear to be a safe approach, as many people believe that technology is essentially value-neutral, without partisan leanings or hidden agendas. But that's a surface illusion; our technologies are fundamentally cultural artifacts, manifestations of our values, beliefs, and intentions.

Foresight—including scenarios—needs to be about people, our desires, our fears, and our emotions. Even when we talk about technological developments, we need to use stories of what it's like to live in, to experience, a world changed by those developments. A world turned BANI. Our values serve as the foundation for our understanding of this.

All of that said, far be it from us to talk at length about the philosophy and meaning of scenarios but not offer a sample of how to undertake BANI-based scenario development.

Archetypes of Scenarios in a BANI Future

There are dozens of ways to build stories of the future. You've probably heard of a few; you may even make use of them. Lots of organizations use derivatives of the Delphi method and trend analysis, and anyone who has played a strategy game has experienced simulations and modeling. One of our favorites is the scenario archetypes method.

Professor Jim Dator, at the University of Hawaii at Manoa's graduate school of Futures Studies, developed the scenario archetypes technique back in 1979. This tool offers a useful heuristic for examining scenario diversity, making sure that forecasts cover as wide an assortment of future outcomes as possible: Growth, Collapse, Discipline (or Constraint), and Transformation. These four archetypes represent the standard variety of narrative forecasts; most scenarios out there can be classified as broadly one of these four. As a result, it's not uncommon for futurists to use the archetypes as a basis for a good spread of scenarios.

Scenario archetypes don't specify the content of a given scenario, just the vector: it's a common mistake to see the Growth scenario as generally positive, for example, but it can be a nightmare if what's growing is something undesirable (like a pandemic infection rate). The archetypes illuminate an array of pathways of change.

The traditional scenario archetypes are especially useful tools to explore VUCA-based forecasts, but they don't seem to fit quite as well in a BANI world. This may reflect the inherent messiness of a BANI Future—the distinctions between (for example) a Collapse future and a Transformation future can be less clear in BANI. Consequently, we've proposed a set of alternative scenario archetypes that better translate the BANI framework into a structured scenario tool.

It's tempting to see a BANI Future as being a manifestation of the Collapse archetype. After all, BANI-classic depictions can easily expand into stories of the world falling apart (see, for example, chapters 2 through 5). But the underlying logic of the BANI framework is that BANI manifests in all of the various ways in which the next period of time (through at least the midpoint of the century, arguably) will unfold. A Growth scenario should show elements of a BANI environment just as readily as a Collapse scenario. Moreover, the ways in which a Growth, Collapse, Discipline, or Transformation scenario plays out should be understood through the BANI lens.

In that spirit, here is a draft set of BANI-focused scenario archetypes, preembedding BANI lenses, both original recipe and positive, into the traditional scenario formats. These new BANI scenario archetypes offer vectors of change that make sense in a world that's brittle, anxiety inducing, nonlinear, and often simply incomprehensible. But we can also create scenarios that explore our potential to be bendable, attentive, neuroflexible, and deeply interconnected.

BANI Scenario Archetypes

Growth Becomes Compounding

Spiraling, worsening crisis, omnicrisis, overload

These are scenarios where situations continue to build, seemingly without control. This archetype parallels but is not identical to Growth—there need not be continuation of any particular factor if the mix of consequences from multiple factors adds up. In most cases, however, newer problematic outcomes derive from the previous ones. Examples would include climate impacts (not just carbon levels), political antagonism, and migration crises. The "urban doom loop" concept is a Compounding scenario, as the worsening of one element undermines the others in a continuing cycle.

Collapse Becomes Disassembly

Isolation, disconnection, atomization, hostility

These are scenarios where the system loses coherence, falling apart in ways that prove broadly disruptive. Examples would include secessionist movements, the possible fracture of the internet into competing standards or controls, and ongoing disruption of logistics. Brexit is an obvious Disassembly scenario, as is the emergence of "cord-cutting" behavior around media consumption. Disassembly can include the embrace of alternative models of organization.

Discipline Becomes Trapped

Muddling through, inertia, endless cycle, survival

These are scenarios where systems continue to exist even in the face of significant failure states. There could be external support mechanisms, cultural factors, or false minima. Examples would include impossible-to-eliminate political hoaxes, postwar social and governance structures, and sunk-cost inertia. The resource curse (disproportionate returns on sales of an unsustainable resource crowding out investment in a more sustainable economy) is a Trapped scenario.

Transformation Becomes Discontinuity

Abrupt shift, singularity, black swan, wild card

These are scenarios where a transformation happens quickly and (for most people) without warning; implicitly, the transformation may have been seen as essentially impossible or highly unlikely. Discontinuity scenarios are often functionally irreversible. Examples would include large-scale natural disasters, abandonment of social or political norms for a rapid power grab, and breakthrough technologies that render industries obsolete. The collapse of guano-based agriculture at the end of the 19th century after the invention of artificial fertilizers, as talked about in chapter 2, is a classic Discontinuity scenario.

Positive BANI Scenario Archetypes

Growth Becomes Reinforcement

Strengthening, rebuilding, buttressing, restoring (especially as is done with art)

These are scenarios where the purpose of adaptation is building resilience or strength into existing systems. This could mean simply the provision of resources (financial, technological, human). It could also be a rethinking and reinvention of the systems, but the focus is on reviving once-functional structures or norms. Attempts to strengthen democracy with ranked-choice voting can be a reinforcement scenario. Reinforcement is more difficult than it might appear; flipping to Compounding is an obvious risk, but this also has the potential to turn into a Trapped scenario.

Collapse Becomes Retrenchment

Divestment, degrowth, graceful failure, focusing

These are scenarios where the purpose of adaptation is consciously paring down elements of a complex system, but with a goal of eventual revival. There is typically a recognition that previous conditions no longer function as needed, but care is taken to make sure that the less- or non-functional elements do not shatter suddenly. The elimination of academic departments at a university in a way that protects existing students can be an example. This is an intentional effort to steer away from a potential Disassembly scenario, but it also runs the risk of ending up as a Trapped scenario if revival is attempted too quickly.

Discipline Becomes Curation

Gardening, long-term planning, sanctuary, "art is to omit"

These are scenarios where careful choices allow for simplifying systems with the goal of long-term presence of the new configuration. This is not battening down the hatches to weather a storm; it's rebuilding without hatches to begin with. One example would be updating regulatory environments by paring away dated conditions, in order to let them better fit a more dynamic path of technology change. Poorly-thought-through changes run a risk of becoming a Disassembly scenario if too much is removed or a Discontinuity scenario if the remaining elements combine in unintended ways.

Transformation Becomes Emergence

Experimentation, synchronicity, rewilding, transcendence

These are scenarios where signs of transformation get recognized and embraced rather than ignored or fought. This requires a light touch, nudging rather than steering. It's a conscious recognition that the results of incomprehensibility and nonlinearity are not always negative, and that the careful restoration of some chaos in an overly controlled or limited system can have real benefits. Experiments with different forms of basic-income guarantees can be an example of this. Discontinuity is the most likely failure state but hasty or forceful efforts to avoid failure might result in a Compounding scenario.

(BANI) Things to Come

Scenario archetypes—traditional or BANI flavored—aren't the only way to build scenarios to explore what BANI Futures could hold. There are multiple books and courses available to learn how to build scenarios and use them for organizational or leadership insights. Institute for the Future (IFTF), a foresight nonprofit over fifty years old and based in Silicon Valley, offers a variety of foresight training and courses, both online and in person. Bob is a former president of IFTF, and both he and Jamais are Distinguished Fellows there. Angela has engaged IFTF multiple times over the last decade.

That's not the only alternative, of course. Creation of BANI scenarios can be as straightforward as asking the following:

What do I/we expect to happen in our BANI Future?

What would it look like if things are *better* than we expect?

What would it look like if things are *worse* than we expect?

What would it look like if things are *weirder* than we expect?

The purpose of this set of questions isn't to produce the most elaborate and creative scenarios but to help train your thinking. Most of us slip easily into thinking about a default, expected future; some of us can expand that to consider what happens if something goes wrong. It's actually harder, in our experience, to get people and organizations to think about *better* futures. In a BANI setting, imagining a better future requires you to think about what kind of actions you can take now to be more BANI+.

And thinking about a *weirder*-than-expected future gives you space to consider how you'd respond to the kinds of futures that seem really unlikely. Weirder in this context can be events with a low likelihood in the short term but a high impact, like another pandemic or a big earthquake. It can also be asking "What happens if the guy or party nobody seems to trust actually wins that election?" or "How would we deal with energy prices tripling?" or "Where would we go if we had to move out of the area?"

All of this, *all of this*, is intended not to reveal the Future to you but simply to encourage you to be aware of different possible outcomes in the chaos of today. The age of chaos is not kind to people who believe only in a single tomorrow. We all need to work on gaining clarity and to work on letting go of certainty.

This especially applies to leaders—so let's dive into BANI leadership.

11
BANI Leadership
Charting the Course

LEADERSHIP: In BANI and BANI+, "leadership" means cultivating clarity amid confusion and disorder. In a world that is brittle, anxious, nonlinear, and incomprehensible, command and control will rarely work over a long period of time. The best leaders won't have all the answers—but they will create the conditions for trust, vision, insight, and resilience. The biggest challenge for leaders in a BANI world is making decisions when what's happening around them makes no sense. That's what this book is about.

BANI bleeds trust. Certainty may be comforting in the short run—even false certainty—but it won't be sustainable. There is little to be certain about in BANI.

Even in a BANI world, however, clarity of direction will be possible. Great leaders will tell great clarity stories that motivate people toward a better future. While rigid plans won't work, leaders will be sense-makers and story architects, weaving diverse perspectives and ideas together in compelling ways. Amid chaos, successful leaders will invite curiosity and calm—with a healing touch. Somehow, they will be both firm and nurturing, strong and humble. They will lead by example, authenticity, and character.

The Age of Leadership

In the BANI Future, clinging to misbegotten leadership models that were conceived in times of greater stability will only deepen the chaos. Still, there are enduring leadership principles that we can build upon.

Even leaders who have thrived in recent years will be tested severely by the BANI Future. Traditional leadership strategies will fall short as leaders scramble to prepare for a future becoming increasingly chaotic. The BANI Future will deliver unimagined dilemmas, even for experienced leaders and leadership.

It's a simple question: In the BANI Future, how do we lead?

The path forward will require a new, adaptive leadership playbook that helps us develop clarity amid chaos—while learning to thrive without any hope of certainty. We need to stretch our thinking about what will constitute leadership in a BANI Future.

Many of us think that trust is the essence of leadership, but in a BANI world, trust is hard to develop and easy to lose. Our understanding of trust and how it can be strengthened must evolve and adapt to meet the emerging conditions. Let's begin by stretching our thinking about fitness for trusted leadership in the BANI Future.

Dr. Nassir Ghaemi, a medical doctor at Tufts and Harvard Medical School, explores how mood conditions like bipolar disorder and depression might actually **help** some leaders be more effective during times of crisis. His book, *A First-Rate Madness: Uncovering the Links between Leadership and Mental Illness*, questions a basic assumption about trusted leadership:

> Most of us make a basic and reasonable assumption about sanity: we think it produces good results, and we believe insanity is a problem. This book argues that in at least one vitally important circumstance *insanity* produces good results and *sanity* is a problem. In times of crisis, we are better off being led by mentally ill leaders than mentally normal ones.[1]

This is less extreme than it may initially sound. Ghaemi's analysis of historic leaders suggests that those who have experienced mental health challenges often have increased empathy, realism, resilience, and creativity. For example, in brittle situations, leaders who have experienced disruptive mental health challenges (such as bipolar disorder) may show more resilience and have more clarity and persistence of direction.

Ghaemi's notion of "depressive realism" (where individuals with depression often see the world more accurately than others from neurotypical backgrounds who have limited mental health experiences) could be very useful for leaders facing the BANI world. People who have fought through mental health challenges may be more prepared to anticipate disruptions and withstand shocks. BANI creator Jamais Cascio, for example, has personal experience with the connections between clinical depression and heightened sensitivity to disruptive change.

In anxious situations, leaders who have experienced anxiety or depression are likely to possess heightened realism and empathy. They may have more clarity of direction and be better able to work with just enough anxiety. Jamais observes that they can be attuned to the more subtle indicators of conditions or actions that can increase anxiety. In his experience, a sensitivity to disruptive change increases his professional need and ability to explore and understand consequences.

In nonlinear situations, those who have experienced mania may be able to foster creativity and see beyond sequential thinking and expected outcomes. They will have experienced a form of the selective nonlinearity we talked about in chapter 8. Consequently, they will be more likely to question dangerous, unexamined assumptions.

With incomprehensible situations, leaders who are *not* neurotypical in their thinking will have a competitive advantage because of their extremely diverse ways of perceiving and judging what's going on around them. They will be used to unusual ways of thinking. They will be more comfortable being uncomfortable.

There are enduring mental health basics that all leaders will need. Dr. David Rock (founder of the NeuroLeadership Institute in New York City) and Dr. Dan Siegel (a psychiatrist and neuroscience expert) have developed a "healthy mind platter" to summarize the essential daily brain activities that are needed for sustainable health and readiness:

1. **Focus time:** Concentration on tasks

2. **Play time:** Spontaneous enjoyable experiences

3. **Connecting time:** Social relationships with others

4. **Physical time:** Exercise and movement, particularly in natural settings

5. **Time in:** Practices such as mindfulness, meditation, and self-reflection

6. **Down time:** Rest and relaxation without specific goals

7. **Sleep time:** Significant blocks of high-quality sleep[2]

In Bob's book *The New Leadership Literacies: Thriving in a Future of Extreme Disruption and Distributed Everything*, he describes the necessity for leaders to both create and sustain positive energy among the people they lead.[3] In a BANI Future, leaders will need to be extremely mentally and physically healthy to perform at the highest levels of leadership. If leaders are going to thrive in a future of extreme disruption, they will need to not only manage their own personal energy; they will need to encourage, model, and reward positive energy in others.

The healthy-living tools for energy management are so much better now than they ever were—and they will get even better over the next decade. Although these tools often take advantage of digital technologies, they aren't all necessarily devices. A better understanding of the connections between the body and the mind already shapes what we consider to be critical capacities. Fitness—physical, mental, and even spiritual (though not necessarily religious)—will be required for top leadership roles.

Mental and physical health will be required for leaders in the BANI Future. Leaders who have overcome mental or physical health issues are likely to be better suited for the chaos of the BANI Future than people who have never faced those challenges. New leadership strategies will be required that build upon and sometimes disrupt what worked best in more stable times.

Leadership Strategies

The following seven leadership strategies will help leaders find solid footing on shifting ground. Each strategy—from fostering a futureback growth mindset to scenario gaming through uncertainty—starts from future possibilities but links them back to insight and actions in the present.

These aren't just tactics; they are transformative strategies designed to bend brittle, reframe anxiety, help the brain learn new tricks, and flip the incomprehensible with full-spectrum thinking. Together, these seven leadership strategies are a resilient guide for navigating the age of chaos.

BANI LEADERSHIP STRATEGIES

1. Think futureback—from the BANI Future back to present choices.

2. Tell authentic stories that flip BANI positive.

3. Develop leadership skills matched to the BANI duture.

4. Organize with clarity of direction—but flexibility of execution.

5. Track and map signals from today that tickle thoughts about BANI futures.

6. Work within legal, ethical, and moral bounce ropes—with firm stanchions.

7. Practice frequent scenario gaming of BANI variants.

Each of the BANI leadership strategies has implications that will help leaders move from foresight to insight to action.

1: Think Futureback—from the BANI Future Back to Present Choices

The present is so noisy, so oppressively and dangerously noisy. In a BANI world, the best leaders will think at least ten years into the future and work backward. We call this "futureback" thinking and—surprisingly—it is easier to get a sense of what's going on by looking ahead ten or more years than it is to figure out what is happening now or what could happen in the future based only on present experience.

When Satya Nadella became CEO of Microsoft, the company was on a downhill slide. It had been an overconfident engineering-driven company and Nadella himself is an engineer, but the story he told was a flip from Microsoft as a "know it all" culture to a "learn it all" culture. He built upon Stanford professor Carol Dweck's research on "growth mindsets" (as compared to "fixed mindsets") and focused on personal growth as essential for financial growth.[4]

Nadella told a compelling story of cultural reinvention and embracing a future that empowers every person and every organization to achieve more. It was an inclusive narrative that expected everyone to innovate, not just the acknowledged geniuses that had always been rewarded at Microsoft. They moved from being perceived as a rather stale Windows-centric legacy provider to a more forward-looking cloud- and AI-driven player. This was both a business and cultural shift in response to a tech industry moving from VUCA to BANI ahead of other industries.

Fortunately, modern neuroscience is becoming practical and relevant to understanding how our brains can help us prepare our minds for leadership. Cognitive philosopher Andy Clark's book *The Experience Machine: How Our Minds Predict and Shape Reality* describes how our minds predict and shape how we will see the BANI Future as it unfolds:

> There is a fundamental drive, instantiated by the brain, to minimize errors in our own sensory predictions. . . . Human minds are not elusive ghostly things. They are seething, swirling oceans of prediction, continuously orchestrated by brain, body, and world. We should be careful what kinds of material, digital, and social worlds we build, because in building those worlds we are building our own minds too.[5]

Nobody can predict the future, but our brains try to do it anyway. Most of us default to a "present-forward" practice, trying to imagine a future through successive "if-then" steps. For simpler issues, this can sometimes be sufficient. But for the BANI world, we need to teach our brains new tricks.

Futureback thinking asks us to imagine a possible future then "look back" at how we got there. What kinds of surprises and changes became necessary to allow that future to happen? What challenges did we have to face? What new opportunities presented themselves? Adding futureback thinking to the growth mindset provides a fresh look—beyond the noisy present.

Fail early, fail often, and fail cheaply—as the mantra of Silicon Valley goes. Thinking futureback provides a context of consequence for your strategy, increasing the likelihood that failing early, often, and cheaply won't come at the expense of failing your communities, shareholders, or other stakeholders. Futureback helps you to choose a direction of change with clarity, while still retaining flexibility regarding how to get there.

2: Tell Authentic Stories That Flip BANI Positive

BANI-flipping leadership stories need to recognize the brittle, anxious, nonlinear, and incomprehensible world *and* flip the current story into a credible and compelling positive future. This will be a delicate balance indeed. Unless we learn BANI-flipping, we may slip into BANI-defaulting where we are so focused on negativity that we tell only BANI-reinforcing stories of dread and fear.

Our brains are wired for stories.[6] If our brains don't hear stories, they make them up. We're so wired for stories that our brains seek to identify patterns in chaos, whether it's recognizing animal shapes in clouds or seeing links between artistic expressions like *The Wizard of Oz* and Pink Floyd's *The Dark Side of the Moon*. Stories help us make sense out of what's going on around us—even if what's going on around us seems incomprehensible. Stories help us connect the dots, connect to others, and imagine better futures—even in a BANI world.

The best stories provide psychological, organizational, and societal glue to hold us together by teaching life lessons. Tribal storytellers were leading with stories before there were books—let alone leadership books. Storytellers teach, inspire, and direct their communities. Today's storytellers must lead while competing with the noisy now. The best leaders will be great storytellers.

Soon after Angela became the first woman CEO of United Way Worldwide she went on a listening tour. The compelling stories she heard helped to bring a higher level of understanding of the complex and expansive network of local United Ways around the world. These stories informed and became an integral part of her communication content and style. She discovered that local solutions are scalable and chose storytelling as an effective vehicle for illustrating the power of community. United Way Worldwide's organizational model allows local affiliates to respond directly to their community's needs based on the resources and priorities of the community. There are no one-size-fits-all solutions for systemic deficits, so it's important that leaders are always prepared to use storytelling as a tool to introduce creativity and collaboration.

Angela's story of adaptive leadership expanded as local communities came together to tackle the COVID-19 pandemic's challenges with a focus on hope, resilience, and grassroots action. She showcased how even small acts of community care could have ripple effects that created waves of community-led recovery.

Angela flipped this BANI-related public health crisis by using the crisis itself to reinforce the organization's mission of strengthening communities by leveraging technology to innovate how the organization provided services. For example, she introduced virtual volunteering to get people involved with reduced risk from the virus. This pivot helped United Way remain relevant and resilient while serving millions of people during the pandemic.

During the pandemic, many families turned to food banks, but traditional hunger relief programs were not designed for a world where people could not leave their homes. The challenge wasn't just food shortages; it was logistics. United Way partnered with DoorDash and Lyft to deliver groceries directly to families. This approach was so successful that over twenty million meals were delivered between 2021 and 2024. This was the basis of a compelling story that flipped BANI experiences positive.

3: Develop Leadership Skills Matched to the BANI Future

The BANI Future will require special skills. Thinking futureback, Bob and his colleagues Jeremy Kirshbaum and Gabe Cervantes have recently finished a series of research projects and a book to identify those new skills, which we summarize and match to the coming challenges of each dimension of BANI: Brittle, Anxious, Nonlinear, and Incomprehensible:[7]

BRITTLE

- **Clarity:** Leaders must be very clear about direction—but very flexible about the specifics of action. The best leaders will hone their clarity but resist certainty. Leadership will continue to be an interactive process. Clarity must be expressed accurately and also understood accurately in the same way to be effective. Leaders define clarity, but those being led will be needed to move from clarity to action. In anxious times, leaders must meet people where they are emotionally and provide reassuring clarity—even when things don't make sense around them.

- **Depolarizing:** Leaders must be able to lower tensions and bridge polarities.

ANXIOUS

- **Human calming:** Leaders must themselves have a sense of centeredness that helps with inner focus of others. The best leaders will have composure under pressure with a grounded presence that resists quick judgment.

- **Strength—with humility:** Leaders must balance understanding, empathy, and assertiveness. A leader's clarity will be valuable only if it is heard accurately by others, and those people are motivated to act.

NONLINEAR

- **Bio-engaging:** Leaders must harness the inherent wisdom of nature to mobilize responses to the climate-disruption urgencies we face as a planet.

- **Dilemma flipping:** Leaders will turn unsolvable problems into opportunities. The best leaders will thrive in the space between judging too soon (the classic mistake of the problem solver or true believer) and deciding too late (the classic mistake of the academic).

INCOMPREHENSIBLE

- **Futureback curiosity:** Leaders will cultivate exploration and mind stretching with the aid of tools like generative

AI (GenAI). The best leaders will think futureback as well as present-forward. Be willing to experiment and pivot when necessary.

- **Immersive learning:** Leaders will foster gameful emotionally laden attention to deliver first-person growing experiences. Young people who grew up learning through video gaming will have a competitive advantage. Ideally, immersive learning experiences should be more difficult than the actual real-world experience being prepared for.

- **Commons creating:** Leaders must seek out shared values. The best leaders will search for common ground and explore alternative paths for collaboration. The most robust commons will combine what Harvard professor of public policy Robert Putnam describes as moving beyond "bonding social capital" (within a group) to create "bridging social capital" (between or among varied groups).[8]

- **Smart mob swarming:** Leaders will organize shape-shifting teams of human and nonhuman agents that surge with coordinated energy.

Over the next decade, we could see increasing use of cognitive enhancement technologies like neural implants or biopharma interventions. GenAI and other forms of machine learning will very likely become integrated with the skills and practices of leadership in ways we are only beginning to understand. Thinking futureback, it is probable that all leaders will be augmented in some way—but the question is how they choose to be augmented.

Many current concerns about GenAI are real. Its power demands are unsustainable. Many large language models are built upon ethically dubious or even illegal use of content from uncompensated and nonconsenting human writers and artists. Increasingly, these models build upon other GenAI models in ways that may degrade the overall quality of the content. Some of these systems are deceptive because they sound so supremely confident, even if they are wrong. Often users have to know the subject matter well enough to know if the output is rational and doesn't just sound good. Finally, many of these GenAI models are biased because they include often-hidden human prejudices and misunderstandings.

Our advice to leaders at this stage is to use GenAI systems for mind stretching. They are marvelous tools for divergence. **But do not trust them.**

Over the next decade, the use of GenAI by leaders will evolve from prompts and answer-finding (often with unsatisfying results) to expansive conversations. Now, many leaders are looking to GenAI for efficiency and speed (with the brittleness that can entail). Sometimes, these results are achieved. A decade from now, GenAI and its successor technologies will be used more for effectiveness (doing the right things) and augmentation. These will be meaning-making tools.

Overall, the concerns about GenAI should be considered in the context of the ways in which humans choose to deploy these highly unusual technologies. Both the wider consequences and the possible benefits must be taken into account.

The future leadership skills we've discussed are not completely new, of course, but there are now specialized capabilities that were not available in the pre-BANI world. GenAI may make possible new forms of augmented leadership that reflect nine of the ten new leadership skills we summarized. The skill of human calming reflects the need for all leaders to go inside themselves—independent of the AI that may stretch their minds—for purpose, meaning, and direction of their leadership.

4: Organize with Clarity of Direction—but Flexibility of Execution

Imagine a traditional organization chart: it looks like a symmetrical hierarchy of rigid metal pipes. Today's organization charts are shown as fixed and inflexible. They look brittle, and many organizations today are brittle. In a BANI Future, organization charts will be animated to match tasks to people with the relevant skills.

The best leaders will have great clarity of direction but great flexibility of execution. They will continuously evaluate who is in the best position to make which decision at what time—based on situation awareness (what's really going on and what is needed) and frequent after-action reviews (what was our goal and what could be improved). It will be easier to develop clarity when you think futureback—especially in the noisy present that is so common in the BANI world.

By flexible, we mean pliable, responsive, and adaptable processes and methods—not rigid or fixed. Imagine a fishnet lying on a dock. Pick up one node in the net and a temporary hierarchy takes shape. Put that node down and pick up another node, and another temporary hierarchy forms. By *intent*, we mean being clear about direction—but not necessarily outcomes. Intent is commitment to a direction of change. Flexible intent opens opportunities to adapt a course of action in response to ever-changing circumstances.

A good example of flexible intent is what Mariana Mazzucato calls "missions." Missions are inherently futureback-targeted projects, with great clarity of outcomes and direction alongside considerable flexibility about how that direction is achieved. The European Union, for example, has a mission to have one hundred carbon-neutral cities, and they have organized many projects to achieve this mission—but these projects will happen in varied ways. Mazzucato's book *Mission Economy* shows how social purpose can guide how public and private actors can work together to cocreate what she calls public value. In her view, public means collaborative efforts in communities, in the public interest.[9]

In the BANI Future, command and control will be too brittle to succeed in the long term.

When Alan Mulally came from Boeing to take over Ford as CEO, the company was losing billions of dollars, and the auto industry was in crisis. Mulally created a distributed authority structure he called "One Ford" that emphasized "accountability through transparency." He set up weekly business-plan reviews from the many distributed parts of Ford, and he opened those meetings to everyone. He argued correctly that the pressure to present when anyone could be in attendance was a more powerful form of accountability than anything he could mandate top down from his role as CEO. These weekly reviews were core to the One Ford story and they "would shine a light on the darkest corners of the company. . . . Now they were being told they were all on the same team, and Mulally expected them to act like it."[10] One Ford was both organized and animated.

Bob was a speaker on the same stage as Mulally for a group of about fifty CIOs from major corporations while Mulally was still CEO of Ford. Mulally embodied the leadership skill we call strength—with humility.[11] He got there early and sat in the back of the room quietly to get a sense of the group. When he was introduced, he went around and shook hands with everyone before going up front to speak. Compare that to how many busy CEOs arrive late or just in time, then leave without really engaging individual people in the group. Mulally told the story of a very distributed One Ford with great clarity. Ford turned down government bailout money, and that became a convincing part of the story. The crisis they faced was real, but so was the turnaround. Of course, the challenges of the BANI world will continue for Ford even after Mulally's departure.

When Angela became president and CEO of United Way Worldwide in 2021, the organization was in a deep, complex, and multilayered crisis. United Way Worldwide is the global center of a federated network of autonomous local United Ways in the United States and internationally. Angela is the CEO but does not have authority over the component parts of the United Way network. In this kind of shape-shifting organizational structure, the focus needs to be on a shared clarity of direction—and this global direction had been lost at United Way Worldwide. It was

Angela's job to meet and listen to some 700 local United Way leaders around the world.

The global United Way clarity story needed to be refreshed and retold in authentic ways. The bright light in an otherwise gloomy landscape was that United Way's performance during the COVID-19 pandemic was exemplary. United Way is active in some 95 percent of communities in the United States, and it was able to connect people in need with services and solutions. Their immediate actions during the COVID crisis told the United Way story so effectively that Angela was able to spread the message globally. The signals were clear, and the stories that were told were compelling as the global United Way network transformed during the crisis.

5: Track and Map Signals from Today That Tickle Thoughts about BANI Futures

As William Gibson first said, "the future is already here, it's just unevenly distributed." We call the indicators of an unevenly distributed future "signals"—very specific happenings in the present that hint at the future. Even signals that fail tend to fail in interesting ways.

In a BANI world, where chaos is the norm, digital tools will offer leaders the ability to track critical signals in real time. These dashboards can provide a visual representation of key data, allowing leaders to make sense out of an overwhelming flow of information and identify patterns.

More than tracking current performance, dynamic dashboards will help detect weak signals and emerging threats so leaders can respond proactively. By integrating a diversity of data sources—both internal and external—dashboards offer a holistic view that is essential for navigating the nonlinear and incomprehensible forces of BANI.

Dynamic dashboards were originally called "decision support systems" and "executive support systems" when they were first introduced in the 1970s and 1980s, but they are finally becoming practical thanks to big-data analytics and big-data visualization.

Investing in dynamic dashboards will promote agility and adaptability as conditions shift. Dynamic dashboards will be customizable and able to evolve and learn with changing conditions and priorities. They can also foster collaboration and transparency if used correctly. It is crucial, however, to strike a balance between data analytics and human judgment. Not every issue that matters can be reliably measured. Dynamics provide context and data for human decision-makers.

Under Alan Mulally, for example, Ford used dynamic dashboards to monitor key performance indicators that were critical to their turnaround. One Ford was a flexive-intent story of transparency and alignment that allowed everyone access to the same data. As GenAI becomes more powerful, practical, and trustable, dynamic dashboards will become even more useful. Organizations will be truly distributed—not just decentralized. Thinking futureback, they will need to operate with flexive intent delivered through swarms of human and AI agents.

6: Work within Legal, Ethical, and Moral Bounce Ropes—with Firm Stanchions

Bounce ropes encircle wrestling rings to keep the wrestlers safe inside the ring in a strong yet flexible way. The stanchions, however, are solid and don't give. It is even possible for a wrestler to bounce off the rope as it flexes back—but the stanchions are anchored and don't move.

In a BANI world, a bounce rope is a much more appropriate analogy than a guardrail. It will be desirable to have some legal and behavioral constraints, but those constraints will have to be flexible as the reality of BANI takes shape in unpredictable ways. Core values and ethical limits—like the dignity of human life—will serve as the strong stanchions holding the bounce ropes in place.

Calls for public policymakers to create highly restrictive guardrails for GenAI, for example, are understandable but naive. Significant controls may seem appealing when not even GenAI developers understand exactly what is going on within these large language models—let alone the implications of large-scale use. But policymakers and elected officials are likely to be un- or (more dangerously) mis-informed about these emerging tools and media, even if they are well intentioned. We expect many unintended consequences from even the most prescient policies. Unexpected, inappropriate, and sometimes malicious actors are likely to step into any vacuum.

Bounce ropes are inherently less brittle than guardrails—which will constrain up to a point before they break. Bounce ropes will be able to absorb and redirect force. In the case of GenAI, such forces are likely to be surprises that are unanticipated by policymakers or even those who created the technologies. A BANI Future needs bounce ropes supported by strong stanchions, backed up by guardrails for the values that are most important to protect.

7: Practice Frequent Scenario Gaming of BANI Variants

Variants of simulation, scenario planning, and gaming will be the best low-risk ways of learning in the future. Games are practical ways for leaders to experience the future before it happens. More specifically, gaming can help leaders develop and test new strategies.

Growing up playing video games could be very helpful for prospective leaders since serious gamers, especially those playing collaborative multiplayer online games, have the chance to immerse themselves in dilemmas and learn advanced social networking skills. Gaming and simulation are low-risk high-return learning media, if used in a constructive fashion. Today's video games sometimes have a bad reputation, particularly among parents. Although video games may sometimes be easy targets for moral panics, the right games can provide mind expansion and leadership-skill development.

Games can help you learn how to succeed in the real world by providing you with a low-risk practice field. Games can help you rehearse so that you don't choke when the pressure is on. Sian Beilock explores why people often fail at routine tasks in her book *Choke: What the Secrets of the Brain Reveal about Getting It Right When You Have To*.[12]

Using fMRI (functional magnetic resonance imaging of the brain), Beilock has shown that the prefrontal cortex of our brains can get in the way, causing us to overthink routine tasks and choke when trying a short putt in golf or a free throw in basketball, or example. The good news is that practice—developing a routine—can help. Experience at performing under pressure helps you develop new ways of coping with pressure and coming through. Gaming gives you a safe way to practice your skills.

Whether games offer first-person adventures or top-down command and control of a battlefield, the player is a big part of the story. Games are animated stories. A player's actions help shape the narrative as it unfolds.

Bob got to visit the US Army's National Training Center at Fort Irwin in the Mojave Desert, a soldier's last stop before going to war. The NTC is about the size of the state of Rhode Island. Bob thought of it as the world's largest video-gaming parlor—with real tanks, real helicopters, and very realistic war gaming. The games at Fort Irwin, which often last two weeks and run twenty-four hours per day, are designed to be harder than real warfare. Players experience being killed, without having to die. Leadership strategies are tested, refined, and tested again. They practice scenario gaming continuously and evaluate alternative strategies.

Our IFTF colleague Jake Dunagan, an experienced scenario gamer, likes to say: "It's better to be surprised in a simulation that blindsided in reality." Jamais has a favorite variant: "It's safer to be disappointed by the future than to be surprised by it."

Beyond the Noisy Now

A futureback view will help leaders find a calm place from which to make their choices about how to engage with the BANI world. In the noisy now, finding this calm place will be difficult for leaders—but it is extremely important.

University of Michigan professor Kentaro Toyama is a self-described former technology utopian who cofounded Microsoft Research India and has many years of experience introducing new digital technologies in developing countries. Over the years, Toyama has become increasingly disappointed and frustrated as the computing technologies he thought would springboard people out of poverty often sit unused in dusty closets. How can leaders avoid the similar missed opportunities as they engage with the BANI world?

The success stories that Toyama did see all had more to do with the mindset and skills of human leaders than with the new technologies themselves. Reluctantly, he concluded that successful use of new technologies for positive social change requires human leaders who can apply a creative mix of distinctly human cognitive skills:

- **Intention** that compels leaders to act with purpose and clarity to align their use of technology with their core human values and long-term goals. What is your clarity of direction as a leader?

- **Discernment** so that leaders can evaluate the available tools and make informed choices that balance innovation, practical value for intended users, and ethics of use. Discernment means making wise decisions. Discernment begins with asking discerning questions—the kind of questions that cannot be answered with just a yes or no.

- **Self-control**, with personal discipline, restraint, and focus that prevents the allure of technology-centric power from overshadowing the need for human-centric leadership.[13]

Self-control means operating within the bounce ropes and adhering to ethical guidelines.

BANI will be boundary stretching, so human leaders must be continuously mindful that the technology will be used in ways that enhance, not detract, from their intention.

Calm human decision-making is critical to successful leadership. But technologies must be activated by human choices. It is up to us humans to make smart, wise, and kind choices. Calm technology will be good, but calm humans will be better.

The leadership strategies proposed in this chapter combine narrative, process, and technology-amplified suggestions. Leadership in the BANI Future will require a clear and compelling story of future direction. It will also require adaptive use of technology without distancing ourselves from our own humanity.

CONCLUSION

BANI and Our Futures

FUTURE: The "Future" refers to the inevitable but uncertain point yet to happen where the consequences of today's decisions will play out. That's why it matters—the future isn't just a vector on a timeline; it's where the implications of our choices become real. Our decisions now, based on the results of our pasts and our experiences of the present, create our futures.

We don't just live in the moment; we live in the space created by past actions. We, in turn, make spaces for the people who will have to grapple with the results of what we do now. Those people may even include us—our choices today make space for our own options tomorrow.

Right now, the coming consequences of the decisions we've already made and the decisions we're making now look pretty BANI. It's up to us to determine *which version* of BANI we create.

The Age of BANI, Revisited

We wrote *Navigating the Age of Chaos* to make clear what BANI means, where it comes from, and what we can do in the midst of it. It is important to all of us to make sure that the origin story for the Age of BANI—or whatever this moment comes to be called—be properly documented. More than that, this book represents a need we all feel to explore a world that each one of us, in our own spheres and histories, has come to recognize as having become something new. There are elements of the BANI Future that differ dramatically from anything any of us has experienced.

The unprecedented scale of some of the crises we now (or will soon) face is startling enough, but what has become clear is the depth of connection between the various catalysts of stress and disruption in our world. It's not just that the elements of this multipocalypse are all hitting us at the same time; it's that the elements reinforce each other. Each of the large-scale issues we as a planet, as a civilization, face makes the others harder to confront. How we deal with the climate, for example, will shape and be shaped by how we deploy artificial intelligence, political rivalries between oligarchs, our nuclear sword of Damocles, and more.

The BANI world and the BANI Future arise from a tangle of forces we too often can't quite wrap our heads around but that will define how our lives play out.

The purpose of this book, then, is to help to unravel the situation, at least a bit. As we said in the early chapters, we are with the BANI world until a better lens comes along; there is no backing out. All we can do in a world of BANI is work to understand the tangle in order to try to untangle it—even if it continues to worsen.

As we write this book, the global chaos we're talking about is only growing in intensity. We have tried to be careful not to let our focus drift to the latest disruption; it's highly likely that by the time you read this book, whatever bits of craziness in today's doomscroll will have been superseded by various new categories of bedlam. And there's no sense of vindication about accurately describing a world falling into greater chaos, only a sense of deep empathy for the billions of people who have to grapple with this BANI Future.

We want this book to be something you can hand to a friend, colleague, or family member trying to figure out how to cope as their world becomes more BANI, whether in the next year or the next decade.

Staring Down the Age of Chaos

As overwhelming as the BANI world and the BANI Future can be, the most difficult task we face is retaining a sense of humanity—resilience, empathy, *hope*—in the midst of it all.

If you've read straight through the book, you might have noticed a distinct difference in scale between the crises and challenges described in the BANI section versus the practices and mindsets articulated in BANI+. You have Brittle risks like cascading satellite destruction and collapsing ice shelves alongside Bendable practices of mindfulness and gratitude. What gives?

Remember what we said at the introduction to the Positive BANI section: "These are not intended as *solutions* for the challenges described by BANI but *responses* that allow us to remain resilient in a BANI world." We've said repeatedly throughout the book that we already know how to deal with most of the threats described in chapters 2–5; the real challenge is getting ourselves to take action. It's true that bendable, resilient clarity isn't going to fix a brittle world, but without it, we will find it far harder to push back against brittle crises.

The same applies across the BANI+ paradigm. The strategic mindsets and individual practices we're encouraged to adopt will help to give us the perspective needed to see how to respond effectively to BANI threats. Being able to see the path forward is absolutely fundamental to dealing with a BANI world. It's why we called this book *Navigating the Age of Chaos*: it's about steering a course through the chaos, whether for yourself, your community, your company, or your world.

More importantly, it's about being able to see that such a course is possible to begin with. It's really hard to keep one's eye on the future when the present can seem so awful. As we finish writing this book, some leaders are telling us that empathy is a sin, trust is for suckers, and those who are different should be shunned. It will be seductively easy to close off, shut down, and focus on protecting just our closest circles. But present choices create the future.

The dilemmas are stark: we can't build better futures if we give up hope.

It's Not the End of the World

We recognize that any discussion of BANI, even those emphasizing the hope and potential of the BANI+ paradigm, stands a good chance of becoming overwhelmed by catastrophism. The myriad examples in this book of planetary systems being dangerously brittle, human communities being despairingly anxious, displays of power being deceptively nonlinear, and, well, *everything* being simply incomprehensible do nothing to dissuade us from a belief that we are, as a planet and species, racing to annihilation. But consider this: we've been through worse—and "we" means both the planet Earth and humanity itself.

Environmental scientists often argue that we are presently going through the "sixth extinction." It's the sixth because Earth has faced five massive extinction events over the past 500 million years of complex life:

- The **Ordovician-Silurian** extinction events, 445–444 million years ago; 42–52 percent of all taxa (categories of life) wiped out.

- The **Late Devonian** extinctions, 372–359 million years ago; 50–70 percent of all taxa.

- The **Permian-Triassic** extinction, 252 million years ago; 62–83 percent of all taxa. (This one is known as the Great Dying. Seriously. Look it up.)

- The **Triassic-Jurassic** extinction, 201 million years ago; 47–73 percent of all taxa.

- The **Cretaceous-Paleogene** extinction, 66 million years ago; 38–40 percent of all taxa. (This is the one that wiped out non-avian dinosaurs.)

And now there's us. To be blunt, human civilization is engaged in ecocide. According to the Intergovernmental Science-Policy Platform on Biodiversity and Ecosystem Services in 2019, of Earth's 8 million plant and animal species, 1 million are threatened with extinction.[1] A 2023 study, calling it a "mutilation of the tree of life," argued that extinctions caused by humans over the past 500 years were 35 times the rate of natural extinctions over the previous million years.[2]

So far, so horrible. And what about humans? There was a genetic bottleneck about 800,000 to 900,000 years ago, where what had been around 100,000 early humans suddenly dropped down to about 1,300, in total.[3] There were similar reductions of human populations approximately 100,000 and 60,000 years ago, each one bringing the human species down to a number of "breeding pairs" measurable in the hundreds. All of these were caused by rapid (on geologic time scales) changes to the planet's environment. In every case, *Homo sapiens* got very lucky not to be wiped out completely.

But here's the thing. Look again at the five natural mass extinctions and the handful of human near extinctions. In each case, over time, life saw a resurgence. We may be in the sixth extinction, but what we're doing to the planet now pales in comparison to past extinction events. And our present world, with over 8 billion people, comes from that small handful of surviving humans—our ancestors, having to face a world that they didn't understand changing all around them.

As apocalyptic as BANI might seem, we will not destroy Earth. We will (probably) not wipe ourselves out. Our "best" efforts now are blips compared to what the planet itself has done. What we will do if we don't act is **make ourselves miserable**. Centuries of misery for humankind and for life on Earth is the inevitable result if our BANI Future is allowed to continue unchecked.

Misery. Take that word in for a moment. A world of misery is a world where everything is entirely, unavoidably BANI. Systems are unrecoverably broken. Everyone we know drowns in despair.

The concentration of power and wealth approaches a singularity. And it all feels so meaningless. It's not the end of the world—but for a lot of people that might actually sound like a welcome alternative.

The creation of the BANI framework came directly out of a desire to avoid that fate. **We are not doomed to an inevitable future of misery.** We have the ability to change the direction of history. We have the tools. We have the knowledge. But do we have the will?

A Future Worth Protecting

Science fiction writer Bruce Sterling once said in a talk, "The future is a process, not a destination."[4] Sometimes that process is understandable, if difficult. Sometimes it can be completely chaotic. But it doesn't stop.

It would be nice to have a little help figuring it all out. In a chaotic world, the desire to be told how to make everything better can be overpowering. Because it speaks so clearly about our present dilemmas, BANI (and BANI+) can sometimes appear to be laying out an unavoidable trajectory for our futures. If you're not paying close attention, it can be easy to mistake clarity for certainty.

But BANI doesn't tell us what disasters will definitively happen, nor does it reveal optimal strategies. What BANI can do for the future is offer a way of looking at the world—a lens—that lets us ask good, important questions about possible disasters and potential strategies. We don't need to have immediate answers for these questions; the important dynamic is that we ask them and really think about what the answers might be.

A lens can show us the world with greater focus and clarity, but it cannot tell us where to go. Instead, the purpose of a lens is to help us see and understand our possible paths ahead and to recognize the urgency with which we need to move. Ultimately it is a tool that can help us see more clearly. To help us navigate.

Foresight is a discipline that demands clarity, as the concepts we immerse ourselves in are often quite messy. Foresight is intensely metaphorical and relies heavily on our abilities to pick out patterns from noise. We're forced to push our *causal cognition* to its limits. We can't truly predict the future, but we can describe what we recognize when we imagine it. Sometimes the patterns we see are deceptive or illusory, derived from what we want or what we fear might happen. Sometimes the patterns we see give us a distant early warning of onrushing transformations. And sometimes, the patterns we see can even give us hope.

The Future is not a separate space; it's a continuous unfolding of the consequences of today. It is a creation of the present. The BANI Future is and will be the continuously evolving result of the BANI world in which we find ourselves now. How BANI manifests in five years or fifteen years will undoubtedly differ considerably from how it manifests today, but the core reality of a world that's Brittle, Anxious, Nonlinear, and Incomprehensible—as well as Bendable, Attentive, Neuroflexible, and Interconnected—will remain. What our tomorrows look like will depend upon how we balance the two forms of BANI today.

The BANI Future, whatever it looks like, emerges directly from the choices we make *and do not make* now in the BANI present. All of the issues we discuss as examples of BANI will continue to evolve in the years to come but will do so in a manner that results from what we do now. Our choices matter.

What artificial intelligence technologies become in a decade hence will almost certainly bear little resemblance to present-day AI, for example, but the guidelines we put in place today—and whether they are as flexible as bounce ropes or as brittle as guardrails—will have had a direct bearing on how tomorrow's AI behaves. And this is true whether those guidelines work or fail.

We can say the same thing for the climate worries, the power and wealth inequalities, the emotional impacts of social media, and the myriad other engines of anxiety that drive the chaos of today. The way these dilemmas will look in ten years will likely differ radically from the way they look now, but that form will be based on what we *do about them today*. **Every decision today is the foundation for the choices we face tomorrow.**

That's a lot of responsibility.

We believe that humankind is able to take on that responsibility and able to build the kind of future that can move us out of the BANI trajectory. The mental models and actionable steps we talk about in BANI+ are all achievable. We can create a future that's bendable and resilient, attentive and empathetic, neuro-flexible and improvisational, interconnected and inclusive—and we can do so with the tools and wisdom we've created already.

We can make a BANI Future a BANI+ world. But it won't happen unless we try.

Navigating the Age of Chaos Discussion Guide

Navigating the Age of Chaos describes how to live in a world of chaos, and the chaos to come. Although many parts of it can be upsetting, the overall purpose of the book is to leave the reader with a greater sense of agency. This will come from the need to set aside existing scripts and habits and examine closely what new points of view and insights will help replace and rebuild mental models and understanding of the world. Readers should recognize a need to increase their resilience in the face of the unexpected, build empathy for those whose lives have been turned upside down by the chaotic future, be willing to experiment with new approaches, and be part of a greater network of people who see the need for a new way forward.

What follows are discussion questions about your experiences in a BANI world. We come at this inquiry from two different perspectives. The first set of questions explores your sense of the BANI/BANI+ frameworks and their specific elements. These questions prompt a deeper discussion into what BANI and BANI+ mean for you and your communities and organizations. The second set of questions comes at this topic from the perspective of the individual, the organization, and the future, putting the BANI/BANI+ elements into a larger context.

Questions about BANI as a Whole

BANI: *How can you recognize the nature of the risks in your world without being overwhelmed by them?*

In what ways can you guide and sustain yourself and your family, community, or organization amid broken systems or problems entirely outside your worldview? What can you do now to make sure you have better answers for these questions in the future? What does a BANI world look like for you, and what can you do to change it?

BANI+: *What kinds of resources—material, cultural, human—are available to you to increase your capacity to face chaos?*

What can you do to gather them? How do you help others gather their own resources? What ways do you have to spot hidden connections or points of influence in a crisis? What do you pay attention to in order to recognize when things aren't working and a new approach is needed? What would it take for you to have the strength and willingness to adapt and evolve?

Questions about Specific BANI Elements

Brittle: *Which systems do you depend on whose failure would be catastrophic to you?*

What kinds of stress do they face, whether from external forces or internal demands? What actors in your environment (people, organizations, cultural movements) might try to increase that stress for their own ends? What are the systems that are so critical that their existence is a basic assumption of your reality? What are the signs, hints, or distant early warnings that one of the systems you depend on is weakening? In what ways do you keep watch over them?

Bendable: *How have you prepared for the potential failure of one or more key systems?*

What kinds of backups, or emergency supplies, or multiple sourcing, or access to whatever would be necessary to continue, do you have if your normal situation suddenly fails? What are your alternative methods? How will your infrastructure adapt quickly to new conditions? What's the status of the people or organizations in your community or network, those you might depend on or who might depend on you? What kinds of necessary preparations do they have? How can you help them think about their futures?

Anxious: *What do you do when it all gets to be too much?*

Who are the people you talk with? What most worries or frightens you now? What's out there on the horizon that seems threatening, even if it's not imminent? How do you distinguish between changes that are difficult but rewarding and changes that are difficult for you but rewarding for someone else? How will you recognize when someone or some system is trying to manipulate your emotions?

Attentive: *Who else might depend on you to be a source of good advice or empathy?*

What might they be going through? What are your own sources of stress, and in what ways can you mitigate them? What parts of the world—large or small—can you improve? How do you relax? How could it help others relax, too?

Nonlinear: *What kinds of precarity do you see around you?*

In what ways are your results proportional to the effort you put in, and how are they not? How do the systems with which you work offer useful feedback? Which parts of your personal or organizational or cultural systems might exhibit unexpected or confusing delays or disconnections? What are the points of influence or surfaces of control in your world that you might take advantage of—or that might be used to take advantage of you?

Neuroflexible: *What are the mental models, scripts, and checklists that you follow?*

What new thing have you done, simply as an experience or practice? What can you learn from your failures and mistakes? What can you learn from the failures and mistakes of others? How could you add creativity and imagination to your work processes? What might you do to change the systems around you to add clarity or transparency?

Incomprehensible: *What simply doesn't make sense to you?*

What aspects of your world seem to make superficial sense but, upon a closer look, are actually quite opaque? What is unthinkable in your world—that is, what do you avoid thinking about, whether it's because you're not supposed to, or the consequences are too harrowing, or it's all just so weird? What tools do you use to help you generate answers? How do you ensure they do so in ways that are reliable and trustable?

Interconnected: *How could you widen your circle of consideration?*

Who are the friends or colleagues or networks able to provide insights and perspectives outside of your experience or paradigm? How do they react when you disagree with them? How do you react when they disagree with you? In what ways can you combine their insights and ideas in novel and surprising ways? What do their own networks of interconnection look like?

Questions about BANI in Your Different Contexts

Individual

1. What does chaos mean to me?
2. How do I see chaos affecting the lives of those around me?
3. In what ways has my life been brittle?
4. How have I learned to be more bendable?
5. How has anxiety affected me?
6. In what ways can I be more attentive?
7. When has nonlinearity surprised me?
8. What can I do to become more neuroflexible?
9. What is incomprehensible to me?
10. Who is part of my circle of interconnection?

Organization

1. How has my organization experienced a BANI world?
2. Do the policies and practices of my organization increase or reduce the chaos of our stakeholders?
3. What's an example of my organization experiencing a brittle system?
4. How could my organization increase its resilience in possible times of stress?
5. In what ways do the policies and practices of my organization rely on anxiety-increasing methods to grow markets or gain attention?

6. How does my organization show awareness of and empathy toward external stresses affecting stakeholders?

7. How can my organization recognize nonlinear and disproportionate systems within itself?

8. How does my organization encourage or punish improvisation and experimentation?

9. In what ways could the policies and practices of my organization make better sense?

10. How does my organization connect with outside people and groups when it comes to ideas and awareness?

The Future

1. What stories of our futures do we tell ourselves?

2. What is my—as an individual or as an organization—"official future"?

3. In what ways do we watch for emerging changes (in policies, in technologies, in the environment) that could have a direct impact on us in the future?

4. In what ways do we watch for emerging changes that could have a direct impact on our surrounding communities or stakeholders?

5. How often do we think about the future?

6. How has my sense of the future changed after reading this book?

7. What are the steps I can take now to increase my (or my organization's) bendability, attentiveness, and ability to improvise, and the size of my circle of interconnection?

8. What's an example of me or my organization taking the future seriously?

9. How can I help others in my circle, network, or community develop better skills for adapting to a BANI Future?

10. What will I do now?

Notes

Introduction

1 Waltraud Glaeser, "Where Does the Term VUCA Come From!," VUCA World, August 1, 2024, accessed January 20, 2025, https://www.vuca-world.org/roles-of-nanus-and-bennis/.

2 David Dunning, "Chapter Five: The Dunning–Kruger Effect: On Being Ignorant of One's Own Ignorance," *Advances in Experimental Social Psychology* 44 (January 1, 2011): 247–296, https://doi.org/10.1016/B978-0-12-385522-0.00005-6.

3 Jamais Cascio, "Facing the Age of Chaos," *Medium*, April 29, 2020, https://medium.com/@cascio/facing-the-age-of-chaos-b00687b1f51d.

Chapter 1

1 Marlize Lombard and Peter Gärdenfors, "Tracking the Evolution of Causal Cognition in Humans," *Journal of Anthropological Sciences* 95 (2017): 219–234, https://doi.org/10.4436/jass.95006.

Chapter 2

1 Niels Eichhorn, "Emancipation in War: The United States and Peru," *The Journal of the Civil War Era*, September 15, 2020, https://www.journalofthecivilwarera.org/2020/09/emancipation-in-war-the-united-states-and-peru/; "The Grim Tale of Guano," *Sarah Albee* (blog), October 2, 2013, https://sarahalbeebooks.com/the-grim-tale-of-guano/.

2 Alvita Akiboh, "The Guano Islands: Bird Turds and the Beginnings of U.S. Overseas Territories," US History Scene, April 10, 2015, https://ushistoryscene.com/article/guano-islands-bird-turds/.

3 Mike Wall, "Kessler Syndrome and the Space Debris Problem," Space.com, July 14 2022, https://www.space.com/kessler-syndrome-space-debris.

4 "How Many Satellites Are in Space?," Nanoavionics.com, May 4, 2023, https://nanoavionics.com/blog/how-many-satellites-are-in-space/.

5 Justine Calma, "Space Collisions Could Become a Bigger Risk Thanks to Greenhouse Gas Pollution," *The Verge*, March 10, 2025, https://www.theverge.com/news/626810/space-collision-satellite-greenhouse-gas-emissions.

6 Dan Milmo et al., "Slow Recovery from IT Outage Begins as Experts Warn of Future Risks," *The Guardian*, July 19, 2024, https://www.theguardian.com/australia-news/article/2024/jul/19/microsoft-windows-pcs-outage-blue-screen-of-death.

7 David Weston, "Helping Our Customers through the CrowdStrike Outage," *Official Microsoft Blog*, July 20, 2024, https://blogs.microsoft.com/blog/2024/07/20/helping-our-customers-through-the-crowdstrike-outage/.

8 Evan Bush, "Comprehensive Study of West Antarctic Ice Sheet Finds Collapse May Be Unavoidable," *NBC News*, October 23, 2023, https://www.nbcnews.com/science/environment/west-antarctic-ice-sheet-collapse-may-unavoidable-study-finds-rcna120993.

9 Alison George, "Antarctica's 'Doomsday' Glacier Is Heading for Catastrophic Collapse," *New Scientist*, September 20, 2024, https://www.newscientist.com/article/2448793-antarcticas-doomsday-glacier-is-heading-for-catastrophic-collapse/.

10 Veronica Root Martinez faculty page: https://law.duke.edu/fac/martinez; Veronica Root Martinez, "The Role of Norms in Modern-Day Government Ethics," *Notre Dame Journal of Law, Ethics & Public Policy* 35 (2021): 771–793, https://scholarship.law.duke.edu/faculty_scholarship/4198/.

11 "Social Media and News Fact Sheet," Pew Research Center, September 17, 2024, https://www.pewresearch.org/journalism/fact-sheet/social-media-and-news-fact-sheet/.

Chapter 3

1 Elahe Izadi, "The Latest News? Not Right Now, Thanks," *Washington Post*, November 24, 2024, https://www.washingtonpost.com/style/media/2024/11/24/news-quitting-shutting-off/.

2 Anne Case and Angus Deaton, "Rising Morbidity and Mortality in Midlife among White Non-Hispanic Americans in the 21st Century,"

Proceedings of the National Academy of Sciences 112, no. 49 (November 2, 2015): 15078–15083, https://doi.org/10.1073/pnas.1518393112.

3 Yasemin Saplakoglu, "'Diseases of Despair' on the Rise across the US," *Live Science*, November 10, 2020, https://www.livescience.com/diseases-despair-rising-us.html; Matthew Garnett, Merianne Rose Spencer, and Julie D. Weeks, "Suicide among Adults Age 55 and Older, 2021," CDC National Center for Health Statistics, *NCHS Health Brief*, no. 483, November 2023, https://www.cdc.gov/nchs/products/databriefs/db483.htm.

4 "Suicide," World Health Organization, August 29, 2024, https://www.who.int/news-room/fact-sheets/detail/suicide.

5 "Opioid Overdose," World Health Organization, August 29, 2023, https://www.who.int/news-room/fact-sheets/detail/opioid-overdose.

6 Wikipedia, s.v. "United States Drug Overdose Death Rates and Totals over Time," accessed December 31, 2024, https://en.wikipedia.org/wiki/United_States_drug_overdose_death_rates_and_totals_over_time. Data collected primarily from https://wonder.cdc.gov/mcd-icd10.html.

7 "Over 3 Million Annual Deaths Due to Alcohol and Drug Use, Majority among Men," World Health Organization, June 25, 2024, https://www.who.int/news/item/25-06-2024-over-3-million-annual-deaths-due-to-alcohol-and-drug-use-majority-among-men; Marissa B. Esser et al., "Deaths from Excessive Alcohol Use—United States, 2016–2021," CDC, *Morbidity and Mortality Weekly Report* 73, no. 8 (February 29, 2024): 154–161, https://www.cdc.gov/mmwr/volumes/73/wr/mm7308a1.htm.

8 Dina Spector, "The Evolutionary Reason Humans Crave Sugar," World Economic Forum, May 8, 2015, https://www.weforum.org/stories/2015/05/the-evolutionary-reason-humans-crave-sugar/.

9 Amrisha Vaish, Tobias Grossmann, and Amanda Woodward, "Not All Emotions Are Created Equal: The Negativity Bias in Social-Emotional Development," *Psychological Bulletin* 134, no. 3 (2008): 383–403, https://doi.org/10.1037/0033-2909.134.3.383.

10 Joshua Benton, "Negative Words in News Headlines Generate More Clicks—But Sad Words Are More Effective Than Angry or Scary Ones," *NiemanLab*, March 20, 2023, https://www.niemanlab.org/2023/03/negative-words-in-news-headlines-generate-more-clicks-but-sad-words-are-more-effective-than-angry-or-scary-ones/.

11 Kyra-lin Hom, "Rage Baiting," *Westside Seattle Herald*, May 25, 2015, https://www.westsideseattle.com/west-seattle-herald/2015/05/25/rage-baiting; "How to Recognise Rage Farming and Keep Yourself Safe from It," *The Hindu*, January 8, 2024, https://www.thehindu.com/sci-tech/technology/how-to-detect-rage-farming-and-keep-yourself-safe-from-it/article67718125.ece.

12 TechDetox Mom, "Enrage to Engage: How Attention Economy Profits from Outrage While Driving Us Crazy," TechDetox, October 25, 2023, https://www.techdetoxbox.com/weapons-of-digital-manipulation/how-attention-economy-profits-from-outrage/.

13 Michalis Mamakos and Eli J. Finkel, "How Trolls Poison Political Discussions for Everyone Else," *Kellogg Insight*, March 1, 2024, https://insight.kellogg.northwestern.edu/article/trolls-poison-political-discussions-for-everyone-else.

14 Zoe Kleinman, "Political Trolling Twice as Popular as Positivity, Study Suggests," *BBC News*, June 21, 2021, https://www.bbc.com/news/technology-57558028.

15 "Cheese Photo Leads to Liverpool Drug Dealer's Downfall," *BBC News*, May 24, 2021, https://www.bbc.com/news/uk-england-merseyside-57226165.

16 Martha W. Buckley and John Marshall, "Observations, Inferences, and Mechanisms of the Atlantic Meridional Overturning Circulation: A Review," *Reviews of Geophysics* 54, no. 1 (2016): 5–63, https://doi.org/10.1002/2015RG000493.

17 "New Study Finds That Critical Ocean Current Has Not Declined in the Last 60 Years," Woods Hole Oceanographic Institute, January 15, 2025, https://www.whoi.edu/press-room/news-release/no-amoc-decline/.

Chapter 4

1 This version is from a 1912 book by James Baldwin—no, not that one—titled *Fifty Famous People: A Book of Short Stories*.

2 Mark Ward, "Deadly Plague Hits Warcraft World," *BBC News*, September 22, 2005, http://news.bbc.co.uk/2/hi/technology/4272418.stm.

3 Jhaan Elker, "World of Warcraft Experienced a Pandemic in 2005. That Experience May Help Coronavirus Researchers," *Washington Post*, April 9, 2020, https://www.washingtonpost.com/video-games/2020/04/09/world-warcraft-experienced-pandemic-2005-that-experience-may-help-coronavirus-researchers/.

4 Richard Dawkins, *The Selfish Gene* (Oxford: Oxford University Press, 1976).

5 Jeremy Salvucci, "An In-Depth Timeline of the GameStop Short Squeeze Saga," *TheStreet*, September 15, 2023, https://www.thestreet.com/investing/stocks/a-timeline-of-the-gamestop-short-squeeze.

6 Zoltan Vardai, "Musk's DOGE Agency Launches Official Website with Dogecoin Logo," *Cointelegraph*, January 21, 2025, https://cointelegraph.com/news/dogecoin-rally-musk-doge-agency-launch.

7 Juliana Menasce Horowitz, Ruth Igielnik, and Rakesh Kochhar, "Views of Economic Inequality," Pew Research Center, January 9, 2020, https://www.pewresearch.org/social-trends/2020/01/09/views-of-economic-inequality/.

8 Thomas Douenne, Oda Sund, Joël van der Weele, "DP19174 Do People Distinguish Income from Wealth Inequality? Evidence from the Netherlands," Centre for Economic Policy Research, June 24, 2024, https://cepr.org/publications/dp19174.

9 Oliver P. Hauser and Michael I. Norton, "(Mis)perceptions of Inequality," *Current Opinion in Psychology* 18 (2017): 21–25, https://doi.org/10.1177/1745691614549773.

10 Barnabas Szaszi et al., "Selective Insensitivity to Income Held by the Richest," *PNAS Nexus*, September 17, 2024, https://doi.org/10.1093/pnasnexus/pgae333.

11 Rachel Louise Ensign, "The U.S. Economy Depends More Than Ever on Rich People," *The Wall Street Journal*, February 23, 2025, https://www.wsj.com/economy/consumers/us-economy-strength-rich-spending-2c34a571.

12 "Yellow Journalism," "Crucible of Empire: The Spanish-American War," PBS, 1999, https://www.pbs.org/crucible/bio_hearst.html.

13 Tara Copp, "Elon Musk's Refusal to Have Starlink Support Ukraine Attack in Crimea Raises Questions for Pentagon," Associated Press, September 11, 2023, https://apnews.com/article/spacex-ukraine-starlink-russia-air-force-fde93d9a69d7dbd1326022ecfdbc53c2.

14 Emily Crockett, "Trump's 2nd Amendment Comment Wasn't a Joke. It Was 'Stochastic Terrorism,'" *Vox*, August 11, 2016, https://www.vox.com/2016/8/10/12422476/trump-second-amendment-hillary-stochastic-terrorism-anti-abortion-violence.

15 Heather Timmons, "Stochastic Terror and the Cycle of Hate That Pushes Unstable Americans to Violence" *Quartz*, October 26, 2018,

https://qz.com/1436267/trump-stochastic-terror-and-the-hate-that-ends-in-violence.

16. Jonathan McGovern, "The Origin of the Phrase 'Will No One Rid Me of This Turbulent Priest?,'" *Notes and Queries* 68, no. 3 (September 2021): 266, https://doi.org/10.1093/notesj/gjab094.

17. Erich Wagner, "Employee Group Urges Centralized Response to Increase in Doxxing and Threats against Federal Workers," *Government Executive*, October 31, 2024, https://www.govexec.com/workforce/2024/10/employee-group-urges-centralized-response-increase-doxxing-and-threats-against-federal-workers/400727/; Sara Kettler, "'Swatting': How a Hoax Can Become Deadly," *A&E True Crime Blog*, January 16, 2024, https://www.aetv.com/real-crime/swatting-results-in-death.

18. Song et al., "Climate Sensitivity Controls Global Precipitation Hysteresis in Changing CO_2 Pathway," *NPJ Climate and Atmospheric Science* 6, no. 156 (September 30, 2023), https://doi.org/10.1038/s41612-023-00484-2.

Chapter 5

1. John Mecklin, "A Moment of Historic Danger: It Is *Still* 90 Seconds to Midnight," *Bulletin of the Atomic Scientists*, January 23, 2024, https://thebulletin.org/doomsday-clock/timeline/.

2. David S. Jonas and Bryn McWhorter, "Nuclear Launch Authority: Too Big a Decision for Just the President," *Arms Control Today*, June 2021, https://www.armscontrol.org/act/2021-06/features/nuclear-launch-authority-too-big-decision-just-president.

3. Hans Kristensen et al., "Status of World Nuclear Forces," *Federation of American Scientists*, March 29, 2024, https://fas.org/initiative/status-world-nuclear-forces/.

4. "Data Page: Estimated Explosive Power of Nuclear Weapons Deliverable in First Strike," Our World in Data, 2024, data derived from Suh (2022), https://ourworldindata.org/grapher/estimated-megatons-of-nuclear-weapons-deliverable-in-first-strike.

5. Elizabeth Yuko, "Why Are Black Communities Being Singled Out as Vaccine Hesitant?," *Rolling Stone*, March 9, 2021, https://web.archive.org/web/20210309201001/https://www.rollingstone.com/culture/culture-features/covid-19-vaccine-hesitant-black-communities-singled-out-1137750/.

6 Jacob Wallace, Paul Goldsmith-Pinkham, and Jason L. Schwartz, "Excess Death Rates for Republican and Democratic Registered Voters in Florida and Ohio during the COVID-19 Pandemic," *JAMA Internal Medicine* 183, no. 9 (July 24, 2023): 916–923, https://doi.org/10.1001/jamainternmed.2023.1154.

7 Kaleigh Rogers, "Where Breitbart's False Claim That Democrats Want Republicans to Stay Unvaccinated Came From," *FiveThirtyEight*, October 1, 2021, https://fivethirtyeight.com/features/where-breitbarts-false-claim-that-democrats-want-republicans-to-stay-unvaccinated-came-from/.

8 Dinah V. Parums, "A Review of the Resurgence of Measles, a Vaccine-Preventable Disease, as Current Concerns Contrast with Past Hopes for Measles Elimination," *Medical Science Monitor* 30 (March 13, 2024): e944436-1–e944436-10, https://doi.org/10.12659/MSM.944436.

9 Matteo Wong, "AI Is an Existential Threat to Itself," *The Atlantic*, June 21, 2023, https://www.theatlantic.com/technology/archive/2023/06/generative-ai-future-training-models/674478/.

10 Anika Zuschke, "Fact vs. Fiction: Strategies to Combat LLM Hallucinations," *Medium*, October 4, 2024, https://medium.com/ai-ippen-media/fact-vs-fiction-strategies-to-combat-llm-hallucinations-cbc6a28918f5.

11 Paul Robinette et al., "Overtrust of Robots in Emergency Evacuation Scenarios," *2016 11th ACM/IEEE International Conference on Human-Robot Interaction (HRI)*, IEEE Xplore, 2016, https://doi.org/10.1109/HRI.2016.7451740.

12 Jamais Cascio, *Hacking the Earth: Understanding the Consequences of Geoengineering* (pub. by author, 2009).

13 Patrick Cain, "Empty Skies after 9/11 Set the Stage for an Unlikely Climate Change Experiment," *Global News*, September 12, 2016, https://globalnews.ca/news/2934513/empty-skies-after-911-set-the-stage-for-an-unlikely-climate-change-experiment/.

14 Fred Pearce, "How Airplane Contrails Are Helping Make the Planet Warmer," *Yale E360*, July 18, 2019, https://e360.yale.edu/features/how-airplane-contrails-are-helping-make-the-planet-warmer.

Part II opener

1 Adapted from "Welcome to Human Dignity and Humiliation Studies (HumanDHS)," Human Dignity and Humiliation Studies, accessed

April 16, 2025, https://www.humiliationstudies.org/whoweare/index1.php.

Chapter 6

1. M. E. P. Seligman, *Learned Helplessness: On Depression, Development, and Death* (San Francisco: W. H. Freeman, 1975).
2. Joel C. Dotterer, CPT, "Commander's Intent: Less Is Better," *Field Manual 100-5*, June 14, 1993, https://www.globalsecurity.org/military/library/report/call/call_98-24_ch1.htm.
3. Bob Johansen, *Full-Spectrum Thinking: How to Escape Boxes in a Post-Categorical Future* (Oakland: Berrett-Koehler, 2020), 107–111.
4. On the United Nations, see Nezir Aydin and Zeynep Cetinkale, "Simultaneous Response to Multiple Disasters: Integrated Planning for Pandemics and Large-Scale Earthquakes," *International Journal of Disaster Risk Reduction* 86, no. 103538 (February 15, 2023), https://doi.org/10.1016/j.ijdrr.2023.103538; on Intel, see Yossi Sheffi, "A Quake Breaks a Supply Chain," in *The Power of Resilience* (Cambridge, MA: MIT Press, 2017), https://web.archive.org/web/20241003125346/https://covid-19.mitpress.mit.edu/pub/84v5elhf/release/1; on the California Telehealth Resource Center, see "Disaster Preparedness, Mitigation, and Recovery in the Digital Age: Enhancing Healthcare Resilience in CA and Beyond," California Telehealth Resource Center, accessed December 20, 2024, https://caltrc.org/news/disaster-preparedness-mitigation-and-recovery-in-the-digital-age-enhancing-healthcare-resilience-in-ca-and-beyond/.
5. "Global Social Media Statistics," DataReportal, accessed April 16, 2025, https://datareportal.com/social-media-users.
6. Tufia C. Haddad, et al., "A Scalable Framework for Telehealth: The Mayo Clinic Center for Connected Care Response to the COVID-19 Pandemic," *Telemedicine Reports* 2, no. 1 (February 24, 2021): 78–87, https://doi.org/10.1089/tmr.2020.0032.
7. Viktor Frankl, *Man's Search for Meaning* (London: Rider, 2004), first published in 1946.
8. See Stephen Hawking, *My Brief History* (New York: Bantam Books, 2013). Also see this book written by his first wife: Jane Hawking, *Travelling to Infinity: My Life with Stephen* (Surrey, England: Alma Books, 2007).
9. Bryan Stevenson, *Just Mercy: A Story of Justice and Redemption* (New York: Spiegel & Grau, 2014).

10   Judith T. Moskowitz, et al., "Positive Affect and Health: A Review," *Annual Review of Psychology* 69, no. 1 (2018): 539–566.

11   Bruce Lee (@brucelee), status post on Twitter (now X), posted by Shannon Lee, Bruce Lee Family Archives, September 11, 2020, https://x.com/brucelee/status/1304344053216096256.

12   For basic introductions to cognitive behavioral therapy, we recommend these three sources: Jeff Riggenbach, *The CBT Toolbox: A Workbook for Clients, Clinicians, and Coaches* (Eau Claire, WI: PESI Publishing, 2021); David Burns, *The Feeling Good Handbook* (New York: Plume, 1999); Seth J. Gillihan, *Cognitive Behavioral Therapy Made Simple: 10 Strategies for Managing Anxiety, Depression, Anger, Panic, and Worry* (Naperville, IL: Callisto Publishing, 2018).

Chapter 7

1   Kamila Jankowiak-Siuda, Krystyna Rymarczyk, and Anna Grabowska, "How We Empathize with Others: A Neurobiological Perspective," *Medical Science Monitor* 17, no. 1 (January 1, 2011): RA18–RA24, https://doi.org/10.12659/MSM.881324.

2   Robert H. Rosen, *Just Enough Anxiety: The Hidden Driver of Success* (New York: Portfolio, 2008), 1.

3   Kate Darling, *The New Breed: What Our History with Animals Reveals about Our Future with Robots* (New York: Henry Holt and Company, 2021), xix.

4   An excellent summary of this story is contained in Adam Galinsky, *Inspire: The Universal Path for Leading Yourself and Others* (New York: HarperCollins Publishers, 2025).

5   Galinsky, *Inspire*, 127.

6   Alan W. Watts, *The Wisdom of Insecurity: A Message for an Age of Anxiety* (New York: Vintage Books, 1951).

7   Watts, *The Wisdom of Insecurity*, 14–15.

Chapter 8

1   Daniel L. Haulman, "KAL Flight 007," Air Mobility Command Museum, accessed December 15, 2024, https://amcmuseum.org/history/kal-flight-007/.

2   David Hoffman, "'I Had a Funny Feeling in My Gut,'" *Washington Post*, p. A19, February 10, 1999, https://www.washingtonpost.com/wp-srv/inatl/longterm/coldwar/shatter021099b.htm.

3 Adam Galinsky, *Inspire: The Universal Path for Leading Yourself and Others* (New York: HarperCollins Publishers, 2025).

4 Galinsky, x.

5 Fred Luskin and Kenneth R. Pelletier, *Stress Free for Good: 10 Scientifically Proven Life Skills for Health and Happiness* (New York: Harper One, 2005).

6 Fred Luskin, *Forgive for Good* (New York: Harper One, 2002), 163.

7 For more of the basics, see Tom Salinsky and Deborah Frances-White, *The Improv Handbook: The Ultimate Guide to Improvising in Comedy, Theatre, and Beyond* (New York: Centinuum, 2011).

Chapter 9

1 "Intertidal Zone," National Geographic Society, October 19, 2023, https://education.nationalgeographic.org/resource/intertidal-zone/.

2 Brian Gaylord et al., "Ocean Change within Shoreline Communities: From Biomechanics to Behaviour and Beyond," *Conservation Physiology* 7, no. 1 (November 18, 2019): coz077, https://doi.org/10.1093/conphys/coz077.

3 Bob Johansen, *Full-Spectrum Thinking: How to Escape Boxes in a Post-Categorical Future* (Oakland: Berrett-Koehler, 2020).

4 Malala Yousafzai, with Christina Lamb, *I Am Malala: The Girl Who Stood Up for Education and Was Shot by the Taliban* (New York: Little, Brown and Company, 2013), 288–289.

5 For an introduction to body-based therapies for resilience, see Bessel Van der Kolk, *The Body Keeps the Score: Brain, Mind, and Body in the Healing of Trauma* (New York: Viking, 2014).

6 Carla Fernandez, *Renegade Grief: A Guide to the Wild Ride of Life after Loss* (New York: Simon & Schuster, 2025).

7 Carla Fernandez, quoted in an interview in Casper ter Kuile's newsletter: "Renegade Grief: Learning from Carla Fernandez," March 6, 2025, https://www.caspertk.com/blog/renegade-grief-learning-from-carla-fernandez.

Chapter 10

1 Herman Kahn and Anthony J. Weiner, "The Use of Scenarios," Hudson Institute, January 1, 1967, https://www.hudson.org/technology/the-use-of-scenarios.

2. Peter Schwartz, *The Art of the Long View: Planning for the Future in an Uncertain World* (New York: Currency Doubleday, 1991).

3. Jamais worked for Global Business Network between 1996 and 1999 so was witness to this firsthand.

4. Thomas Nagel, *The View from Nowhere* (Oxford: Oxford University Press, 1989); Jay Rosen, "The View from Nowhere: Questions and Answers," *PressThink*, November 10, 2010, https://pressthink.org/2010/11/the-view-from-nowhere-questions-and-answers/.

Chapter 11

1. Nassir Ghaemi, *A First-Rate Madness: Uncovering the Links between Leadership and Mental Illness* (New York: Penguin, 2011), 2.

2. D. Rock et al., "The Healthy Mind Platter," *NeuroLeadership Journal* 4 (2012).

3. Bob Johansen, *The New Leadership Literacies: Thriving in a Future of Extreme Disruption and Distributed Everything* (Oakland: Berrett-Koehler, 2017).

4. Carol S. Dweck, *Mindset: The New Psychology of Success* (New York: Random House, 2006).

5. Andy Clark, *The Experience Machine: How Our Minds Predict and Shape Reality* (New York: Pantheon Books, 2023), 216.

6. Kendall Haven, *Story Smart: Using the Science of Story to Persuade, Influence, Inspire, and Teach* (Santa Barbara, CA: Libraries United, 2014).

7. Bob Johansen, Jeremy Kirshbaum, and Gabe Cervantes, *Leaders Make the Future: 10 New Skills to Humanize Your Leadership with Generative AI*, 3rd ed. (Oakland: Berrett-Koehler, 2025).

8. Robert D. Putnam, *Bowling Alone: The Collapse and Revival of American Community* (New York: Simon & Schuster Paperbacks, 2000). For a deeper analysis of the varied literature on this topic, see Tristan Claridge, "Functions of Social Capital—Bonding, Bridging, and Linking," Social Capital Research, 2018.

9. Mariana Mazzucato, *Mission Economy: A Moonshot Guide to Changing Capitalism* (New York: Penguin Books, 2022).

10. Bryce Hoffman, *American Icon: Alan Mulally and the Fight to Save Ford Motor Company* (New York: Crown, 2013).

11. One of the ten future leadership skills introduced in the third edition of *Leaders Make the Future* (Oakland: Berrett-Koehler, 2025).

12 Sian Beilock, *Choke: What the Secrets of the Brain Reveal about Getting It Right When You Have To* (New York: The Free Press, 2010).

13 Kentaro Toyama, *Geek Heresy: Rescuing Social Change from the Cult of Technology* (New York: Public Affairs Books, 2015), 129–132, 253. These are the three "Pillars of Wisdom" identified by Professor Toyama in his analysis of why it is so difficult to make effective and scalable use of technology for social and economic development. Toyama is a computer scientist and international development researcher at the University of Michigan School of Information.

Conclusion

1 "Nature's Dangerous Decline 'Unprecedented'; Species Extinction Rates 'Accelerating,'" Intergovernmental Science-Policy Platform on Biodiversity and Ecosystem Services, May 6, 2019, https://www.ipbes.net/news/Media-Release-Global-Assessment.

2 Gerardo Ceballos and Paul R. Ehrlich, "Mutilation of the Tree of Life via Mass Extinction of Animal Genera," *Proceedings of the National Academy of Sciences* 120, no. 39 (September 18, 2023): e2306987120, https://doi.org/10.1073.

3 Wangjie Hu et al., "Genomic Inference of a Severe Human Bottleneck during the Early to Middle Pleistocene Transition," *Science* 381, no. 6661 (August 31, 2023), https://doi.org/10.1126/science.abq7487.

4 Jamais heard him say this in person, but the original source can be found here: Bruce Sterling, "The Singularity: Your Future as a Black Hole," The Long Now Foundation, June 11, 2004, https://longnow.org/seminars/02004/jun/11/the-singularity-your-future-as-a-black-hole/.

Bibliography

Aydin, Nezir, and Zeynep Cetinkale. "Simultaneous Response to Multiple Disasters: Integrated Planning for Pandemics and Large-Scale Earthquakes." *International Journal of Disaster Risk Reduction* 86, no. 103538 (February 15, 2023). https://doi.org/10.1016/j.ijdrr.2023.103538.

Baldwin, James. *Fifty Famous People: A Book of Short Stories*. Living Book Press, 1912.

BBC News. "Cheese Photo Leads to Liverpool Drug Dealer's Downfall." May 24, 2021. https://www.bbc.com/news/uk-england-merseyside-57226165.

Beilock, Sian. *Choke: What the Secrets of the Brain Reveal about Getting It Right When You Have To*. New York: The Free Press, 2010.

Benton, Joshua. "Negative Words in News Headlines Generate More Clicks—But Sad Words Are More Effective Than Angry or Scary Ones." *NiemanLab*, March 20, 2023. https://www.niemanlab.org/2023/03/negative-words-in-news-headlines-generate-more-clicks-but-sad-words-are-more-effective-than-angry-or-scary-ones/.

Buckley, Martha W., and John Marshall. "Observations, Inferences, and Mechanisms of the Atlantic Meridional Overturning Circulation: A Review." *Reviews of Geophysics* 54, no. 1 (2016). https://doi.org/10.1002/2015RG000493.

Burns, David D. *The Feeling Good Handbook*. New York: Plume, 1999.

Burns, David D. *Feeling Good: The New Mood Therapy*. New York: Harper, 1999.

Burns, David D. *Feeling Great: The Revolutionary New Treatment for Depression and Anxiety*. Eau Claire, WI: PESI Publishing & Media, 2020.

Bush, Evan. "Comprehensive Study of West Antarctic Ice Sheet Finds Collapse May Be Unavoidable." *NBC News*, October 23, 2023. https://www.nbcnews.com/science/environment/west-antarctic-ice-sheet-collapse-may-unavoidable-study-finds-rcna120993.

Cain, Patrick. "Empty Skies after 9/11 Set the Stage for an Unlikely Climate Change Experiment." *Global News*, September 12, 2016. https://globalnews.ca/news/2934513/empty-skies-after-911-set-the-stage-for-an-unlikely-climate-change-experiment/.

California Telehealth Resource Center. "Disaster Preparedness, Mitigation, and Recovery in the Digital Age: Enhancing Healthcare Resilience in CA and Beyond." Accessed December 20, 2024. https://caltrc.org/news/disaster-preparedness-mitigation-and-recovery-in-the-digital-age-enhancing-healthcare-resilience-in-ca-and-beyond/.

Calma, Justine. "Space Collisions Could Become a Bigger Risk Thanks to Greenhouse Gas Pollution." *The Verge*, March 10, 2025. https://www.theverge.com/news/626810/space-collision-satellite-greenhouse-gas-emissions.

Cascio, Jamais. "Facing the Age of Chaos." *Medium*, April 29, 2020. https://medium.com/@cascio/facing-the-age-of-chaos-b00687b1f51d.

Cascio, Jamais. *Hacking the Earth: Understanding the Consequences of Geoengineering*. Published by the author, 2009.

Case, Anne, and Angus Deaton. "Rising Morbidity and Mortality in Midlife among White Non-Hispanic Americans in the 21st Century." *Proceedings of the National Academy of Sciences* 112, no. 49 (November 2, 2015): 15078–15083. https://doi.org/10.1073/pnas.1518393112.

Ceballos, Gerardo, and Paul R. Ehrlich. "Mutilation of the Tree of Life via Mass Extinction of Animal Genera." *Proceedings of the National Academy of Sciences* 120, no. 39 (September 18, 2023): e2306987120. https://doi.org/10.1073.

Claridge, Tristan. "Functions of Social Capital—Bonding, Bridging, and Linking." Social Capital Research, 2018.

Clark, Andy. *The Experience Machine: How Our Minds Predict and Shape Reality*. New York: Pantheon Books, 2023.

Copp, Tara. "Elon Musk's Refusal to Have Starlink Support Ukraine Attack in Crimea Raises Questions for Pentagon." Associated Press, September 11, 2023. https://apnews.com/article/spacex-ukraine-starlink-russia-air-force-fde93d9a69d7dbd1326022ecfdbc53c2.

Crockett, Emily. "Trump's 2nd Amendment Comment Wasn't a Joke. It Was 'Stochastic Terrorism.'" *Vox*, August 11, 2016. https://www.vox.com/2016/8/10/12422476/trump-second-amendment-hillary-stochastic-terrorism-anti-abortion-violence.

Darling, Kate. *The New Breed: What Our History with Animals Reveals about Our Future with Robots.* New York: Henry Holt and Company, 2021.

DataReportal. "Global Social Media Statistics." Accessed April 16, 2025. https://datareportal.com/social-media-users.

Dawkins, Richard. *The Selfish Gene.* Oxford: Oxford University Press, 1976.

Dotterer, CPT, Joel C. "Commander's Intent: Less Is Better." *Field Manual 100-5*, June 14, 1993. www.GlobalSecurity.org.

Douenne, Thomas, Oda Sund, and Joël van der Weele. "DP19174 Do People Distinguish Income from Wealth Inequality? Evidence from the Netherlands." Centre for Economic Policy Research, June 24, 2024. https://cepr.org/publications/dp19174.

Duckworth, Angela. *Grit: The Power of Passion and Perseverance.* New York: Scribner, 2016.

Dunning, David. "Chapter Five: The Dunning–Kruger Effect: On Being Ignorant of One's Own Ignorance." *Advances in Experimental Social Psychology* 44 (January 1, 2011): 247–296. https://doi.org/10.1016/B978-0-12-385522-0.00005-6.

Dweck, Carol S. *Mindset: The New Psychology of Success.* New York: Random House, 2006.

Elker, Jhaan. "World of Warcraft Experienced a Pandemic in 2005. That Experience May Help Coronavirus Researchers." *Washington Post*, April 9, 2020. https://www.washingtonpost.com/video-games/2020/04/09/world-warcraft-experienced-pandemic-2005-that-experience-may-help-coronavirus-researchers/.

Engelbart, Douglas C. "Augmenting Human Intellect: A Conceptual Framework." Stanford Research Institute Summary Report Air Force Office of Scientific Research (AFOSR-3223), 1962. https://www.dougengelbart.org/pubs/augment-3906.html.

Ensign, Rachel Louise. "The U.S. Economy Depends More Than Ever on Rich People." *The Wall Street Journal*, February 23, 2025. https://www.wsj.com/economy/consumers/us-economy-strength-rich-spending-2c34a571.

Esser, Marissa B., Adam Sherk, Yong Liu, and Timothy S. Naimi. "Deaths from Excessive Alcohol Use—United States, 2016–2021." *CDC, Morbidity and Mortality Weekly Report* 73, no. 8 (February 29, 2024): 154–161. https://www.cdc.gov/mmwr/volumes/73/wr/mm7308a1.htm.

Fernandez, Carla. *Renegade Grief: A Guide to the Wild Ride of Life after Loss.* New York: Simon & Schuster, 2025.

Frankl, Viktor. *Man's Search for Meaning*. London: Rider, 2004. First published in 1946.

Galinsky, Adam. *Inspire: The Universal Path for Leading Yourself and Others*. New York: HarperCollins Publishers, 2025.

Garnett, Matthew, Merianne Rose Spencer, and Julie D. Weeks. "Suicide among Adults Age 55 and Older, 2021." CDC National Center for Health Statistics, *NCHS Health Brief*, no. 483, November 2023. https://www.cdc.gov/nchs/products/databriefs/db483.htm.

Gaylord, Brian, Kristina M. Barclay, Brittany M. Jellison, Laura J. Jurgens, Aaron T. Ninokawa, Emily B. Rivest, and Lindsey R. Leighton. "Ocean Change within Shoreline Communities: From Biomechanics to Behaviour and Beyond." *Conservation Physiology* 7, no. 1 (November 18, 2019): coz077. https://doi.org/10.1093/conphys/coz077.

George, Alison. "Antarctica's 'Doomsday' Glacier Is Heading for Catastrophic Collapse." *New Scientist*, September 20, 2024. https://www.newscientist.com/article/2448793-antarcticas-doomsday-glacier-is-heading-for-catastrophic-collapse/.

Ghaemi, Nassir. *A First-Rate Madness: Uncovering the Links between Leadership and Mental Illness*. New York: The Penguin Press, 2011.

Gillihan, Seth J. *Cognitive Behavioral Therapy Made Simple: 10 Strategies for Managing Anxiety, Depression, Anger, Panic, and Worry*. Naperville, IL: Callisto Publishing, 2018.

Glaeser, Waltraud. "Where Does the Term VUCA Come From!" VUCA World. Accessed January 20, 2025. https://www.vuca-world.org/roles-of-nanus-and-bennis/.

Haddad, Tufia C., Rebecca N. Blegen, Julie E. Prigge, Debra L. Cox, Greg S. Anthony, Michelle A. Leak, Dwight D. Channer, Page Y. Underwood, Ryan D. Williams, Rhapsody D. Hofschulte, Laura A. Christopherson, Jordan D. Coffey, Sarvam P. TerKonda, James A. Yiannias, Brian A. Costello, Christopher S. Russi, Christopher E. Colby, Steve R. Ommen, and Bart M. Demaerschalk. "A Scalable Framework for Telehealth: The Mayo Clinic Center for Connected Care Response to the COVID-19 Pandemic." *Telemedicine Reports* 2, no. 1 (February 24, 2021): 78–87. https://doi.org/10.1089/tmr.2020.0032.

Haidt, Jonathan. *The Anxious Generation: How the Great Rewiring of Childhood Is Causing an Epidemic of Mental Illness*. New York: Penguin Press, 2024.

Harvard Health Publishing. "Somatic Therapy: A New Approach to Mental Health." Accessed March 10, 2025. https://www.health.harvard.edu.

Haulman, Daniel L. "KAL Flight 007." Air Mobility Command Museum. Accessed December 15, 2024. https://amcmuseum.org/history/kal-flight-007/.

Hauser, Oliver P., and Michael I. Norton. "(Mis)perceptions of Inequality." *Current Opinion in Psychology* 18 (2017): 21–25. https://doi.org/10.1177/1745691614549773.

Haven, Kendall. *Story Smart: Using the Science of Story to Persuade, Influence, Inspire, and Teach.* Santa Barbara, CA: Libraries United, 2014.

Hawking, Jane. *Travelling to Infinity: My Life with Stephen.* Surrey, England: Alma Books, 2007.

Hawking, Stephen. *My Brief History.* New York: Bantam Books, 2013.

The Hindu. "How to Recognise Rage Farming and Keep Yourself Safe from It." January 8, 2024. https://www.thehindu.com/sci-tech/technology/how-to-detect-rage-farming-and-keep-yourself-safe-from-it/article67718125.ece.

Hoffman, Bryce. *American Icon: Alan Mulally and the Fight to Save Ford Motor Company.* New York: Crown, 2013.

Hoffman, David. "'I Had a Funny Feeling in My Gut.'" *Washington Post*, p. A19, February 10, 1999. https://www.washingtonpost.com/wp-srv/inatl/longterm/coldwar/shatter021099b.htm.

Hom, Kyra-lin. "Rage Baiting." *Westside Seattle Herald*, May 25, 2015. https://www.westsideseattle.com/west-seattle-herald/2015/05/25/rage-baiting.

Horowitz, Juliana Menasce, Ruth Igielnik, and Rakesh Kochhar. "Views of Economic Inequality." Pew Research Center, January 9, 2020. https://www.pewresearch.org/social-trends/2020/01/09/views-of-economic-inequality/.

Hu, Wangjie, Ziqian Hao, Pengyuan Du, Fabio Di Vincenzo, Giorgio Manzi, Jialong Cui, Yun-Xin Fu, Yi-Hsuan Pan, and Haipeng Li. "Genomic Inference of a Severe Human Bottleneck during the Early to Middle Pleistocene Transition." *Science* 381, no. 6661 (August 31, 2023). https://doi.org/10.1126/science.abq7487.

Humiliation Studies. "Welcome to Human Dignity and Humiliation Studies (HumanDHS)." Accessed April 16, 2025. https://www.humiliationstudies.org/whoweare/index1.php.

Intergovernmental Science-Policy Platform on Biodiversity and Ecosystem Services. "Nature's Dangerous Decline 'Unprecedented'; Species

Extinction Rates 'Accelerating.'" May 6, 2019. https://www.ipbes.net/news/Media-Release-Global-Assessment.

Izadi, Elahe. "The Latest News? Not Right Now, Thanks." *Washington Post*, November 24, 2024. https://www.washingtonpost.com/style/media/2024/11/24/news-quitting-shutting-off/.

James, Scott. *Prepared Neighborhoods: Creating Resilience One Street at a Time*. Bainbridge Island, WA: Prepared Neighborhoods, 2017.

Jankowiak-Siuda, Kamila, Krystyna Rymarczyk, and Anna Grabowska. "How We Empathize with Others: A Neurobiological Perspective." *Medical Science Monitor* 17, no. 1 (January 1, 2011): RA18–RA24. https://doi.org/10.12659/MSM.881324.

Johansen, Bob. *Full-Spectrum Thinking: How to Escape Boxes in a Post-Categorical Future*. Oakland: Berrett-Koehler, 2020.

Johansen, Bob. *The New Leadership Literacies: Thriving in a Future of Extreme Disruption and Distributed Everything*. Oakland: Berrett-Koehler, 2017.

Johansen, Bob, Jeremy Kirshbaum, and Gabe Cervantes. *Leaders Make the Future: 10 New Skills to Humanize Your Leadership with Generative AI*, 3rd ed. Oakland: Berrett-Koehler, 2025.

Jonas, David S., and Bryn McWhorter. "Nuclear Launch Authority: Too Big a Decision for Just the President." *Arms Control Today*, June 2021. https://www.armscontrol.org/act/2021-06/features/nuclear-launch-authority-too-big-decision-just-president.

Kahn, Herman. *Thinking about the Unthinkable*. New York: Horizon Press, 1962.

Kahn, Herman, and Anthony J. Weiner. "The Use of Scenarios." Hudson Institute, January 1, 1967. https://www.hudson.org/technology/the-use-of-scenarios.

Kettler, Sara. "'Swatting': How a Hoax Can Become Deadly." *A&E True Crime Blog*, January 16, 2024. https://www.aetv.com/real-crime/swatting-results-in-death.

Kleinman, Zoe. "Political Trolling Twice as Popular as Positivity, Study Suggests." *BBC News*, June 21, 2021. https://www.bbc.com/news/technology-57558028.

Kristensen, Hans, Matt Korda, Eliana Johns, Mackenzie Knight, and Kate Kohn. "Status of World Nuclear Forces." *Federation of American Scientists*, March 29, 2024. https://fas.org/initiative/status-world-nuclear-forces/.

Kross, Ethan. *Shift: Managing Your Emotions—So They Don't Manage You.* New York: Crown, 2025.

Lee, Bruce (@brucelee). Status post on Twitter (now X), posted by Shannon Lee, Bruce Lee Family Archives, September 11, 2020. https://x.com/brucelee/status/1304344053216096256.

Lombard, Marlize, and Peter Gärdenfors. "Tracking the Evolution of Causal Cognition in Humans." *Journal of Anthropological Sciences* 95 (2017): 219–234. https://doi.org/10.4436/jass.95006.

Luskin, Fred. *Forgive for Good.* New York: Harper One, 2002.

Luskin, Fred. *Forgive for Love.* New York: Harper One, 2007.

Luskin, Fred, and Kenneth R. Pelletier. *Stress Free for Good: 10 Scientifically Proven Life Skills for Health and Happiness.* New York: Harper One, 2005.

Malone, Thomas W. *Superminds: The Surprising Power of People and Computers Thinking Together.* New York: Little, Brown and Company, 2018.

Mamakos, Michalis, and Eli J. Finkel. "How Trolls Poison Political Discussions for Everyone Else." *Kellogg Insight*, March 1, 2024. https://insight.kellogg.northwestern.edu/article/trolls-poison-political-discussions-for-everyone-else.

Marion, Bruno. *Chaos: A User's Guide.* Published by the author, 2014.

Martinez, Veronica Root. "The Role of Norms in Modern-Day Government Ethics." 35 *Notre Dame Journal of Law, Ethics & Public Policy* 35 (2021): 771–793. https://scholarship.law.duke.edu/faculty_scholarship/4198/.

Mazzucato, Mariana. *Mission Economy: A Moonshot Guide to Changing Capitalism.* New York: Penguin Books, 2022.

McGovern, Jonathan. "The Origin of the Phrase 'Will No One Rid Me of This Turbulent Priest?'" *Notes and Queries* 68, no. 3 (September 2021): 266. https://doi.org/10.1093/notesj/gjab094.

Mecklin, John. "A Moment of Historic Danger: It Is *Still* 90 Seconds to Midnight." *Bulletin of the Atomic Scientists*, January 23, 2024. https://thebulletin.org/doomsday-clock/timeline/.

Miller-Karas, Elaine. *Building Resilience to Trauma: The Trauma and Community Resiliency Models.* New York: Routledge, 2023.

Milmo, Dan, Julia Kollewe, Ben Quinn, Josh Taylor, and Mimi Ibrahim. "Slow Recovery from IT Outage Begins as Experts Warn of Future Risks." *The Guardian*, July 19, 2024. https://www.theguardian.com/australia-news/article/2024/jul/19/microsoft-windows-pcs-outage-blue-screen-of-death.

Morton, Oliver. *The Planet Remade: How Geoengineering Could Change the World*. Princeton: Princeton University Press, 2015.

Moskowitz, Judith T., et al. "Positive Affect and Health: A Review." *Annual Review of Psychology* 69, no. 1 (2018): 539–566.

Murphy, Mary C. *Cultures of Growth: How the New Science of Mindset Can Transform Individuals, Teams, and Organizations*. New York: Simon & Schuster, 2024.

Nagel, Thomas. *The View from Nowhere*. Oxford: Oxford University Press, 1989.

Nanoavionics. "How Many Satellites Are in Space?" May 4, 2023. https://nanoavionics.com/blog/how-many-satellites-are-in-space/.

National Geographic Society. "Intertidal Zone." October 19, 2023. https://education.nationalgeographic.org/resource/intertidal-zone/.

Our World in Data. "Data Page: Estimated Explosive Power of Nuclear Weapons Deliverable in First Strike." 2024. Data derived from Suh (2022). https://ourworldindata.org/grapher/estimated-megatons-of-nuclear-weapons-deliverable-in-first-strike.

Parums, Dinah V. "A Review of the Resurgence of Measles, a Vaccine-Preventable Disease, as Current Concerns Contrast with Past Hopes for Measles Elimination." *Medical Science Monitor* 30 (March 13, 2024): e944436-1–e944436-10. https://doi.org/10.12659/MSM.944436.

PBS. "Yellow Journalism." "Crucible of Empire: The Spanish-American War." 1999. https://www.pbs.org/crucible/bio_hearst.html.

Pearce, Fred. "How Airplane Contrails Are Helping Make the Planet Warmer." *Yale E360*, July 18, 2019. https://e360.yale.edu/features/how-airplane-contrails-are-helping-make-the-planet-warmer.

Pew Research Center. "Social Media and News Fact Sheet." September 17, 2024. https://www.pewresearch.org/journalism/fact-sheet/social-media-and-news-fact-sheet/.

Pietersen, Willie. *Leadership: The Inside Story*. Irvington, New York: Rivertowns Books, 2024.

Putnam, Robert D. *Bowling Alone: The Collapse and Revival of American Community*. New York: Simon & Schuster Paperbacks, 2000.

Redstone, Ilana. *The Certainty Trap: Why We Need to Question Ourselves More—and How We Can Judge Others Less*. Durham, NC: Pitchstone Publishing, 2024.

Riggenbach, Jeff. *The CBT Toolbox: A Workbook for Clients, Clinicians, and Coaches*. Eau Claire, WI: PESI Publishing, 2021.

Ritchie, Hannah. *Not the End of the World: How We Can Be the First Generation to Build a Sustainable Planet.* New York: Little, Brown Spark, 2024.

Robinette, Paul, Wenchen Li, Robert Allen, Ayanna M. Howard, and Alan R. Wagner. "Overtrust of Robots in Emergency Evacuation Scenarios." *2016 11th ACM/IEEE International Conference on Human-Robot Interaction (HRI).* IEEE Xplore, 2016. https://doi.org/10.1109/HRI.2016.7451740.

Rock, D., D. J. Siegal, S. A. Y. Poelmans, and J. Payne. "The Healthy Mind Platter." *NeuroLeadership Journal* 4 (2012).

Rogers, Kaleigh. "Where Breitbart's False Claim That Democrats Want Republicans to Stay Unvaccinated Came From." *FiveThirtyEight*, October 1, 2021. https://fivethirtyeight.com/features/where-breitbarts-false-claim-that-democrats-want-republicans-to-stay-unvaccinated-came-from/.

Rosen, Jay. "The View from Nowhere: Questions and Answers." *PressThink*, November 10, 2010. https://pressthink.org/2010/11/the-view-from-nowhere-questions-and-answers/.

Rosen, Robert H. *Just Enough Anxiety: The Hidden Driver of Success.* New York: Portfolio, 2008.

Salinsky, Tom, and Deborah Frances-White. *The Improv Handbook: The Ultimate Guide to Improvising in Comedy, Theatre, and Beyond.* New York: Centinuum, 2011.

Salvucci, Jeremy. "An In-Depth Timeline of the GameStop Short Squeeze Saga." *TheStreet*, September 15, 2023. https://www.thestreet.com/investing/stocks/a-timeline-of-the-gamestop-short-squeeze.

Saplakoglu, Yasemin. "'Diseases of Despair' on the Rise across the US." *Live Science*, November 10, 2020. https://www.livescience.com/diseases-despair-rising-us.html.

Schwartz, Peter. *The Art of the Long View: Planning for the Future in an Uncertain World.* New York: Currency Doubleday, 1991.

Seligman, M. E. P. *Learned Helplessness: On Depression, Development, and Death.* San Francisco: W. H. Freeman, 1975.

Sheffi, Yossi. "A Quake Breaks a Supply Chain." In *The Power of Resilience.* Cambridge, MA: MIT Press, 2017. https://web.archive.org/web/20241003125346/https://covid-19.mitpress.mit.edu/pub/84v5elhf/release/1.

Song, Se-Yong, Sang-Wook Yeh, Richard P. Allan, Shang-Ping Xie, Soon-Il An, and Hyo-Seok Park. "Climate Sensitivity Controls Global

Precipitation Hysteresis in Changing CO_2 Pathway." *NPJ Climate and Atmospheric Science* 6, no. 156 (September 30, 2023). https://doi.org/10.1038/s41612-023-00484-2.

Spector, Dina. "The Evolutionary Reason Humans Crave Sugar." World Economic Forum, May 8, 2015. https://www.weforum.org/stories/2015/05/the-evolutionary-reason-humans-crave-sugar/.

Sterling, Bruce. "The Singularity: Your Future as a Black Hole." The Long Now Foundation, June 11, 2004. https://longnow.org/seminars/02004/jun/11/the-singularity-your-future-as-a-black-hole/.

Stevenson, Bryan. *Just Mercy: A Story of Justice and Redemption*. New York: Spiegel & Grau, 2014.

Suh, Kyungwon. "Nuclear Balance and the Initiation of Nuclear Crises: Does Superiority Matter?" *Journal of Peace Research* 60, no. 2 (March 2022): 337–351. https://doi.org/10.1177/00223433211067899.

Szaszi, Barnabas, Hooman Habibnia, Josephine Tan, Oliver P. Hauser, and Jon M. Jachimowicz. "Selective Insensitivity to Income Held by the Richest." *PNAS Nexus*, September 17, 2024. https://doi.org/10.1093/pnasnexus/pgae333.

TechDetox Mom. "Enrage to Engage: How Attention Economy Profits from Outrage While Driving Us Crazy." TechDetox, October 25, 2023. https://www.techdetoxbox.com/weapons-of-digital-manipulation/how-attention-economy-profits-from-outrage/.

Tetloc, Philip E., and Gardner, Dan. *Super Forecasting: The Art and Science of Prediction*. New York: Broadway Books, 2015.

Timmons, Heather. "Stochastic Terror and the Cycle of Hate That Pushes Unstable Americans to Violence." *Quartz*, October 26, 2018. https://qz.com/1436267/trump-stochastic-terror-and-the-hate-that-ends-in-violence.

Toyama, Kentaro. *Geek Heresy: Rescuing Social Change from the Cult of Technology*. New York: Public Affairs Books, 2015.

Vaish, Amrisha, Tobias Grossmann, and Amanda Woodward. "Not All Emotions Are Created Equal: The Negativity Bias in Social-Emotional Development." *Psychological Bulletin* 134, no. 3 (2008): 383–403. https://doi.org/10.1037/0033-2909.134.3.383.

Van der Kolk, Bessel. *The Body Keeps the Score: Brain, Mind, and Body in the Healing of Trauma*. New York: Viking, 2014.

Vardai, Zoltan. "Musk's DOGE Agency Launches Official Website with Dogecoin Logo." *Cointelegraph*, January 21, 2025. https://cointelegraph.com/news/dogecoin-rally-musk-doge-agency-launch.

Wagner, Erich. "Employee Group Urges Centralized Response to Increase in Doxxing and Threats against Federal Workers." *Government Executive*, October 31, 2024. https://www.govexec.com/workforce/2024/10/employee-group-urges-centralized-response-increase-doxxing-and-threats-against-federal-workers/400727/.

Waldinger, Robert, and Marc Schulz. *The Good Life: Lessons from the World's Longest Scientific Study of Happiness*. New York: Simon & Schuster, 2023.

Wall, Mike. "Kessler Syndrome and the Space Debris Problem." Space.com, July 14, 2022. https://www.space.com/kessler-syndrome-space-debris.

Wallace, Jacob, Paul Goldsmith-Pinkham, and Jason L. Schwartz. "Excess Death Rates for Republican and Democratic Registered Voters in Florida and Ohio during the COVID-19 Pandemic." *JAMA Internal Medicine* 183, no. 9 (July 24, 2023): 916–923. https://doi.org/10.1001/jamainternmed.2023.1154.

Ward, Mark. "Deadly Plague Hits Warcraft World." *BBC News*, September 22, 2005. http://news.bbc.co.uk/2/hi/technology/4272418.stm.

Watts, Alan W. *The Wisdom of Insecurity: A Message for an Age of Anxiety*. New York: Vintage Books, 1951.

Weston, David. "Helping Our Customers through the CrowdStrike Outage." *Official Microsoft Blog*, July 20, 2024. https://blogs.microsoft.com/blog/2024/07/20/helping-our-customers-through-the-crowdstrike-outage/.

Wikipedia. "United States Drug Overdose Death Rates and Totals over Time." Accessed December 31, 2024. Data collected primarily from https://wonder.cdc.gov/mcd-icd10.html. https://en.wikipedia.org/wiki/United_States_drug_overdose_death_rates_and_totals_over_time.

Wong, Matteo. "AI Is an Existential Threat to Itself." *The Atlantic*, June 21, 2023. https://www.theatlantic.com/technology/archive/2023/06/generative-ai-future-training-models/674478/.

Woods Hole Oceanographic Institute. "New Study Finds That Critical Ocean Current Has Not Declined in the Last 60 Years." January 15, 2025. https://www.whoi.edu/press-room/news-release/no-amoc-decline/.

World Health Organization. "Opioid Overdose." August 29, 2023. https://www.who.int/news-room/fact-sheets/detail/opioid-overdose.

World Health Organization. "Over 3 Million Annual Deaths Due to Alcohol and Drug Use, Majority among Men." June 25, 2024. https://www.who.int/news/item/25-06-2024-over-3-million-annual-deaths-due-to-alcohol-and-drug-use-majority-among-men.

World Health Organization. "Suicide." August 29, 2024. https://www.who.int/news-room/fact-sheets/detail/suicide.

Yousafzai, Malala, with Christina Lamb. *I Am Malala: The Girl Who Stood Up for Education and Was Shot by the Taliban*. New York: Little, Brown and Company, 2013.

Yuko, Elizabeth. "Why Are Black Communities Being Singled Out as Vaccine Hesitant?" *Rolling Stone*, March 9, 2021. https://web.archive.org/web/20210309201001/https://www.rollingstone.com/culture/culture-features/covid-19-vaccine-hesitant-black-communities-singled-out-1137750/.

Zuschke, Anika. "Fact vs. Fiction: Strategies to Combat LLM Hallucinations." *Medium*, October 4, 2024. https://medium.com/ai-ippen-media/fact-vs-fiction-strategies-to-combat-llm-hallucinations-cbc6a28918f5.

Acknowledgments

Institute for the Future has been very supportive as we have written this book. All three of us have worked with IFTF in various ways over the years. IFTF is a continuous source of inspiration and ideas, and the IFTF leadership team, led by executive director Marina Gorbis, has been consistently encouraging of our efforts. We are very appreciative to be part of the IFTF community.

Upon the publication of the original BANI essay, immediate interest came from Wade Roush at the *Soonish* podcast. Wade was the first person to give Jamais a public platform to talk about BANI. Soon afterward, Isabelle Sailer in Switzerland offered Jamais a chance to speak with a group of interested and focused decision-makers, helping him to refine his thinking. A massive thanks to the both of them for seeing the value of this idea so early.

A big thank you to colleague and friend Christopher Rice for an early and extremely useful peer review of the first draft of this book.

Jamais first encountered "The future is uncertain, and yet we must act" back in 1996, said by Erika Gregory, now president of Horizon 2045. Many thanks to her for coming up with such an evocative turn of phrase.

Delice Brown, executive communication strategist at United Way Worldwide, has been enormously valuable to the development of this book. She's a collaborative sojourner looking to make sense of this BANI world, and we are glad for her help.

Our editor Steve Piersanti has believed in this project from the beginning. He has helped us imagine what this book can become and shape it to reach wider audiences. The BK production team has made this book possible on a global scale.

Scott James, the founder of Bainbridge Prepares on Bainbridge Island, Washington, was very helpful as we developed the BANI+ chapters. His work on preparedness is a model for communities preparing for all aspects of the BANI Future. Scott's book *Prepared Neighborhoods: Creating Resilience One Street at a Time* is a great summary of this perspective.

Finally, a note from Bob: As I was writing this book with Jamais and Angela, I was also finishing the 3rd edition of *Leaders Make the Future: 10 New Skills to Humanize Leadership with Generative AI*. As part of this futureback exploration of augmented leadership, I began using a customized version of ChatGPT designed by my coauthor Jeremy Kirshbaum. I've nicknamed it Stretch, because I use it to stretch my thinking. I have Stretch running on a separate screen next to me as I write. I have ongoing conversations about the ideas I'm exploring. I use it to diverge, not to converge. I don't trust Stretch for answers. Stretch is sometimes overconfident—even if wrong. Stretch is very good, however, at helping me stretch my mind and explore alternatives. Stretch comes to life in conversation, with lots of back and forth. Stretch has become a useful medium that I use to stretch my writing, but I use it with caution.

Index

A

accountability through transparency, 180
action
  climate change response, 78–79
  future as result of past, 187, 189
  vs. passivity, 189
  to reduce future harm, 25
  amid uncertainty, 16, 19, 153–154
active empathy, 106, 107, 112, 114, 145
activism, 145
adaptability, 89, 90, 107, 108, 120, 168, 171, 179
advocacy scenarios, 159
agency, 7, 112, 131
aging, 118
agricultural revolution, 29
AI (artificial intelligence)
  and BANI Future, 20
  and dynamic dashboards, 182
  guardrails for, 183
  image/video creation by, 49
  incomprehensibility and, 76–78
  leaders' use of, 176–178
  overreliance on, 78
  and probabilistic identifiers, 51
  robot ethics, 112–114
Airbnb, 108
alcoholism, 44, 45
algorithmic manipulation, 48, 63–64, 75, 93–94
ALS (amyotrophic lateral sclerosis), 97
AMOC (Atlantic meridional overturning circulation), 52–54
Andropov, Yuri, 127
animals, respect for, 112–113
anticipatory history, 154, 156
antivaccine misinformation, 74–76
anxiety
  aging and, 118
  attentiveness and, 106–111
  clarity vs., 124
  defined, ix, 41
  and despair, 44–47
  empathy and, 105
  as engine of BANI, 10, 42
  of grief, 148

  of incomprehensibility, 71
  as inevitable, 107, 111
  intentional increase of, 47–48, 50
  leadership amid, 176
  and loss of control, 18, 43–44
  of marginalized groups, 45–46
  mental health and, 169
  narratives of, 23–24
  nonlinearity and, 60
  and passivity, 43
  questions for exploring, 197
  and rage-farming, 47–49
  skills for coping with, 116–118
  systemic, 13
archetypes, scenario, 160–165
arrogant ignorance, 6, 38, 137
athleticism, 141–142
AT Protocol, 93–94
attention hijacking, 48
attentiveness
  and adaptability, 107–108
  defined, 105
  and empathy, 11, 84, 105, 106
  organizational examples of, 108–111
  personal examples of, 111–115
  as Positive BANI, ix, 7, 84
  questions for exploring, 197
  skill building, 116–118

B

BANI (Brittle, Anxious, Nonlinear, Incomprehensible)
  and AI, 77
  anxiety and, 10, 42, 107
  BANI lens benefits, 8–9, 21–23, 155, 192
  brittleness of, 27–29, 31, 32–33, 39–40
  climate emergency as, 35
  defined, vii, ix
  despair about, 44, 191–192
  distressing reality of, 24–25
  and Earth survival, 191
  emerging era of, 5–8
  flipping BANI Positive, 171, 173–175
  as fraught, 6
  incomprehensibility in, 70
  leadership amid, 167, 171–186

BANI (*continued*)
and learned helplessness, 89
and loss of control, 43–44
of Nazi Germany, 95–96, 143
nonlinearity in, 57, 59–61
organizational/institutional, 199–200
overwhelm about, 81–82
as participatory panopticon, 50–52
personal/individual context, 199
Positive BANI response to, viii, x, 7–8, 83–84, 154, 189
questions for exploring, 151–152, 195–201
responsibility for, 19
scenario archetypes for, 161–163
scenario world-building, 11, 165
vs. VUCA, vii
the world as, 10, 13, 14, 17–19, 188
BANI Future
anxiety in, 107
brittleness of, 40, 90
countering helplessness of, 89
deep thinking about, 19
elements of, 20
grief in, 148
hope in, 54
leadership in, 168
multiple crises of, 17, 188
narratives of, 23–24
negative thinking about, 102
as noninevitable, 85
as nonlinear, 120, 121
overwhelm about, 81–82
present-time decisions and, 193
present-time hints of, 181–182
questions for exploring, 200–201
reality of, 25
real vs. fake in, 49
scenario archetypes for, 161–163
scenario mapping, 151, 165–166
uncertainty in, 131
Becket, Thomas, 66
Beilock, Sian, 184
belief, extreme, 91, 102
bendability
and clarity, 88–89
defined, 87
and flexive intent, 89–91
personal, 95–99
as Positive BANI, ix, 7, 84
questions for exploring, 197
resilience of, 11, 84, 88
skill-building, 99–103
for social media, 93–94
for telemedicine, 94–95
and "What if?," 88
Bennis, Warren, 2
Bentham, Jeremy, 50

bias
and AI hallucinations, 77, 177–178
disconnection and lack of, 160
systemic racism, 45, 98–99
binary thinking, 138
biological systems, 61
bipolarity, 168–169
Black communities, 45–46, 74
black swan concept, 136
Blockbuster, 122
Bluesky Social PBC, 93–94
brainstorming solutions, 132
Brief History of Time, A (Hawking), 98
brittleness
abrupt failure and, 13, 27, 28, 32, 35
in BANI term, ix
vs. bendability, 88, 92–93
brittle norms, 37–38
danger/damage of, 10
defined, 27
examples of, 29–30, 31–35
experience of, 5–6
and failure of reliability, 17–18
human, 38–40
hyperefficiency of, 32
leadership amid, 175–176
narratives of, 23–24
nonlinearity and, 60
questions for exploring, 196
as ubiquitous, 31–33
Brown, Gordon, 145
Bulletin of the Atomic Scientists, 73
butterfly effect, 58

C

calmness, 129, 176, 186
Cascio, Jamais, vii, 5, 8, 9, 21, 80, 83, 169
Case, Anne, 44
Cassandra complex, 46
catastrophe/crises
and agency, 7
AMOC, 52–54
anxiety and, 42, 105–106
BANI and understanding of, 9
calm amid, 129
cascading, 34, 35, 39, 54, 58, 60, 188
CrowdStrike crisis, 33–35
enhanced communication in, 109
global extinctions, 190
Kessler syndrome, 33
optimism and, 85
polycrises, 20–21
preparation for, 91, 130
purpose/goals in, 115
pushing back against, 11
responses to, 91–92, 133
causal cognition, 16, 155, 193
cause and effect

breakdown of, 10, 18
climate hysteresis and, 67
and human cognition, 16
nonlinearity and, 66–68
CEO average income, 64–65
certainty, 131, 137, 149, 166, 192
Cervantes, Gabe, 175
change
  anxiety as engine of, 111
  butterfly effect, 58
  chaos vs., 15
  clarity about direction of, 91
  culture and comprehension of, 5–6
  and grief, 148
  for harm reduction, 55
  language for describing, 3
  neuroflexibility for, 119
  nonlinear, 59, 120, 121
  options for response to, vii, 7
  and understanding, 24
Chanthawong, Ekapol (Coach Ek), 114–115
chaos
  and anxiety, 41, 42, 54
  as BANI, 13, 17
  clarity and, 121–122
  decision-making amid, 15
  defined, 15
  future of, 19
  of incomprehensibility, 148
  and interest in BANI, 9
  leadership amid, 167
  vs. legacy structures, 2
  navigating, 189
  overwhelm/disconnect about, 21
  in personal lives, viii
  of polycrises, 2, 17, 188
  recognizing patterns in, 8, 71–72
  responses to, ix, 22–23
  of social media, 93
  and uncertainty, 166
charitable contributions, 120
chemtrails, 80–81
Choke (Beilock), 184
clarity
  about purpose, 110
  vs. anxiety, 124
  bodily, 147
  vs. certainty, 8, 166, 192
  and change, 121, 123–124
  and chaos, 121–122
  and flexible execution, 178–181
  and flexive intent, 90–91
  of leadership, 167, 175–176
  mental health and, 169
  resilient, 88–89, 102
climate emergency
  AMOC and, 52–54

and BANI Future, 20
climate hysteresis, 67
despair about, 47
and geoengineering, 79–81
as human caused, 35
and Kessler syndrome, 33
lack of response to, 78–80
multiple crises of, 17
nonlinearity and, 59, 67–68
reducing harm of, 55
and systemic brittleness, 31–32
West Antarctic Ice Sheet (WAIS), 36–37
cognition, human
  and biological hijacking, 47–48, 63
  causal cognition, 16, 155, 193
  and desire for certainty, 91
  and empathy, 106
  leadership and, 172–173, 185
  neuroflexibility, 119–121
  and practicing actions, 184
  and storytelling, 158–159, 174
  technological enhancements to, 177
cognitive empathy, 106
Cold War era, vii, 3, 72, 127
Collapse, 161, 162, 164
commons, creating the, 177
communication, 98, 109, 174
communities
  attentiveness in, 116
  in BANI world, viii
  brittleness vs., 39
  charitable contributions in, 120
  crowdsourcing in, 125
  grieving in, 148
  initiatives in crises, 109–111
  interconnection via, 148
  listening widely in, 135–138, 139–140, 174
  resilience in, 99
  at the Special Olympics, 142
compassion, 130
Compounding, 162, 164, 165
concentration camps, 95–96, 111, 126, 143
confidence, unwarranted, 6
conspiracy theories, 75, 80–81
constraints, flexible, 182–183
contrails, 80, 81
control
  anxiety and loss of, 18, 43–44
  and command, 90, 167, 179
  and digital deception, 51–52
  passivity and lack of, 89
  wealth and, 65–66
  of the weather, 80–81
coping skills, 101, 102
Corbett-Helaire, Kizzmekia "Kizzy" Shanta, 144–145

232 INDEX

Corrupted Blood, 62–63
counterintuitive thinking, 120
COVID-19 pandemic
  abrupt failures in, 28, 30–31
  Airbnb adaptability in, 108
  antivaccine movement, 74–76
  and awareness of BANI, 8
  behavioral choices in, 62–63
  brittleness revealed by, 31
  and diseases of despair, 45
  inflation in, 67
  lack of preparation for, 91–92
  and limits of VUCA, 4–5
  Moderna vaccine, 144–145
  nonlinearity of, 18, 59, 61–63
  telemedicine and, 94
  United Way initiative, 109–111, 181
  virtual volunteering in, 174–175
creative solutions, 132
crowdsourcing, 125, 141
CrowdStrike crisis, 17, 33–35
cruelty, human, 143
cryptocurrencies, 64
Curation, 164
curiosity, 176–177
cybersecurity systems, 34

D

dangers
  of arrogant ignorance, 6, 137
  brittle failure points, 32–33
  of generative AI, 177
  of hurting people, 39–40
  polycrises of, 78
  questions for exploring, 196
Darling, Kate, 112–114
data
  and AI hallucinations, 76–78
  conflicting/incomplete, 71
  data stream poisoning, 51–52
  dynamic dashboards of, 181–182
  information overload, 69
Dator, Jim, 161
Dawkins, Richard, 63
deaths of despair, 44–45
Deaton, Angus, 44
decision-making
  and anxiety, 43
  amid chaos, 15
  despair about, 43–44
  dynamic dashboards for, 181–182
  fatigue/paralysis about, 41, 43
  fragmented/isolated, 60
  future as shaped by, 187, 189, 193–194
  futureback thinking for, 185
  human capacity for, 16
  and incomprehensibility, 18
  informed, 12, 139

amid instability, 4, 5, 19
nonlinearity and, 57
and pandemic spread, 62–63
preparation for quick, 130
and scenario world-building, 11
stress of difficult, 41
depression, 168–169
despair, 44–47, 82, 191–192
digital deception, 51
dignity, 112
dilemmas
  flipping, 176
  for future leaders, 72
  managing vs. solving, 100
  problems vs., 22–23
  unfixable BANI, 83
disabilities, intellectual and physical, 141–142
Disassembly, 162, 164
discernment, 185
Discipline (or Constraint), 100–101, 114, 161, 163, 164
Discontinuity, 163, 164, 165
diseases of despair, 44–45
disruptions
  BANI era, 5–8
  and BANI Future, 20, 126
  and brittle system breakdown, 27
  celebration of, 39
  of climate change response, 78–79
  collective peaking of, 20–21
  COVID-19 pandemic, 4–5
  disrupting the, 11
  and human/AI relationship, 78
  neuroflexibility amid, 122
  overwhelm by, 22–23
  sensitivity to, 169
  VUCA era, 2–5
diverse views, listening to, 135–138
doomscrolling, 42–43
Doomsday Clock, 73
drug abuse, 44, 45
Duke University, 78
Dunagan, Jeff, 184
Dunning-Kruger effect, 6
Dweck, Carol, 172
dynamic dashboards, 181–182

E

echo chambers, 75
economies of scope, 92
education for girls, 145–146
efficiency, 32, 35
Ellisor, Darren, 129, 130
Emergence, 165
emotional empathy, 106
emotional health, 115
emotions, positive, 100, 116

empathy
  active, 107, 108, 110, 111, 112, 114, 145
  attentiveness and, 11, 84, 105, 106
  amid chaos, 189
  vs. despair, 46
  emotional and cognitive, 106
  mental health and, 169
  robots and teaching of, 113
  skill building, 116–117
  at Unified Sports, 142
Equal Justice Initiative, 98, 99
escalate to de-escalate, 73, 127
ethical behavior, 37, 112–114, 182–183
Ever Given ship, 31
executive income, 64–65
exercise, physical, 100–101, 103
Experience Machine, The (Clark), 173
extinctions, global, 190–191

F

Facebook, 38, 94
"Facing the Age of Chaos" (Cascio), 8
failure, 133, 164, 184
faith, 91, 96–97, 101–102
fear, 4, 42–43, 47–48, 61
Fernandez, Carla, 148
finances
  2008 financial crisis, 4
  biological hijacking for profit, 48
  cost of sea level rise, 37
  COVID-era inflation, 67
  CrowdStrike crisis, 34
  cryptocurrencies, 64
  executive income, 64–65
  and overreliance on AI, 77–78
  See also wealth disparities
First-Rate Madness, A (Ghaemi), 168
fitness, 100–101, 103, 170–171
flexibility. *See* bendability; neuroflexibility; resilience
flexive command, 90
flexive intent, 89–91, 179, 182
Ford, 179–180, 182
foresight planning, 155–156, 160, 165, 193
forgiveness, 131
fossil fuels, 30, 67–68, 79–80
Frankl, Viktor, 95–97, 111, 126–127, 131, 143
full-spectrum thinking, 138, 141–142
Full-Spectrum Thinking (Johansen), 90
future
  deep thinking about, 19
  defined, 187
  despair about, 46
  harm reduction for, 25
  as imagined by humans, 16
  investment in, 111

  mental predictions of, 173
  as nonlinear, 120
  and present-time fear, 43
  present-time hints of, 181–182
  scenario mapping of, 153, 165–166
  as shaped by the present, 187, 189, 193
  uncertainty of, vii
  See also BANI Future
futureback thinking, 90, 171–186, 172, 176–177, 179
futurists, vii, 5, 22, 46, 72, 136, 139, 156–158, 161

G

Galinsky, Adam, 115
GameStop, 64
gaming, 125, 183–184
geoengineering, 79–80
Ghaemi, Nassir, 168–169
Gibson, William, 181
Gilbert, Martin, 96
girls/women, rights of, 145
Global South, 8, 45, 185
goals, 90, 147
gratitude, 100, 103, 116
Great Influenza of 1918–1919, 91–92
greenhouse gas, atmospheric, 67–68, 79–80
grief, 148
Growth, 131, 161, 162, 163
growth vs. fixed mindsets, 172
guano industry, 29–30
Gumby cartoons, 89, 90

H

H1N1 virus, 92
H5N1 bird flu, 61
Haber-Bosch process, 30
hallucination, AI, 76–78
happiness, 100
harm reduction
  action to serve, 25
  climate hysteresis and, 67–68
  hope and, 54
  lessening anxiety, 105, 112
  nonlinearity and, 68
Hawking, Stephen, 97–98
health, 100–101, 103, 170–171
helplessness, 89
Henry II, King, 66
hope, 54, 95, 115, 149, 189
human beings
  BANI and risks to, 13
  behavior of, and pandemic spread, 62
  brittleness of, 38–40
  cognitive abilities of, 16
  emotional response to chaos, 22–23
  ethical behavior of, 37

human beings (*continued*)
  hijacking biology of, 47–48
  humanity of, 112
  mass extinctions of, 190–191
  meaning-making by, 112
  participatory panopticon of, 50–52
  relations with robots, 113
  responsibility of, 194
  values of, 160
humility, 180
Hurricane Sandy, 36–37
hyperefficiency, 32, 35
hysteresis, climate, 67

I

I Am Malala (Yousafzai), 145
ice sheet melting, 36–37, 53
identification, 51
illusion vs. reality, 49, 51
imbalance, nonlinear, 57–58
impartiality, 160
improvisation. *See* neuroflexibility
improvisation, theater, 132–133
inclusivity, 11, 84, 137, 142, 146, 172
incomprehensibility
  and AI, 76–78
  of anthropogenic climate change, 78
  anxiety of, 71
  in BANI term, ix
  of COVID-19, 144
  defined, 69, 70
  and functionality, 70
  and lack of sense-making, 10, 18, 71
  leadership amid, 176–177
  listening widely to lessen, 135–138
  loneliness of, 147
  narratives of, 23–24
  nonlinearity and, 60–61
  of political divisions, 70–71
  questions for exploring, 198
  systemic, 13
Indigenous communities, 45–46
inequality, 1
information. *See* data
infrastructure, 31, 92
injustice, systemic, 45, 98–99
insanity/sanity, 168–169
Institute for the Future (IFTF), viii, 8, 94, 165, 184
intellectual disabilities, 141–142
intention, 185
interconnection
  in brittle systems, 28–29
  and cascading collapse, 60
  via community, 148
  defined, 135
  of diverse systems, 137–138
  and inclusivity, 11, 84

  and listening widely, 135–138
  organizational examples of, 138–142
  personal examples of, 143–146
  as Positive BANI, ix, 8, 84
  questions for exploring, 198
  skill building for, 147–149
  and teamwork, 115
The Intergovernmental Science-Policy Platform on Biodiversity and Ecosystem Services, 191
international politics, 65–66
intertidal zones, 137–138
isolation, 60

J

Johansen, Bob, viii, 9–10, 83, 90, 94, 117, 139, 175
joy, 100, 116
judgment, suspending, 133
Just Enough Anxiety (Rosen), 107
Just Mercy (Stevenson), 98

K

Kahn, Herman, 72, 74, 155
Kessler syndrome, 33, 39
Kirshbaum, Jeremy, 175
knowability, 4, 6
Knudstorp, Jørgen Vig, 123

L

large language models (LLMs), 77, 177
leadership
  via active empathy, 114–115
  and arrogant ignorance, 6
  in a BANI world, viii, ix, 4, 11, 12, 151, 167, 171–186
  brittle norms for, 37
  calm, 129
  and climate hysteresis, 68
  data sources for, 181–182
  feedback for, 124
  with flexible execution, 178–181
  and flexive intent, 90
  fundamental dilemma for, 72
  gaming practice for, 184
  and health, 170–171
  and incomprehensibility, 71
  leader/stakeholder connection, 109, 124
  and mental health, 168–169
  and storytelling, 174–175
  use of AI, 176–178
  use of technology, 185
  wide listening by, 149
learned helplessness, 89
learning, immersive, 177
Lee, Bruce, 101
legal constraints, 182–183
LEGO, 123–216

Lindner, Evelin, 85
Linser, Jo, 85
listening, 105, 132, 136, 139, 174
logotherapy, 111, 127
low-probability events, 136
Luskin, Fred, 131

M

MAD (mutual assured destruction), 127
Malala Fund, 146
malinformation, 49–50
Mandela, Nelson, 107
Man's Search for Meaning (Frankl), 96
marginalized communities, 45–46
Martinez, Veronica Root, 37
Mayo Clinic, 94–95
Mazzucato, Mariana, 179
McMillian, Walter, 98–99
meaning-making, 96, 111, 126–127, 131, 143–144
meditation, 114
memecoins, 64
memes, 62, 63
men's health, 44–45
mental exercises, 101
mental flexibility. *See* neuroflexibility
mental health, 110, 115, 126, 168–171
metapocalypse. *See* polycrises
Microsoft, 34, 172
Microsoft Research India, 185
mindfulness, 100, 103, 114, 116, 117
misery, 191–192
misinformation, 49, 74
Mission Economy (Mazzucato), 179
missions, 179
MIT Media Lab, 112, 125
Moderna COVID-19 vaccine, 144–145
monocultures, 32–33, 34
Moody's Analytics, 65
Mornell, Pierre, 100
Morton, Oliver, 80
Moskowitz, Judith, 99–100, 148
movement, 100–101
Mulally, Alan, 179–180, 182
myths, 157
  See also narratives

N

Nadella, Satya, 172
Nagel, Thomas, 160
Nanus, Burt, 2
narratives
  BANI for exploring, 23–24
  of BANI Future, 23–24
  deceptive digital, 51–52
  to flip BANI Positive, 171, 173–175
  four Index1 types of, 161
  and gaming practice, 184
  of inclusion, 172
  and incomprehensibility, 72
  purpose via, 115
  scenarios as, 153
  "This is a world in which," 156–159
  understanding via, 156–157
natural disasters, 31–32, 36–37
Nature Human Behaviour, 48
Nazi Germany, 95–96, 111, 126, 143
negative thought, 102
Netflix, 122–123
neurodivergence, 141, 169
neuroflexibility
  defined, 119
  forgiveness as, 131
  as improvisation, 11, 84
  for nonlinearity, 119–121, 133
  organizational examples of, 121–126
  personal examples of, 126–130
  as Positive BANI, ix, 7, 84
  questions for exploring, 198
  real-time regulation for, 147
  skill building, 130–133
New Leadership Literacies, The (Johansen), 170
news
  avoiding the, 43
  doomscrolling, 42–43
  malinformation, 49–50
  and rage-baiting, 48–49
  from social media, 38
  wealth and control of, 65
nonlinearity
  in a BANI world, 4, 59–61
  and brittleness, 60
  as cause/effect imbalance, 10, 18, 57–58
  defined, ix, 57
  examples of, 59, 121–130
  leadership amid, 169, 176
  narratives of, 23–24
  neuroflexibility for, 119–121
  nontraditional pathways in, 136
  organizational examples of, 121–126
  positive, 120
  and power disparities, 64–66
  questions for exploring, 197
  skills for coping with, 130–133
  systemic, 13
normative scenarios, 159
norms, 2, 28, 37–38
Northwestern University, 99, 100, 103, 116, 147
nuclear war, 72–74, 127, 128

O

ocean current circulation, 52–54
omnicrisis. *See* polycrises
One Ford, 180, 182

On Thermonuclear War (Kahn), 72
opioid abuse, 45
optimism, 12, 85
orthogonal thinking, 120
overwhelm
  about BANI Future, 81–82
  anxiety and, 106–107, 117, 118
  by catastrophism, 190
  community to lessen, 149
  information overload, 69

P

pandemics
  preparation for, 91–92
  spread of, 61–63, 76
  See also COVID-19 pandemic
panopticon, participatory, 50–52
passivity, 43, 78, 89, 159
path dependence, 67
patience, 111
patterns
  cognitive impulse toward, 91
  collapse of familiar, 2
  for decision-making, 16
  misunderstanding of, 71–72
Peru, 29–30
pessimism, 12, 85
Petrov, Stanislav, 127, 128
Pew Research, 38
physical health, 100–101, 103, 170–171
pivots, quick, 121, 129
Planet Remade, The (Morton), 80
polarization, 38, 138, 176
politics
  and the antivaccine movement, 75–76
  brittle systems of, 32
  and COVID-era inflation, 67
  divisive US, 70–71
  ethical leadership, 37–38
  of geoengineering, 81
  international, 65–66
  post-2015, 1
  post–Cold War instability, 3
  and rage-baiting, 48
  wealth disparities and, 65–66
polycrises
  and anxiety, 42, 105–106
  in BANI world, 2, 21
  depth of, 188
  and Kessler syndrome, 33
Poor Richard's Almanack (Franklin), 58
Positive BANI (Bendable, Attentive, Neuroflexible, Interconnection)
  actions for, 166, 194
  defined, 7–8
  flipping BANI Positive, 171, 173–175
  foundation of, 82
  leadership for, 171

as necessary, 85
paradigm shift of, 11
questions for exploring, 195–201
resilience skills for, 99–103
as response to BANI, 83–84, 189
scenario archetypes for, 163–165
scenario world-building, 11
Positive VUCA (Vision, Understanding, Clarity, Agility), 83
possibility space, 7
power/wealth
  and BANI Future, 20
  and ethical leadership, 38
  wealth and political power, 65–66
practicing resilience, 101, 133
pride, 112
privacy camouflage, 51–52
privacy intrusions, 50–51
probabilistic identifiers, 51
problem/solution thinking, 7, 83
Proceedings of the National Academy of Sciences, 44
purpose
  clarity about, 110
  flexible, 89–91, 96
  resilience via, 112
  shared goals, 115
Putnam, Robert, 177

R

racism, institutional, 45, 98–99
rage-farming, 47–49
Reagan, Ronald, 127
reality vs. falsehood, 49, 51
reappraisals, positive, 103, 130, 132, 144
redundancy, lack of, 32, 35
Reinforcement, 163, 164
Renegade Grief (Fernandez), 148
resilience
  ability and, 142
  active, 189
  attentiveness skills, 116–118
  in BANI world, 189
  bendability skills, 99–103
  bodily, 147
  examples of personal, 95–99
  and flexible constraints, 182–183
  and flexible execution, 178–181
  interconnection skills, 147–149
  in leadership, 168, 171
  to lessen anxiety, 107
  and meaning-making, 131
  neuroflexibility skills, 130–133
  in Positive BANI, 84
  and purpose, 112
  See also bendability
resources
  for facing chaos, 196

guano industry, 29–30
  nonlinearity and need for, 60
  resource curse, 29
responsibility, 19, 194
Retrenchment, 164
robotics, 112–114, 124–215
Rock, David, 170
"The Role of Norms in Modern-Day Government Ethics" (Martinez), 37
Rosen, Jay, 160
Rosen, Robert, 107

S

safety, psychological, 105
Sanger, Larry, 141
sanity/insanity, 168–169
SARS virus, 62
satellite system collapse, 33
savoring life, 116
scenario archetypes method, 160–165
scenario planning
  of a BANI Future, 151
  BANI leadership via, 11
  and bendability, 88
  defined, 153
  Herman Kahn and, 72, 155
  historic use of, 155
  improvisational, 133
  logical possibility in, 156–158, 166
  neutrality in, 159–160
  for Positive BANI, ix
  preparation via, 130
  purpose of, 153
  scenario archetypes method, 160–165
  scenario gaming, 183–184
  setting as focus in, 159
  technology in, 160
  "This is a world in which," 156–159
  understanding via, 154–155
sea level rise, 36–37
self-compassion, 130, 132
self-control, 114, 185
Seligman, Martin, 89
senselessness, 71
September 11 attacks, 4, 90
Shriver, Eunice Kennedy, 141–142
Shults, Captain Tammie Jo, 129–130
Siegel, Dan, 170
Silicon Valley, 165, 173
simulation, 125, 183–184
situational awareness, 117
slave labor, 29
social media
  and the antivaccine movement, 76
  and BANI Future, 20
  biological hijacking by, 47–48
  and lack of social opprobrium, 38
  nonlinearity of, 59, 63–64
  and polarization, 38
  AT Protocol and, 93–94
  use of anxiety, 41
  virality in, 62, 63, 64
socioeconomic systems. *See* structures, legacy
somatic therapy, 147
Special Olympics, 141–142
Sterling, Bruce, 192
Stevenson, Bryan, 98
stochastic terrorism, 66
storm surges, 36–37
storytelling, ix, 156–157
streaming services, 122
strength
  brittleness as illusory, 27, 38–39
  Growth and, 163
  and humility, 176, 180
  personal, 147
stress
  in a BANI world, 100
  breakdown from, 40
  coping with, viii
  of grief, 148
  as natural/inevitable, 102
  resilience skills for, 99–103
  See also anxiety
structures, legacy
  abrupt value changes in, 29–30
  BANI and breakdown of, 17–19
  brittleness of, 28, 31–32, 123
  brittle vs. bendable, 92–93
  chaos vs., 2
  hyperefficiency in, 32
  of leadership, 168
  listening beyond, 136–138
  and nonlinear change, 123
  post–Cold War instability of, 3–4
  systemic racism in, 45
Suez Canal crisis, 31
suicide, 43, 44, 45
Superhost Relief Fund, 108–109
supply chains, 92
surveillance, ubiquitous, 50–51

T

Taleb, Nassim Nicholas, 136
Taliban, 145
teamwork, 115, 130
technology, 160, 185
telemedicine, 94–95
terrorism, stochastic, 66
theatrical improv, 132–133
thermal geoengineering, 79–80
thermohaline circulation, 52–54
thermonuclear war, 72–74
Thwaites Glacier, 36
TikTok, 63, 64, 94

Timmons, Heather, 66
tipping points, 32–33
tone deafness, 117
Toyama, Kentaro, 185
Transformation, 161, 163, 165
transparency, accountability through, 180
Trapped, 163, 164
trauma, 145, 148
trust, 72, 105, 133
Twitter, 93–94

U

uncertainty
  action amid, 16, 153–154
  anxiety and, 117
  and brittleness, 28
  and consequence, 43
  embracing, x
  of the future, vii, 91, 153–155
  vs. negative certainty, 131
understanding
  of anxiety, 107
  via BANI, 155
  BANI and breakdown of, 19
  the future, 153–155
  and incomprehensibility, 69–70
  via narrative, 24
  nontraditional pathways to, 135–138
  partial, 139
  via stories, 153, 174
  wealth disparity, 64
  via wide knowledge circles, 141
unexpected events, 119
Unified Sports, 142
United States
  Cold War bipolarity, 3, 127
  Guano Islands Act, 30
  opioid abuse in, 45
  political divisions in, 70–71
  wealth disparities in, 64–65
United Way Worldwide, viii, 108, 109–111, 133, 139–140, 174, 180
unthinkable realities, 72–74
US Air Force, 80
US Army National Training Center, 184
US Army War College, 2, 90
USSR, 3, 127

V

vaccination, 74–76
values, human, 160
video gaming, 125

virality, 61–62, 63, 145
viruses, spread of, 61
VUCA (Volatile, Uncertain, Complex, and Ambiguous)
  BANI vs., vii
  no returning to, 7
  outgrowing of term, 2–5, 6
  Positive VUCA, 83
  scenario archetypes for, 161

W

Wales, Jimmy, 141
warfare
  nuclear, 72–74, 127, 128
  power and, 65–66
Watts, Alan W., 117–118
wealth disparities
  and BANI Future, 20
  brittle system of, 30
  and political power, 65–66
  in the United States, 64–65
weather, 53, 80–81
"Weather as a Force Multiplier: Owning the Weather in 2025," 80
West Antarctic Ice Sheet (WAIS), 36–37
wide listening, 135–138, 139
Wikipedia, 141–142
wildcard events, 136
Williams, Angela F., viii, 9, 109, 133, 139, 174, 180
Windows startup process, 34
Wisdom of Insecurity, The (Watts), 117
world, the
  as BANI, 16, 17–19
  global extinctions, 190
  as knowable, 4
  Positive BANI and understanding, 11
  "This is a world in which" scenarios, 156–159
World Health Organization, 45
World of Warcraft, 62

X

X (Twitter), 93–94

Y

"Yes, and," 132
Yousafzai, Malala, 145–146

Z

Zuckerberg, Mark, 39

About the Authors

Jamais Cascio

Jamais Cascio has worked as a futurist for over three decades, but he usually refers to himself as an "easily distracted generalist." He has given talks about deepfakes to the Arab Media Forum, the politics of geoengineering to the US National Academies of Science, and the possibility of hope amid global chaos to the World Bank. He's written and spoken around the world about the ethics of cognitive enhancement, the carbon footprint of cheeseburgers, and the critical need to deal with climate change. He explored the disruptive potential of networked mobile cameras (i.e., mobile phones) in his work three years before the iPhone came out. A nuclear policy NGO twice sought him out to write scenarios of the future of global security.

Jamais worked as a computer network administrator and as a (paper and dice) game designer. He spent a couple of years in Hollywood as an adviser for science fiction television shows and was the lead writer for an award-winning climate and culture blog back when there were blogs. He's appeared in enough television and film documentaries to warrant his own IMDb page. *Foreign Policy* magazine listed him as one of their Top 100 Global Thinkers in 2009; the University of Advancing Technology awarded him an honorary doctorate of science (ScD) in 2017.

He's chatted with Al Gore about the animated series *Futurama* and with Michio Kaku about the possibility of "boiling space-time." He was name-checked in an issue of the *Avengers* comic book. He's actually touched a moon rock.

Institute for the Future has had him in their network long enough to consider him a Distinguished Fellow. He created BANI as a way of talking about the future of trust and international power for an IFTF event. It turns out that being an easily distracted generalist is the perfect training for working as a futurist.

Jamais has a bachelor's degree in anthropology (focusing on evolution) and history (focusing on revolutions). He did his graduate work in international politics, although he wrote his master's thesis on consociational democracy in Lebanon. He never got around to finishing his actual PhD.

Amid all of this, he's had one constant: Janice Cripe, his wife of thirty-three years, along with their cats.

Bob Johansen

Bob Johansen has worked for more than fifty years as a professional futurist—with remarkable accuracy. He was one of the first social scientists to study the impact of the internet on both human and organizational behavior, dating back to when it was called the Arpanet. He also has a deep interest in the future of religion, spirituality, and values.

Bob served as president of Institute for the Future (IFTF) from 1996–2004. He now invests his time writing books, delivering (mostly virtual) talks and workshops, and working with IFTF sponsors. Bob is an IFTF Distinguished Fellow.

He is author or coauthor of more than a dozen previous books, including the following:

- *Electronic Meetings*
- *Teleconferencing and Beyond*

- *Leading Business Teams*
- *Groupware*
- *GlobalWork*
- *Upsizing the Individual in the Downsized Organization*
- *Leaders Make the Future (three editions)*
- *The Reciprocity Advantage*
- *The New Leadership Literacies*
- *Office Shock*

An interdisciplinary social scientist by training, Bob has a bachelor of science degree from the University of Illinois (which he attended on a basketball scholarship) and a PhD from the Graduate School of Northwestern University. In addition, he has a divinity school degree from Crozer Theological Seminary, where he focused on world religions. Bob and his wife, Robin, a constitutional lawyer, met as undergraduates and have been married more than fifty years.

Angela F. Williams, JD, MDiv, President and Chief Executive Officer, United Way Worldwide

Angela F. Williams is president and CEO of United Way Worldwide (UWW). With more than thirty years of leadership experience in the nonprofit and corporate sectors, Angela brings her innovative vision and a long history of purpose-driven work to her role at United Way Worldwide.

Angela is bivocational, serving as an ordained minister, attorney, and civil society executive. She jointly integrates her faith and professional expertise into many aspects of her community-impact work and cites her faith as a source of optimism and belief that everyone deserves to live in thriving communities.

In recognition of her bold leadership and impact, Angela was named a 2025 *USA Today* Woman of the Year, a national distinction celebrating women who have made significant contributions to their communities and industries by breaking barriers and uplifting others.

Angela has also been featured in the 2022 and 2024 editions of the *NonProfit Times* Power and Influence Top 50 list, the *Forbes* 2021 List of Women Over 50 Creating Social Change at Scale, *Inside Philanthropy*'s list of the 50 Most Powerful Women in U.S. Philanthropy, and *Virginia Business*'s Virginia 500 Power List of Prominent Leaders for Nonprofits/Philanthropy. She is also the recipient of a 2021 *CEO Today* Healthcare Award.

Before joining United Way, Angela was president and CEO of Easterseals, the nation's leading nonprofit provider of life-changing disability services. She also served on active duty in the US Air Force Judge Advocate General's Corps for more than six years; led as an executive vice president, general counsel, and chief administration officer at YMCA of the USA; served as an interfaith liaison for the Bush-Clinton Katrina Fund; was special counsel on criminal law for Sen. Edward M. Kennedy on the Senate Judiciary Committee staff; and worked as a prosecutor on the DOJ Civil Rights Division's National Church Arson Task Force and as an assistant US attorney.

Angela earned a bachelor's degree in American government from the University of Virginia, a juris doctor from the University of Texas School of Law, and a master of divinity, cum laude, from the Samuel DeWitt Proctor School of Theology, Virginia Union University. She lives with her husband, Reverend Roderick Williams, in the Washington, DC, area. Both are deeply committed to community service through compassionate ministry and mentorship.

About Institute for the Future

Institute for the Future (IFTF) is an independent nonprofit research and education organization based in Palo Alto in California's Silicon Valley. Founded in 1968, IFTF is the longest running futures research organization in the world. IFTF works with a wide range of organizations across all sectors to help them become more future ready by learning how to apply foresight toward making more informed decisions today.

IFTF was established by former RAND Corporation and SRI International researchers with grants from the Arthur Vining Davis Foundation and the Ford Foundation. IFTF continues today to maintain the original vision—to develop leading-edge futures research, foresight methodologies, and tools to share broadly with leaders and organizations of all kinds.

As a leader in foresight training and executive education programming, the IFTF Foresight Essentials Program provides a comprehensive portfolio of strategic foresight training and tools based on over five decades of proven practices and methods. IFTF tools foster the mindset and skills that enable individuals and organizations to anticipate future forces, identify emerging needs, and develop future-ready strategies like those written about in this book. We will be using *Navigating the Age of Chaos* to frame a wide range of strategic foresight we are pursuing at IFTF.

Bob is donating his proceeds from this book to IFTF and its programs for nonprofit leaders, as he has for all his previous books.

To learn more, or sign up for one of IFTF's courses on strategic foresight, visit iftf.org/foresight essentials.

About United Way Worldwide

As CEO of United Way Worldwide, Angela F. Williams knows that building a sustainable and impactful future for everyone requires a foundational understanding of the challenges. She understands that none of us can master what we do not understand. *Navigating the Age of Chaos* is one of the most comprehensive looks at where we are collectively as a society. Although we don't know the future, we are informed by the past and the present. The BANI world is a quagmire of confusion, making it difficult to navigate without a functional framework of understanding.

Navigating the Age of Chaos does more that shape a narrative; it is an important tool for defining reality. United Way Worldwide is an organization that believes in building platforms for the effective communications required to solve some of our most difficult problems. The BANI framework will be an important reference tool for thought leadership and bringing some level of clarity to the very complex variables challenging our baseline understanding of the world. The hope is to bring new perspectives and broader understanding of why the current BANI reality is not fixed. Every future-focused leader must learn new ways to articulate hope and opportunity in order for humanity to thrive.

Mrs. Williams is donating her proceeds from this book to United Way Worldwide to ensure this storied legacy will continue to build resilient and thriving communities throughout the world.

United Way (UW) mobilizes communities to action so all can thrive. True to their founding spirit, UW's approach is to actively listen and respond to difficult community challenges by bringing advocates, donors, and volunteers together. UW helps communities conceptualize and build out sustainable solutions through partnership and collaboration.

United Way Worldwide (UWW) is a global nonprofit that reaches across tens of thousands of communities throughout the world, reaching millions of people with impactful, innovative, and scale programs. UWW brings 137 years of experience addressing common community needs such as housing, education, employment, nutrition, and access to health care. Operating as a force for good, UWW provides community-accessible solutions that address the needs of individuals and families at all stages of life, from infants to seniors.

To learn more about United Way, visit unitedway.org.

Berrett–Koehler Publishers

Berrett-Koehler is an independent publisher dedicated to an ambitious mission: *Connecting people and ideas to create a world that works for all.*

Our publications span many formats, including print, digital, audio, and video. We also offer online resources, training, and gatherings. And we will continue expanding our products and services to advance our mission.

We believe that the solutions to the world's problems will come from all of us, working at all levels: in our society, in our organizations, and in our own lives. Our publications and resources offer pathways to creating a more just, equitable, and sustainable society. They help people make their organizations more humane, democratic, diverse, and effective (and we don't think there's any contradiction there). And they guide people in creating positive change in their own lives and aligning their personal practices with their aspirations for a better world.

And we strive to practice what we preach through what we call "The BK Way." At the core of this approach is *stewardship,* a deep sense of responsibility to administer the company for the benefit of all of our stakeholder groups, including authors, customers, employees, investors, service providers, sales partners, and the communities and environment around us. Everything we do is built around stewardship and our other core values of *quality, partnership, inclusion,* and *sustainability.*

We are grateful to our readers, authors, and other friends who are supporting our mission. We ask you to share with us examples of how BK publications and resources are making a difference in your lives, organizations, and communities at bkconnection.com/impact.

Dear reader,

Thank you for picking up this book and welcome to the worldwide BK community! You're joining a special group of people who have come together to create positive change in their lives, organizations, and communities.

What's BK all about?

Our mission is to connect people and ideas to create a world that works for all.

Why? Our communities, organizations, and lives get bogged down by old paradigms of self-interest, exclusion, hierarchy, and privilege. But we believe that can change. That's why we seek the leading experts on these challenges—and share their actionable ideas with you.

A welcome gift

To help you get started, we'd like to offer you a **free copy** of one of our bestselling ebooks:

bkconnection.com/welcome

When you claim your **free ebook**, you'll also be subscribed to our blog.

Our freshest insights

Access the best new tools and ideas for leaders at all levels on our blog at ideas.bkconnection.com.

Sincerely,

Your friends at Berrett-Koehler